A Grimoire of Italian Witchcraft

Practical Spells & Rituals of the Old Religion

About the Author

Raven Grimassi (1951-2019) was a prolific occult author who had written more than twenty books on various magical, pagan, and occult topics. He is best known for his work in popularizing the branch of Italian witchcraft known as Stregheria and was an active member of the pagan community for decades. He died March 10, 2019 and is survived by not only his books, but also his loving wife Stephanie who continues to make magic in his name.

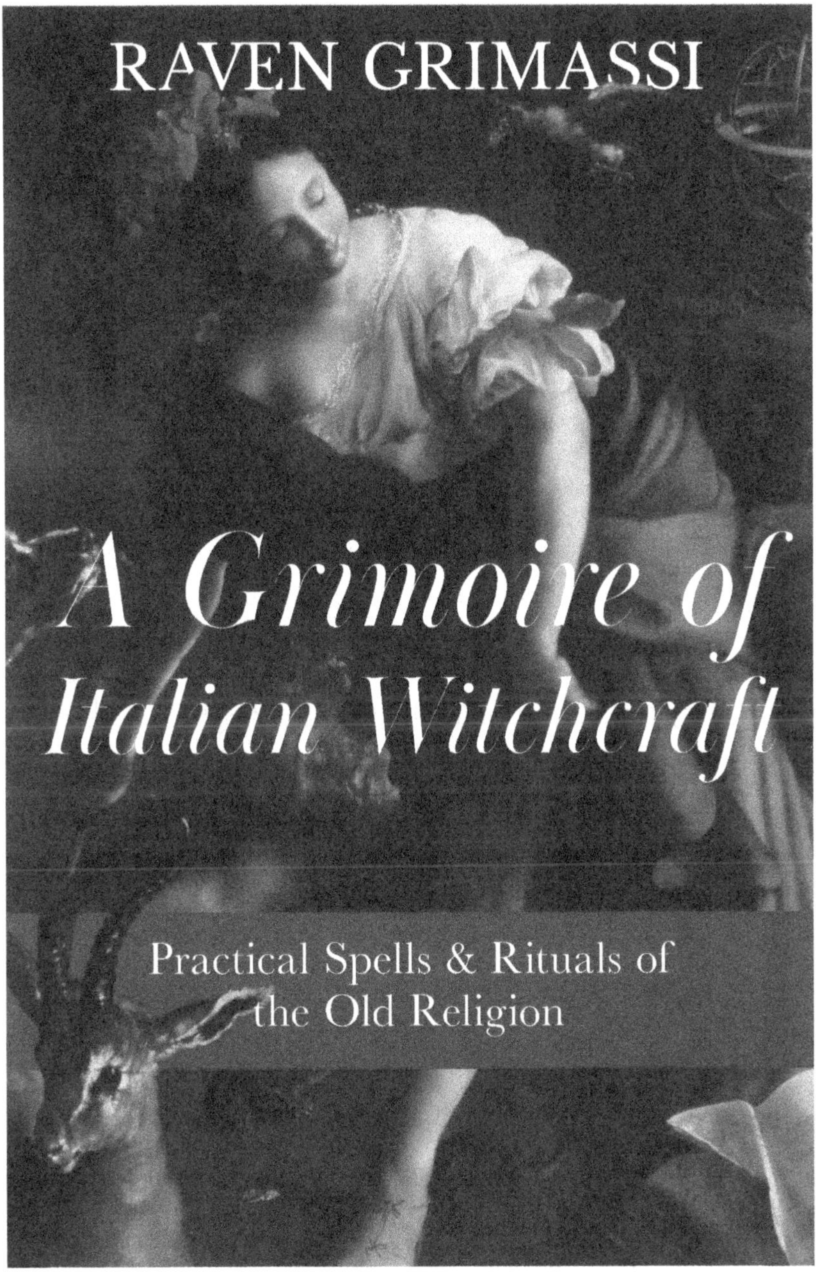

RAVEN GRIMASSI

A Grimoire of Italian Witchcraft

Practical Spells & Rituals of the Old Religion

Chicago, IL

Paperback ISBN: 978-1-964537-58-0
eBook ISBN: 978-1-968185-47-3

Library of Congress Control Number on file.

Published by:
Crossed Crow Books, LLC
518 Davis St, Suite 205
Evanston, IL 60201
www.crossedcrowbooks.com

Printed in the United States of America.
IBI

Table of Contents

CHAPTER ONE

A Look at Italian Witchcraft

Many images come to mind when we think about Italian Witchcraft and Italian Witches. We might imagine the little old lady who reads fortune-telling cards, mixes potions, or sells charms. We also might imagine the beautiful Enchantress, the powerful Sorceress, or the mystical figure seen walking at night in an old cemetery. All of these evoke something of the Witch, and all of them have very distant roots in the Witchcraft of Old Italy.

In Modern Italy, the notion of the Witch is a blend of several ideas. For the average person, she is mistaken for someone in league with the Judeo-Christian Devil-figure of Satan. However, there are also those in mainstream society who see her as simply a person using magick and foretelling the future. This all falls into the category of *Stregoneria,* which is the modern word for "Witchcraft" in the contemporary Italian language. This word highlights the Witch as a sorceress.

For the purposes of this text and its material, we use the word *Stregheria* along with this concept. The word is an archaic one in the Italian language and first appears in writing in the work of Girolamo Tartarotti, who was an Italian Abbot and philosopher in the mid-to-late 1700s. The last common usage of the word *Stregheria* in Italy seems to be in the late 1800s and is found in the writings of several folklorists, including Charles Godfrey Leland. Over time, the word was replaced with the word *Stregoneria,* which also displaced the old meaning.

In Tartarotti's writings, he uses both words, *Stregoneria* and *Stregheria,* to denote Witchcraft. However, his use of *Stregoneria* is in terms of magick only, and his use of *Stregheria* is when he is addressing something religious and organized. Tartarotti wrote, in his book *The Nightly Meeting of Witches,* that Witchcraft is the survival of an ancient Cult of the goddess Diana:

> *The witches of our time are derived from, and are the offspring of, the ancient ones, who were followers of Diana, and Erodiade, and that their crime is witchcraft, just as it was in the past.*
>
> *[Che le nostrè Streghe sono una derivazione , e propagine dell' antiche seguaci di Diana, e di Erodiade, e che il delitto dell' une e dell' altre in sostanza è lo stesso.]*

> *The assembly of modern witches is nothing less than the ancient ones, and because of this succession they enjoy all the rights and privileges of their ancestors.*
>
> *[Le moderne streghe adunque, che non sono da meno dell' antiche, nelle ragioni delle quelle succedettero, debbono per conseguenza godere tutti I diritti e privilege, che quelle godevano.]*[1]

Tartarotti found himself in serious trouble with the Church over his view, because the Church taught that Witches worshipped Satan, not Diana. He was therefore forced to write a retraction that was in keeping with the position of the Church. This book was titled *Apologies—Nightly Meetings of the Witches* and contradicted his earlier view. Fortunately, both versions still exist for comparison, but, sadly, they have never been translated into English.

While some folklorists in Italy during the nineteenth century did discover Witches who venerated Diana, they also discovered Witches who did not. The latter appear to venerate saints, and much of their magickal work embraces elements of Catholicism. This may be connected to the Cult of Saints that was very popular in Italy during the Middle Ages and Early Renaissance periods.

1 Girolamo Tartarotti, *Del Congresso Notturno delle Lammie: Of the Nightly Meeting of Witches* (Giambatista Pasquali, 1749).

This no doubt had a strong influence on people in those times and contributed to displacing the Old Gods among the general populace.

Author Eliza Osborn Putnam Heaton wrote about her encounter with an interesting Witch in Sicily—or was she?—in 1920. The book is titled *By-Paths in Sicily* and it features a woman named Vanna who refers to herself as a Christian, but is clearly linked to non-Christian mystical involvements. For example, she talks about Faery-beings that companioned her from childhood and she wears the "Elf Locks" that signify her as one of their followers. These beings are called the "Ronni."

About Vanna's Elf Locks, Heaton wrote:

> *Pulling out the pins, she let down this mass, undoing with her fingers the upper part of two braids, and releasing a scant lot of gray old woman's hair that hung loose and ragged to her shoulders. Starting from this short mane and falling to Vanna's feet, even lying on the floor, dropped two tails that, felted with dust, had more the look of strands of sheep's wool than of what they were in fact, matted locks of her own hair.*
>
> *These tails were the "trizzi." Never cut, never combed, treated with the respectful neglect which is their proper care, they marked Gna Vanna as a person living under a spell; the protégée from birth of the mysterious "women of the outside" ... here fearsome pixy locks set Vanna apart as one who, taught by witches, possessed some at least of the seven faculties of the witch...*[2]

Another author, Lina Gordon, wrote of another type of Witch, one who lives in isolated villages. In her book *Home Life in Italy,* Gordon writes:

> *The witch of flesh and blood, to whom the disappointed lovers go to weave strange spells and brew love potions, live in*

2 Eliza Osborn Putnam Heaton, *By-Paths in Sicily* (E.P. Dutton & Co., 1920) 16.

> *quiet back streets in the towns or are to be found in isolated hill villages. One old fortune-teller, a real strega, I found at Carrara...dressed in a patched gown, a tawney kerchief on her head, beneath which fell a few wisps of white hair.*[3]

Gordon depicts this Witch as primarily a fortune-teller using cards, but also as one who had psychic abilities. There is nothing in Gordon's description that suggests any religious elements (Pagan or Christian). Why Gordon refers to her specifically as a Witch versus a simple fortune-teller is not made known in the book.

Another fortune-teller Witch, but one who clearly practiced Witchcraft, was a woman named Maddalena Taluti. She lived in Florence, Italy in the late 1800s and was the source of much of the Witchcraft material produced by folklorist Charles Godfrey Leland. His most popular work is titled *Aradia: Gospel of the Witches.*

Maddalena provided Leland with material that demonstrated the connection of Witchcraft to the goddess Diana. It is from her that the figure of Aradia first appears in public writings. Aradia is depicted as Queen of the Witches, Queen of the Faeries, and as a teacher of Witchcraft to suppressed peasants in Feudal Italy.

Another type of Witch that we must note is the one to who people go to for unpleasant resolutions. Often, people with no other resources to turn to for justice, vindication, or even revenge call upon this type of Witch. She deals in what some may call the "Dark Arts," which includes cursing.

Here, we can see that not all Witches adhere to the principle of "Harm None" in their practices of Witchcraft. One law of the Old Craft is this: "We never harm the innocent. We define 'innocent' as someone who does not provoke us. Provoke us and you lose the protection of being innocent because you no longer are."

There were good reasons to fear the Witch throughout the centuries. The average Italian Witch is not a "turn the other cheek" type of Witch.

---

3 Linda Duff Gordon, *Home Life in Italy: Letters from the Apennines* (Methuen, 1908).

One popular folk magick item that has distinct roots in Italian Witchcraft is the Lemon Spell. It can used be used for good or bad, for gain of loss. In old lore, the lemon is the fruit of the Moon. As noted earlier, colored pins are used to place magick in the lemon.

The lemon is divided into different zones. The zone on the left represents a male figure, and the zone on the right denotes a female. A pin marks the subject or subjects of the spell.

The center of the lemon is named to represent the intent of the spell. For example, one can name it "health" or "prosperity," and so on. The center can be divided into different representations as well. The color of the pin is named for what it represents. For example, red can be passion, blue calming, yellow stimulating, and so on. It is your choice. Black pins typically represent a harmful intent. In this light, when receiving a pinned lemon as a gift, always examine it for hidden black pins.

In the Old Custom, threads are tied to the pins, thereby connecting the power/intent of the pins together. This is, in effect, the weaving of the spell, the entanglement of the magick. This is done on either the Dark Moon or Full Moon—a personal choice.

A lesser-known connection of the lemon is that it represents the heart of the person being worked on. It is the "spirit heart," as opposed to the physical heart. The juice of the lemon represents the etheric blood. This usage of the lemon has an effect on the vitality of the person. It was often used either to rid a person of an ailment or to cause an ailment—the idea behind this being what flows out and why.

Another usage of lemon is to cut it in half, then place a symbolic item on one half. The halves are then joined back together, fixed in place with cord or wire, and then roasted over a fire. The magickal idea here is that this puts the intent into the *heart* of the person, and the fire transforms it into reality.

Italian culture absorbed various elements of folk magick and folklore. Even among families that identify as "Catholic," we find magickal practices. One example is the removal of the Evil Eye, which is a curse that brings bad luck or ill health. Another practice is that of hanging various herbs in the kitchen. One old practice is the giving of a rue plant for prosperity and health, which must never be refused, as it will bring calamity. The Lemon Spell we already encountered is also a very common bit of folk magick.

In most cases, such practices do not indicate a practice of Witchcraft per se, but instead often point to continued folk magick practices within the general population. However, some of these practices *are* rooted in Witchcraft. This makes it difficult to discern whether grandma was a Witch, or just a practitioner of Catholic-based sorcery! In Italy, Catholicism clearly adopted magickal ideas about plants, symbols, and charms that have no roots in Christian theology.

Oral tradition tells us that, during the time of the Inquisition, some Witches took on the veneer of Catholicism. This was done in attempt to escape detection and arrest. Part of this deception involved the display of saint imagery. Here, we find that some Witches assigned various saints as veneers to hide the Old Gods behind them. The goddess Diana was painted over to become the Virgin Mary in appearance. This allowed open veneration to continue to take place without fear of ending up in the hands of the Inquisition. In a future chapter, we look at other saint images that disguise the spirits and deities of the Old Religion, Italian Witchcraft.

Being A Witch

Folklorist Charles Leland encountered several Witches during his time in Italy. Maddalena was only one, but, for his writings, she was a particularly important Witch. Leland points out that there are at least a couple of ways to become a Witch. The first is being born into a Witchcraft family—this is called "being of the blood." Another way, he notes, involves studying the things of Witchcraft and keeping the company of Witches.

In modern times, one step to becoming a Strega, or reawakening the Strega within, is to perform the rite of dedication. It is a formal declaration and is one that draws the attention of Otherworld beings that are the forces and intelligences working behind the scenes in Italian Witchcraft. Sometimes, it takes more than one performance to successfully dedicate.

The Rite of Dedication

At midnight, when the Moon is full, go out into an open field or a clearing within the woods, and take with you a vessel of water, another of wine, and a mixing bowl. Take also a small red bag containing a sprig of rue as your amulet and a pinch of salt.

Pour some wine and water into the bowl and add the pinch of salt. Remove your clothing and kneel beneath the Moon. Dip the sprig of rue into the bowl of liquid and anoint yourself with it in the manner of the pentacle: forehead, right nipple, left shoulder, right shoulder, left nipple, forehead.

Then, cup the sprig of rue in your palms and lift it up towards the Moon, saying:

"Hear me O' Diana, Goddess of the Moon,
Queen of all Witches,
for I bear the symbols of The Old Religion.
Hear me then,
and think yet even for a moment
upon this worshipper who kneels before you.

For I have heard the Strega's story,
and I believe the words of the Holy Strega.
When she spoke of your beauty in the night sky,
when she bid us seek and find you above all others.

Here, as the Full Moon shines upon me,
receive me, O' Diana.
Receive me as your child
and grant me the powers of those who follow you.
For I believe in the gifts of Aradia
which you promised to all who follow in the Old Ways."

Anoint yourself again with the rue dipped in the bowl and say:

"Diana, beautiful Diana,
Goddess of the Moon and beyond,
Queen of all Witches,
Goddess of the Dark Night and of all Nature,
if you will grant me your favor
then I ask a token sign from you.

Let there be heard the sound of a dog,
the neigh of a horse,
the croak of a frog,
or the call of a raven."

Anoint yourself a third time with the sprig of rue, saying:

"In the name of Diana,
so may it be."

Gather up the items and place the rue back into the red bag. Sit quietly beneath the Full Moon and listen to the sounds of the night. If you hear any of the sounds requested, then Diana has granted you her favor and you are then one of the Strega. Traditionally, the sound must be heard before the Sun rises. If it was not, then you may try again on the next Full Moon. Sometimes the sound is heard while sitting beneath the Moon, and sometimes it was heard while returning home.

Once you enter into the Ways of the Strega, then the rue sprig is a potent charm that will grant you the powers promised by Aradia. Keep it in a red bag.

Chapter Two

The Divine in Italian Witchcraft

In this chapter, we will explore the two facets of divinity within Italian Witchcraft. One is rooted in pre-Christian Greco-Roman culture, and the other in Italian Catholicism. Some forms of Italian Witchcraft integrate the two together into one system. While they share a common root, there are significant differences. Whether those differences mean that one of them is not truly "Witchcraft" is the primary debate, but not one that we will take on here. Some of the confusion lies in whether or not Witchcraft is just a magickal practice, or a religion that also uses magick.

To gain a wide view and to better understand Italian Witchcraft, let us start at the beginning, meaning let us look at the oldest writings. In the Ancient Greek writings, we find the Witch known as Medea. She is depicted as a priestess of the goddess Hecate. She uses an altar and evokes a variety of primal forces for her magickal spells and rites.

"Night, most faithful keeper of our secret rites;
Stars, that, with the golden moon, succeed the fires of light;
Triple Hecate, you who know all our undertakings,
and come, to aid the witches' art,
and all our incantations:
You, Earth, who yield the sorceress herbs of magic force:
You airs and breezes, pools and hills,
and every watercourse."

What is remarkable about this passage is that captures primal ideas about harnessing the powers of Nature, ideas that were formed in the prehistory of Southern Europe. These are very deep roots to the past. What is most noteworthy for the purposes of this chapter is the depiction of the Witch in a religious role, a priestess of Hecate. As we will see in the appendix for this chapter, Hecate is a goddess that has long been associated with Witches and Witchcraft.

The religious connection continues on over the centuries and is later found in the ancient writings of Horace. He identifies the goddess Diana with Witchcraft, and, when viewing other writers in antiquity, a triformis goddess appears. She is a triple goddess comprised of Hecate, Diana, and Proserpina. Symbolic representations of this triple goddess are found much later in an Italian Witch charm known as the "cimaruta."

On the charm, the Crescent Moon represents Diana. The serpent on the crescent symbolizes Proserpina, an Underworld aspect of the Goddess. The key is symbolic of the goddess Hecate, as one of her depictions is the guardian of gates, doorways, and portals. This connection tied her to the entrance of the Underworld and, later, to a goddess associated with the dead. However, in her earliest appearance in ancient literature, she is a goddess who grants victory, success, and abundance.

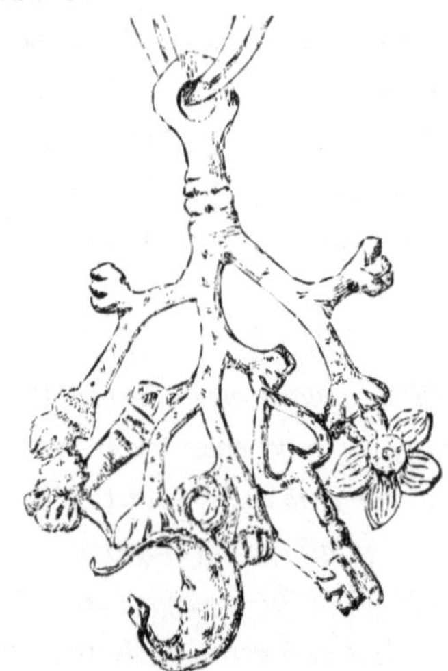

With the rise of Christianity, things begin to drastically change. In the early centuries, the Church tried to crush the worship of Diana. Church sermons were directed against involvement with goddess, and a Church law known as the "Canon Episcopi" (written in the tenth century) essentially outlaws the Cult of Diana.[4] The doctrine contained within this canon teaches that Diana is a false image used by the Devil to trick people into worshipping him.

In the seventeenth century, we find the writings of Girolamo Tartarotti, who holds the view that Witchcraft is the survival of the ancient Cult of Diana.[5] He is admonished by the Church, which teaches that Witches worship the Devil, and Tartarotti is forced to write a retraction. This comes in the form of a book titled *Apologia*

4 "Canon Episcopi," *Council of Ancyra* (314 BC).

5 Girolamo Tartarotti, *Del Congresso Notturno delle Lammie: Of the Nightly Meeting of Witches* (Giambatista Pasquali, 1749).

del Congresso Notturno delle Lammie.[6] Once Diana is successfully removed from Witchcraft, the religious element continues on throughout the Middle Ages and Renaissance periods in the erroneous form of Devil worship.

We know that Europe had no personification of evil in pre-Christian times, and that Satan was an import into Europe from the Middle East. For the majority of Witches, the Devil had little appeal. What did have appeal is the "Cult of Saints," which embraced patron saints that had a variety of influences or powers. This theme was not unlike the Pagan idea of spirits that served in the same way. During the era of persecution by the Inquisition, it was much safer to venerate saints than to venerate the Old Gods. According to oral tradition, some families keep the veneer, while others, over the course of time, moved on to worship the saints. In this, the connection to Paganism became all but lost, and Catholic-based practices moved in to fill the void.

There are a variety of saints who became the outer form for the Old Gods. Some popular examples are Saint Francis (the veneer for the Lord of Animals), Saint John Gualbert (veneer for woodland grove spirit), and Saint Giles (veneer for the Lord of the Woods). Various forms of the Madonna or Virgin Mary were also popular. Some are veneers for Artemis, while others are veneers for ancient Mother figures.

One old Witches' code for Marian symbolism is tied to the clothing worn by Saint Mary. When she is depicted with roses, she is the Goddess of Love. If standing upon a crescent, she is the Moon Goddess, and when wearing a cloak with stars imprinted, she is the Celestial Goddess. When depicted holding an infant, she is the Great Mother who gives birth to the Sun.

In modern times, we also find Saint Barbara as Athena and, on the somewhat darker side, we find Saint Marta Dominadora. She is usually called upon to stop another person from harassing or harming someone. Saint Marta is also called upon to stop gossip, lies, backstabbing, and slander.

---

6 Girolamo Tartarotti, *Apologia del Congresso Notturno delle Lammie: Apology for The Nightly Meeting of the Witches* (Presso Simone Occhi, 1751).

Some Italian Witches also call upon the Archangels: Uriel, Raphael, Michael, and Gabriel. They are often called upon for protection and, in some systems, they are evoked to guard the four directions: North, East, South, and West.

Among the lesser-known workings with saint-figures is the connection to the rose. The rose has long been a symbol of the Inner Mysteries, secrecy, and mystical revelation. It is no surprise that this Ancient Pagan-era symbolic flower found its way into the Christian Mythos. From this arose within Catholicism such figures as "Our Lady of the Roses" and "Rosa Mystica" (the latter is of particular significance). The earliest tale relates how, on a snowy winter's day, a female figure appeared to a peasant man and produced a rose growing from beneath the snow.

The rose is a very old symbol of relationship, connection, and bestowment. This is still reflected in the modern custom of giving roses to loved ones. Roses are also given to confirm an earned success (one example being a beauty contest). They are also typically present at a wedding. All of this speaks to a special connection to a person or an event.

Secret societies in the past (and in the present) used the rose as a symbol of secrecy. The Ancient Latin phrase *sub-rosa,* which translates to "beneath the rose," means "to remain silent." Members of secret societies kneel beneath a rose to take an oath of initiation. This is one of the things that connect the rose to mystical themes.

In Witchcraft, roses have been used for dream-working purposes that grant access to inner worlds. In this light, the rose is a type of key that opens portals to other realities. This also makes the rose a mystical symbol and, by extension, we can connect it with the Divine. One way is to see the rose as a meeting place between us and the Divine. In this way, you can use an image of the Divine without personifying it. Through this view, you can be neutral between a Pagan connection and a Christian connection.

One technique that is useful (when not wishing to connect to a cultural representation) is to set up a shrine or an altar to the basic concept of the Divine. Later on, you may wish to choose a personification, but, for now, a symbolic connection can serve the same function. Simply designate an area for the sole purpose of veneration. Place a rose in a vase on the center of the area, and place a candle in front of it. Place an incense holder to one side of the rose, and have some rose incense available. You can later add other items that you feel drawn to, but, for now, just use the rose, candle, and incense.

When you want to establish a connection, light the candle and incense and gaze upon the rose for a few moments. When you feel ready, speak these words:

"Symbol of the Divine,
mystical rose,
embrace me with your essence,
encircle me with your fragrant spirit,
blossom my mind, body, and spirit with your unfolding,
and impart to me your greater vision."

Touch the rose with the fingertips of your left hand, then touch your forehead and heart. This is an affirmation. Remain with the rose for a few moments.

You may or may not ever want to formally attach a religious or spiritual nature to your Witchcraft, but this simple alignment with the rose symbol keeps your options open.

Chapter Three

Between the Worlds

In the Old Religion of Italy, the world of spirits and elementals was believed to overlap with that of humankind. A portal or doorway was believed to exist at the point in which these two worlds touched. It was, in effect, a place between the worlds. This secret place was considered to be magickal, transcending the laws of mundane nature. Here, anything and everything was possible.

In the cosmology of the ancients in Italy, the portal was set in the northeast direction. The Temple of the goddess Diana was built on the northeast shore of Lake Nemi, in the Alban Hills east of Rome. Here, it marked the meeting place of the two worlds. The reflection of the Full Moon upon the lake could be seen from the temple as the Moon ascended the hills. In association with the reflection of the Moon, the lake came to be known as "Diana's Mirror."

In Ancient Italian Witchcraft, ritual circles were created by Diana's Witches, which symbolized the lake and its magickal orientation. The ritual circle also symbolized the Full Moon drawn down to the Earth. The entrance to the circle was established in the northeast quarter, and all celebrants entered and exited the ritual circle through that point.

According to oral tradition, on the site of Lake Nemi, Watchtowers were set among the hills at the four cardinal points of the compass: North, East, South, and West. These served to observe not only the rising and setting of the Moon, but also the patterns of the stars. The movement of torch signs passed signals to the priestesses at the temple below, announcing the Moon's position on the horizon (the Temple of Diana was surrounded by hills). This allowed them time to make the necessary preparations for the ritual observance at the first appearance of the Moon.

The religious focus of this tradition at Nemi was upon the goddess Diana and her consort. The tradition practiced at Nemi evolved from an earlier cult that originated in the northern region of Tuscany. This earlier cult worshipped the goddess Uni and her consort Tinia. The universe over which they ruled was comprised of sixteen "houses" (four in each of the four quarters). The Gods of Destiny dwelled in the North. In the East were the major Gods, in the South dwelled the astral entities, and in the West were the beings of the Underworld. Tinia and Uni also ruled over a hierarchy of powerful spirits that exerted power and influence over the Earth.

The following is a list of the Old Gods of Tuscany and their Roman correspondences:

Tuscan	**Greek/Roman**
Teramo	Mercury
Nortia	Fortuna
Aplu	Apollo
Losna	Diana/Luna
Turanna	Venus
Pano	Pan
Maso	Mars
Silviano	Silvanus
Esta	Vesta
Sentiero	Terminus

Tuscan	Greek/Roman
Faflon	Bacchus
Tesana	Aurora
Spulviero	Aeolus
Fanio	Faunus
Alpena	Flora
Tituno	Vulcan
Verbio	Verbius
Dusio	Eros
Jano	Janus
Meana	Fata

Over the centuries, with the collapse of the Etruscan Empire and the eventual rise of Christianity, the Old Gods of the Etruscans dwindled. Among the rustics, these former gods eventually came to be regarded as powerful spirits. They were evoked for many purposes and became part of a peasant religion. The lore associated with this peasant religion became part of everyday life in Tuscany, where Witchcraft traditions survived the changes that influenced a great many regions. The lore of Tuscany is so pervasive that even the average Catholic in Italy possesses some degree of it.

In the peasant tradition of Tuscany, Teramo is a messenger spirit who is evoked to carry requests and send spells. Losna is the spirit of the Moon and is evoked to aid in all works of magick. Turanna has influence over matters of love. Among the rustics, everything outside the mundane is the result of either a spirit's or a Witch's action. There is one reason why everyday life incorporates ties to the Old Ways.

In Italian Witchcraft, the basic elemental forces are revered, and conscious entities are associated with the seemingly magickal properties of the elements. Likewise, Nature is viewed filled with spirits that inhabit objects and places. The Fauni and Silvani are spirits of the woods, the Falletto are wind spirits, the Monachetto are Gnome-like spirits, and the Linchetto are Elf-like spirits.

In Tuscan Witchcraft, the North Quarter is a place of great power. The elemental beings of the North are called Pali. In the South are the Settiani, who are spirits of Elemental Fire. In the West, there are the Manii, who are spirits of Elemental Water. In the East are the Bellari, viewed in their original concept as Nature spirits, overseeing productivity and fertility. Through the interaction of all of these beings, vegetation flourishes, rains fall, and life cycles continue. These spirits are the inner forces of Nature.

Closely linked to the belief in these spirits is a large tradition of magickal cures, incantations, spells, and rites for attracting love, banishing evil, and assuring physical comforts. All of these have been passed down through old family lines where the belief that Witches are born again to their descendants is quite strong. Even though non-Witches know portions of the lore, hereditary Witch clans closely guard the secrets of the practical art.

It was in the region of Old Tuscany that Aradia, a legendary teacher of the Old Religion, was born. According to legend, she was taught the Old Religion from a very early age by her aunt and grew up in the consciousness of a different world. Hers was a world steeped in the Witch lore of Tuscany, a world that allowed her the freedom to explore the inner and outer realities. In time, she came to be called "the Holy Strega."

Assured of her future and having found favor with the Old Gods, Aradia founded covens in the Alban Hills region near the ancient Lake of Nemi. It was here that Aradia blended her own spirituality with her understanding of the Old Ways. In time, she brought about a revival of the Old Religion, which embraced peasant and noble alike. A likely historical reference to such an event can be found in the sixteenth century writings of the Italian Inquisitor Bernardo Rategno.

In his work titled *Tractatus de Strigibus* (written in 1508 AD), Rategno writes that a "rapid expansion" of the "Witches sect" had begun 150 years prior to his time.[7] Rategno studied many transcripts from the trials of the Inquisition concerning Witchcraft. Tracing back over the years, he pinpointed the beginnings of the Witch trials and noted their sharp increase over a period of years. Following a thorough study of these records (kept in the Archives of the Inquisition at Como, Italy), Rategno fixed the time of this Witches' revival somewhere around 1358, the latter half of the fourteenth century.

The Otherworld

In the cosmology of Italian Witchcraft, there are three Realms of Existence: The Overworld, Middleworld, and Underworld. The Overworld is the sky and starry heavens. The Middleworld is the Realm of Mortal Kind, and the Underworld is the dimension that lies beyond. It is often referred to as the Otherworld, which consists of the faery or elven lands and the Realm of the Spirits of the Dead.

The image of a tree is used to symbolize the three Realms seen as one manifestation of existence, although they exist on different levels and, therefore, in different dimensions.

The upper branches of the tree extend into the Overworld and represent the Celestial Realm. The trunk of the tree symbolizes the Material World where the mineral, plant, and animal "kingdoms" manifest in solid form. Beneath the trunk, we see the roots that extend into the Faery or Elven Realm, the magickal Otherworld of myth and legend. Beneath this is the Underworld, the Realm of the Spirits of the Dead. It is here that departed spirits from the Material Realm pass and reside until they reincarnate or rise into the Overworld. In some cases, they may reside in the Faery Realm (depending upon rapport and alignment with this dimension).

According to legend, there was time long ago when mortals and the immortals had direct contact in the Middleworld. This theme is remembered in the symbol of the faery door on the trunk

7 Bernardo Rategno, *Tractatus de Strigibus,* 1508.

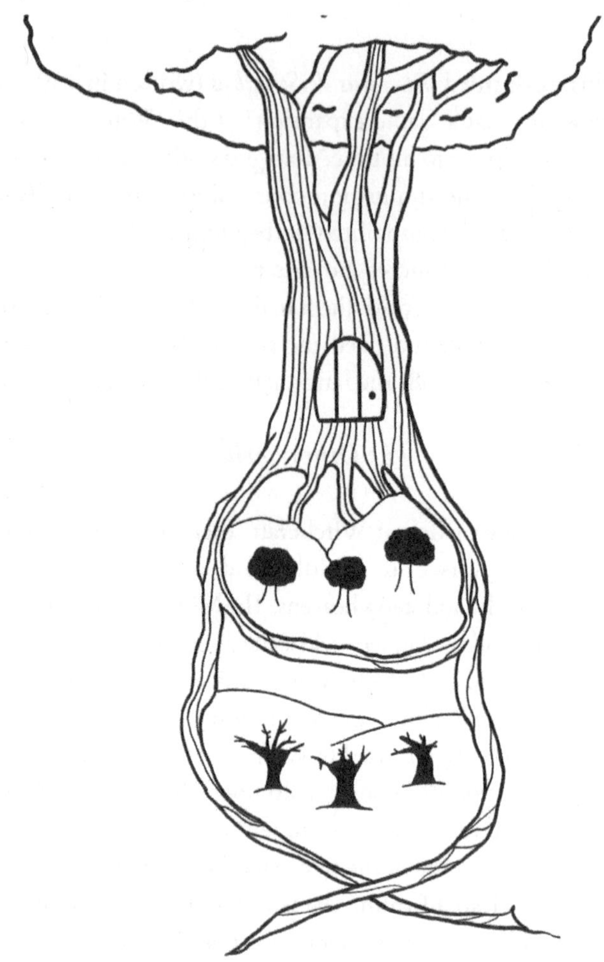

of the tree, which represents the doorway to and from the worlds. As humankind withdrew from Nature and began to create cities, viewing the natural world as solely a resource, the portal between the worlds began to thicken and close. In time, the memories of those beings from the Otherworld faded into the distorted tales of legend. As the saying goes, history became myth, myth became legend, and that which should have never been lost was lost. The world slipped into shadow, and humans hacked down the trees, tunneled into the earth, spread their civilization in all directions, and tried to become the masters of Nature. But, in the deep woods, hills, and meadows that remained, the Old Spirits continued on, companioned by the Witch who shunned the cities and lived among the herb-clad hills.

The Lasa and Lare

In the Old Religion of Italy, there are certain spirits called the Lasa who are both protectors and preservers of the Old Ways. In Roman mythology, they were later called "Lare" and were viewed as ancestral spirits who guarded both home and family. Upon the hearth of each home, a small Lare shrine (or "house") was placed. Each Lare shrine had a receptacle for offerings, which consisted of wine, honey, milk, and flowers.

The focal point of a family is their home and, in ancient times, the focal point of a house was the hearth (the Latin word *hearth* means "focus"; the hearth held the fire that provided heat and was the area where meals were prepared). A prayer was said to the Lare every morning, and special offerings were made at family festivals. These spirits were originally gods of the cultivated fields, worshipped by each household at the crossroads where its allotment joined those of others. Later, they were worshipped in the home, and the household Lar (singular of Lare) was viewed as the center of the family and the familial cult. The image of the Lar was usually a youthful figure dressed in a short tunic, holding in one hand a drinking horn, and in the other a cup.

As noted in Chapter One: "A Look at Italian Witchcraft," the Lare were originally Guardians of demarcations, an association that originated with the establishment of plots of farmland. The connection of the Lare to the fields is rooted in Etruscan religion, a concept drawn by the Romans. In early Etruscan times, these spirits were called the "Lasa," which were spirits of uncultivated fields. There is evidence to conclude that the Lasa were most likely associated with spirits of the dead as well. In Tuscany, the name Lasa still applies to various spirits.

In Italian Witchcraft, the Lare represent not only ancestral ties, but are spirits who protect and preserve the Old Religion (as well as its followers). The Lare element contributed to the survival of the Old Religion during the violent persecution of Witches in the period of the Inquisition. This is due, in part, because the Lare maintain a strong family connection, and this aided the hereditary Witches of Italy to retain a cohesive Tradition down through the centuries. Generation after generation has remembered and honored the previous generations, passing on the ancient traditions of the Old Religion.

Even today, among the mainstream populace, some elements of the Ancient Witches' sect still exist in popular folk magick and folk healing traditions. The Italian tradition of the good Witch Befana who fills stockings hung on the hearth is a living remnant of the Old Religion. It is interesting to note that children write their wishes upon bits of paper that they place in the hearth fire to be carried up the chimney (connecting Fire, Lare, and Befana).

For the purposes of this lesson, there is the preparation of a Lasa shrine and a Lare house. Those of you who are of Italian heritage will most likely wish to construct a Lare house. Those of you who are not of Italian heritage will most likely wish to construct a Lasa shrine. The Lare house will connect Italians with the Pagan current emanating from pre-Christian Southern European religion through their own family lines. A Lasa shrine will connect anyone with the essence of the Old Ways, stemming from Southern European Paganism, regardless of ethnic background.

Lare are invoked on all important family occasions, such as departures, marriages, births, and funerals. Traditionally, on such occasions, their shrines are decorated with a garland, and offerings of incense, fruit, and wine are placed before the shrine. A new bride, in Roman times, when carried across the threshold of her new home, gave offerings to the Lare and placed a coin upon the shrine.

Preparation of a Lare House or Lasa Shrine

Select a suitable shrine structure in which to house the Lare or Lasa spirits. Place it upon a wall (or over a mantle) in the West or East alignment of the home. Set an image to represent the spirit within the opening of the temple structure (doorway/portal). Set a small offering bowl upon the ledge of shrine and, next to this, place an uncooked fava bean (if selecting a Lare house) or a sprig of rue, a key, and some salt (if selecting a Lasa shrine).

Light some incense of pine, sandalwood, or a similar "earthy" scent. Pass the smoke beneath the shrine so that the smoke rises up through and around the shrine. While doing this, say:

"Spirits of the Ether, awaken,
gather the Ancient Ones here,
who were of Old called (Lare/Lasa).
Bless this shrine in the names of (give deity names of god & goddess),
As it was in the time of our beginning,
so is it now,
so shall it be."

At this point, the shrine has been blessed and consecrated. Give an offering to the spirits, placing it within the offering bowl. Sit quietly before the shrine and visualize a small, soft blue light around the Lare or Lasa image. In time, you will actually see this light come and go within the shrine and, perhaps, there may be even more than just a single light. This is assuming that you give an offering at each Full Moon and all family occasions, such as birthdays, marriages, and so forth. Light a candle each time you sit before the shrine. Make requests or ask for assistance in personal matters; work to establish a rapport.

Chapter Four

Making Contact

In the previous chapter, we looked at the "Otherworldly" aspects of spirits and deities. It is from these dimensions (and their associated beings) that we can draw upon power with which to work our magick and also empower our rites. It is therefore essential to learn the techniques through which we can establish rapport with various spirits and deities and, thus, be able to call upon them for assistance. In a mundane sense, we know that we must have a rapport with friends and family in order to ask for favors and help in general. This is also the case in our relationships with non-physical beings.

In Italian Witchcraft, the spirit flame is one of the main tools used to make contact with the non-physical dimensions. Essentially, it is used to connect with Divinity and, once properly prepared, it represents the presence of Divine Consciousness. Another tool used to connect with Divinity (as well as with the inner-divine nature of anything) is the Rite of Union. This chapter contains information on both of these tools so that you can use them for your own spiritual development.

Essentially, the spirit flame and the Rite of Union are methods of interfacing with the source from which the Divine Spark within you was generated. Both are outward expressions of an inner experience. The physical aspects are the means of mental focus and emotional investment, both of which are necessary to bring about the spiritual connection. This is an aspect of the Law of Three, which declares that a three-fold manifestation must take place in order for the material and physical domains to join.

The Law of Three also addresses the invocation of mind, body, and spirit. One act causes a triple manifestation. For example, if you perform an act of kindness for another person, it makes you feel good. What happens biologically is that your endocrine system secretes "reward" chemicals that cause a feeling of elation, which results in a mental and physical sense of well-being (what some people describe as an "inner warm glow"). When the mind and body are feeling good, this affects the state of the indwelling spirit or soul. Therefore, from one single act, there arises a three-fold response. The same is true of performing an act that is unkind, and, from this, arises a negative three-fold response. In either case, the mind, body, and soul are affected.

Italian Spirits

In Italian folklore, the non-physical world is populated by a host of beings, along with the various gods. They are introduced here in this section out of a love of Italian folklore. The following are some of the Nature spirits commonly associated with old Italy. Here, we shall examine some of the Elven class of spirits known as "the Massariol," "the Fauni," and "the Silvani." In Italy, the latter of these are what we group together as "the goat people." The Fauni are field spirits having power over animals. The Silvani are Elves who guard herd animals, as well as house and land boundaries. These Elves appear rather Pan-like and have very large genitals. The goat people prefer light, airy woods and fields and can best be seen when breezes move through the vegetation. They are not unfriendly to humans (unless they abuse animals), but are known to be somewhat mischievous.

The Massariol are known as "the little farmers." They are about a foot high and dress in red costume, including a large hat. Massariol usually spend their time in gardens and barnyards, caring for plants and animals. The male Elves have a certain fancy for human women and sometimes change into grooming articles in order to be close to their bodies. The Massariol have a cheerful disposition and are helpful to humans.

The Italian Fata are spirits of the woods and water. They are beautiful, gentle, and kind. The Fata are excellent shapeshifters and often appear as old men or women. Sometimes, they will change into young women or various small animals. There are many stories in which someone stopped to help an old woman or an animal, only to discover a Fata. Those who helped a Fata in disguise were richly rewarded, but anyone who was cruel risked their health and fortune.

The Lauru is a Folletto spirit with twinkling black eyes, long, curly hair, and clothes of fine velvet. They tend to be somewhat mischievous and enjoy teasing human children. When treated with respect, the Lauru may reveal hidden treasures or supply the winning lottery numbers. Like most Italian spirits, the males love human women and seek to seduce them (usually in dreams). According to peasant folklore, a pair of a ram or bull's horns, when hung over a doorway, will keep the Lauru away.

All Folletto travel in the wind and can be seen at play causing swirls in the dust (or "knots of winds" in Italian). They are said to be somewhat like butterflies and are almost always moving about. Traditionally, the Folletto are friendly towards humans, but can be mischievous and annoying at times. It is not uncommon for the Folletto to lift up a woman's dress in the wind or knock over objects with a sudden gust. They are magickal beings and have a particular attraction to sexual situations. In Northern Italy, certain Folletto are called the *Basadone* ("woman-kisser") and are known to steal kisses from women with a passing breeze. The female spirit is known as a "Folletti," which is also the term for the group as a whole.

Another type of Folletto is a spirit called the "Linchetto." Actually, they belong to the Elven race and are specifically Night Elves. Linchetto are native to the Tuscan region of Italy, which was the Old Etruscan Kingdom. These Elves are said to cause nightmares and noises in the night. Linchetto are said to hate disorder and will not dwell in any such element. One old technique to drive away the Linchetto was to spill seeds upon the floor, surrounding the bed. The Night Elf would come and try to pick up the seeds, usually leaving in frustration. Another technique was to place a lock of curly hair over the bed. The Linchetto would try all night to straighten it, then flee in despair.

The Charm of the Stone

In the old Witch lore, we find a spell involving a round stone. If the stone has a hole through its center, then it is particularly potent. According to this lore, the stone brings good fortune to whoever finds one and carries it upon the body. A spell to invoke a helpful spirit to abide with the stone is part of the tradition.

Upon obtaining the stone, the person looks up into the sky and tosses the stone up three times (catching it with each toss). Next, the following words are spoken:

"Spirit of good auspice,
who I call to aid me,
know I had great need of you.
Spirit of the Red Fairy,
because you come to aid me in my need,
I pray you not abandon me:
I beseech you to enter now this stone,
so I may carry you with me,
and when anything is needed by me,
I can call upon you: be what it may,
and do not abandon me by night or day.
And in the morning, when all spirits go to their repose,
return here to take your rest in this stone.
I pray you abide here as your home,
and always grant me good fortune and success.
In my pocket I shall keep safe this stone,
and you and I will share good company in the days ahead."

Exercises for Establishing Rapport

To begin the work of establishing rapport, you should begin with the Rite of Union. To do this, you must find a temple-style image designed to work as a "portal" upon which you can place whatever symbol you wish to "commune" with. For example, if you wish to establish a rapport with one of the Folletto, then you simply copy or print such image and trim it to fit between the pillars of the temple.

Place the temple drawing on a wall and perform the Rite of Union while facing the composite image.

Pictures of a god or goddess can also be employed in this manner, as can anything with which you desire to establish rapport. Using the portal with an image is also excellent for simple meditation or devotional work. Later, you will use the portal as a doorway to your Astral Temple, which you will construct in a future chapter. The Rite of Union should also be performed to the spirit flame, which can also be used for meditation and devotional work.

Offerings to spirits and deities are also an important element of establishing rapport. In this chapter, you will find a format for offerings. The most time-honored offerings consisted of grains, wine, cakes, or a mixture known as "nectar."

The Grigori

In Italian Witchcraft, the entities who guard the ritual circle's portals are known as "the Grigori." According to oral tradition, this word is an archaic dialect, a form related to the Modern Italian word *grigi* or *grigiastro,* which means "gray" or "grayish." This comes from an ancient legend in which the Grigori appear in a gray mist or fog. In this sense, the Grigori can be referred to as the "Gray Ones."

In Aegean/Mediterranean lore, the color gray is often associated with wisdom. One example is the Graea, who were three sisters born with gray hair. With each passing year, the sisters grew in wisdom. Some commentators believe they are the prototype for the Witch figure in ancient tales. Hesiod first mentions them in his poem called "Theogony," where the sisters are depicted as wise and beautiful. It is interesting to note that the earliest Witches to appear in ancient writings of Southern Europe are young beautiful women such as Circe and Medea. The idea of an ugly and elderly Witch does not arise until close to the Christian era.

In essence, the Grigori are beings that guard the portals that link the worlds together, and they are sometimes referred to as "the Watchers." They are viewed as a spiritual race that once existed in physical form, but have since evolved into beings of energy. The Grigori are associated with the four quarters: North, East, South, and

West. In this regard, they are also associated with the four elements of Earth, Air, Fire, and Water. They are not, however, elemental spirits or beings. They are also linked to each solstice and equinox, as well as to a specific star.

In the early stellar cults of Mesopotamia, there were four "royal" stars (known as "Lords") which were called "the Watchers." The Star Aldebaran, when it marked the Vernal Equinox, held the position of Watcher of the East. Regulus, marking the Summer Solstice, was Watcher of the South. Antares, marking the Autumn Equinox, was Watcher of the West. Fomalhaut, marking the Winter Solstice, was Watcher of the North. Today, each one of these stars is said to "rule" over one of the four fixed signs common to Astrology: Aldebaran—Taurus, Antares—Scorpio, Regulus—Leo, Fomalhaut—Aquarius.

In Charles Leland's book *Aradia; Gospel of the Witches,* he recounts the tale of "The Children of Diana, or how the fairies were born" in which it is stated that Diana created "the great spirits of the stars."[8] In another legend titled "How Diana made the Stars and the Rain," Leland writes that Diana went "to the fathers of the Beginning, to the mothers, the spirits who were before the first spirit."[9] Italian Witches believe that the Grigori are such an ancient race, and this reference may well speak of them.

The Grigori are ritually evoked at the cardinal points of the ritual circle: North, East, South, and West. Here, they guard and witness the rites performed before them. In the first-degree initiation ceremony, the new initiate is taken to the four quarters and formally introduced to each of the Grigori. Each of the quarters is envisioned as a Watchtower guarded by the Grigori. The concept of the Grigori may be an expanded view of archaic beliefs connected to the Lare spirits.

As noted in Chapter One: "A Look at Italian Witchcraft," in archaic Roman religion, small towers were built at the crossroads, and an altar was set before the Lare. Offerings were given to these spirits of the crossroads. The Lare were associated with these towers and with demarcation in general, as well as seasonal themes related

8 Charles Godfrey Leland, *Aradia, Gospel of the Witches* (David Nutt, 1899) 121.

9 Leland, *ibid.* 18.

to agriculture. As also noted, the ancient writer Ovid referred to the Lare as the "Night Watchmen" (which strongly suggests a connection between the Lare and the Grigori as Watchers).

Grigori Alignments

One method of establishing a connection with the Grigori is to create an inner alignment. This can be accomplished through the performance of ritual postures. The magickal principle of "like attracts like" is at the core of this exercise. To perform the alignment, use the following postures to guide you in how to stand at each quarter. Use the guided mental imagery given with each posture in the following sections.

It should be noted that Grigori are without male or female gender. However, because the Italian language assigns gender to individual words, the names of the Grigori appear as though they are male and female names. To think of them in this way has no basis in their nature.

TAGO is the name of the Grigori of the Northern Gate. The posture is one of solidity, strength, and foundation. To begin your alignment, stand facing North. Take up the position pictured here as you stand:

Speak the name of the Grigori out loud. Once you have spoken the name, close your eyes and picture the base of a rocky cliff. As you see this in your mind's eye, picture that the face of the cliff opens and from inside emerges the Grigori, who then stands before you in the same exact position as your body. Remain silent, bow you head, and place the palm of your left hand over your heart. Speak the name Tago once again. Wait a few moments and allow yourself to receive whatever communication may come from Tago. When you are ready, lower your left hand down to your side, and picture the Grigori returning back into the base of the cliff.

BELLARIA is the name of the Grigori of the Eastern Gate. The posture is one of weightlessness, elevation, and transmission. To begin your alignment, stand facing East. Take up the position pictured here as you stand:

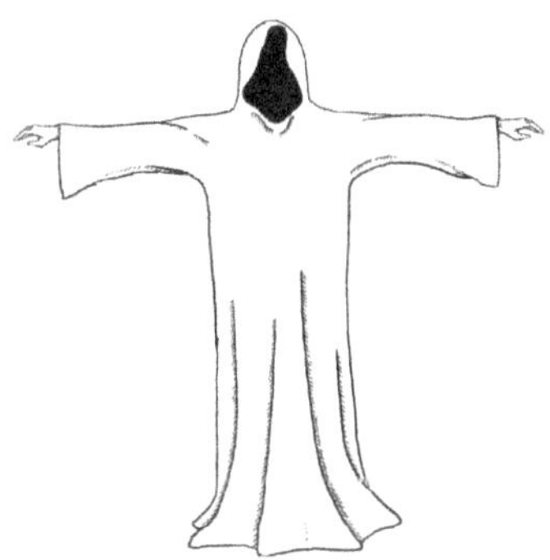

Speak the name of the Grigori out loud; once you have spoken the name, close your eyes and picture yourself on top of a rocky cliff with the wind blowing against your body. As you see this in your mind's eye, a large cloud approaches, and from inside emerges the Grigori, who then stands before you in the same exact position as your body. Remain silent, bow your head, and place the palm of your left hand over your heart. Speak the name Bellaria once again. Wait a few moments and allow yourself to receive whatever communication may come from Bellaria. When you are ready, lower your left hand down to your side, and picture the Grigori returning back into the cloud.

SETTRANO is the name of the Grigori of the Southern Gate. The posture is one of force, vitality, and transformation. To begin your alignment, stand facing South. Take up the position pictured here as you stand:

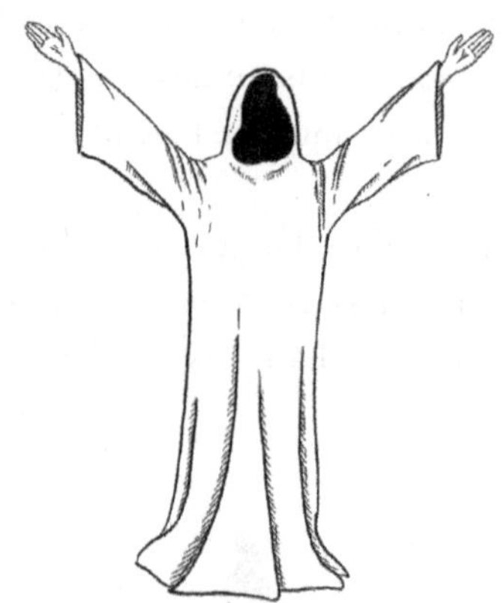

Speak the name of the Grigori out loud. Once you have spoken the name, close your eyes and picture a pit in front of a rocky cliff. As you see this in your mind's eye, picture that, from the pit, a blast of fire rises up in front of you. From inside the flames emerges the Grigori, who then stands before you in the same exact position as your body. Remain silent, bow you head, and place the palm of your left hand over your heart. Speak the Settrano once again. Wait a few moments and allow yourself to receive whatever communication may come from Settrano. When you are ready, lower your left hand down to your side, and picture the Grigori returning back into the fire.

MEANA is the name of the Grigori of the Western Gate. The posture is one of depth, reception, and inner-movement. To begin your alignment, stand facing West. Take up the position pictured here as you stand:

Speak the name of the Grigori out loud; once you have spoken the name, close your eyes and picture the base of a rocky cliff that meets the ocean. As you see this in your mind's eye, picture a wave crashing against cliff and, from inside the foam, emerges the Grigori, who then stands before you in the same exact position as your body. Remain silent, bow you head, and place the palm of your left hand over your heart. Speak the Meana once again. Wait a few moments and allow yourself to receive whatever communication may come from Meana. When you are ready, lower your left hand down to your side, and picture the Grigori returning back into the waves.

Numen and Mana–The Occult Power Within

According to the ancient teachings, there dwells within all objects a conscious power known as the *numen,* which, in archaic Roman religion, was an indwelling consciousness. In some non-Italian traditions, this is referred to as "mana," although, in actuality, mana is not quite the same thing as numen. The two are similar, except regarding consciousness as a sentient being. Mana is traditionally viewed as a type of raw energy or force that may be collected and employed for magickal purposes. Numen is an indwelling force that is both energy and consciousness together. Numen has an "awareness" of both itself and its surroundings. It is numen that gives a place that certain "feel," and it is numen which responds within an object when it "feels" right to the touch (such as a person experiences when choosing a crystal or some other tool).

When ancient occultists established the magickal correspondences commonly associated today with herbs, crystals, and other material forms, it was the emanation of specific indwelling numen that caused them to make those connections. This is why herbs and crystals can possess certain magickal properties; it is the power of their numen spirit. The numen must be communicated with, usually through visual imagery and/or tonal sounds (vibration), in order to establish the link necessary to employ the numen's power. Otherwise, all you end up with is a pretty lump of mineral formation and a pile of dead plant material.

In essence, the *numen* can be thought of as "the Divine Spark" within all matter. It is not, however, a living soul or spirit unto itself, but simply a reflection of Divine Consciousness. In some respects, it may be thought of as a "Divine Imprint" or a "contagious" energy-form left by the hand of the "Source of All Things." Mana, on the other hand, is more like radiation or heat emanating from an object—void of independent action and limited to its effect upon other objects by proximity.

It is one of the arts of Witchcraft to pass mental images (thought-forms) into the numen, so that a magickal rapport is established between the Witch and the crystal or herb, etc. Once this is done, then the object may be employed according to the desire or need of the Witch, as is customary with spellcasting and the like. For herbs, it is best to start with the seed and continue with the mental imagery as the sprout appears and the plant grows to fullness.

In this way, the numen of the herb can form and condense the necessary magickal effect that is desired of it. For crystal work, one must first awaken the crystal before passing mental images to it, or the effect is weakened and the "charge" is diminished in length. Traditionally, the crystal is tapped with a stone (or another crystal) three times while gazing upon the Full Moon in order to awaken it. The term "awaken" in context with this article means to align it to the person who possesses the crystal. During an initiation ceremony, the initiator can tap the initiate's crystal with their own crystal three times, and can then "pass the power" to the initiate in the final stages of the initiation. There is a certain beauty in possessing a crystal that has received the "charge" from an initiator's crystal (whose own crystal received it from another, and so on).

The Spirit Flame

In Italian Witchcraft, the focal point of the altar is called the *spirit flame.* A bowl is placed upon the center of the altar and is filled with a special liquid, which will burn with a blue flame. The appearance of the blue flame represents the presence of Divinity within the ritual setting. The use of fire as a sacred symbol is one of the most ancient of practices.

In ancient times, fire was a mysterious force. It provided warmth and protection, and was an extremely valuable possession. When people lived in villages and towns, crude lamps were used to provide light. Fuel for these lamps was expensive and, therefore, had to be used sparingly. Light was only present at night for short periods and was a time for family gathering. Today, with the convenience of modern lighting, it is difficult to appreciate how precious light (and heat) can really be. In time, light became a symbol of all that was positive in human life.

Aradia associated the flame as the "soul" of the Old Religion. Among her followers, the spirit flame image became a symbol of the Old Ways. Even today, its symbol appears as a sacred sign of our religion.

It is an essential part of setting up the altar, and prescribed gestures and words of evocation are used to empower it as a vessel for Divine presence. Traditionally, the bowl that will bear the flame is placed upon the pentacle. The four elemental tools are then placed around the bowl to each of the cardinal positions. The altar candles, which represent the God and Goddess, are set to the far left and right corners of the altar. Together, with the spirit flame, they will form a triangle of light.

To experience the spirit flame, try the following: obtain some good quality cologne (or Strega liqueur) and pour it in a small bottle, preferably of green glass, and set it out under the Full Moon for several hours (three is fine). Be sure that the bottle is well sealed. When you bring it in, pour some of it out into a small bowl, filling it about halfway. Extinguish all lights, then trace a circle over the bowl to symbolize the Full Moon with your ritual knife, then a Waxing and Waning Crescent Moon, and say:

"In the name of Great Goddess
and by these sacred signs,
be thy essence of magick!"

Now the fluid is ready to ignite. When you light it, say:

"Anima antiquus excitare."

A beautiful blue flame will gently appear and dance upon the surface of the liquid. Now, simply sit and look upon the flame. Do not extinguish it, but allow it to go out on its own. Experience it. The flame can be used to bless objects and empower tools by passing them through the flame three times. Feel free to experiment with it, but remember to treat it with respect, for it is a sacred essence.

The Rite of Union

This rite is performed to the sunrise in adoration of the God (through observance of His symbol) and to the Full Moon in adoration to the Goddess (through observance of Her symbol). It may also be done at any other time which you feel "union" would be appropriate.

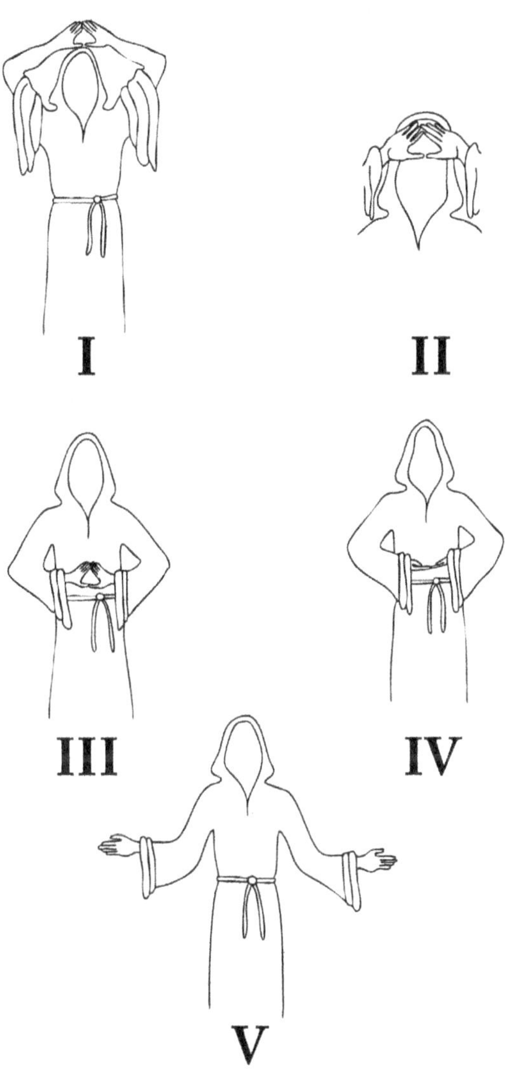

Standing or kneeling before the Light (or symbol), raise hands as in position one, saying:

"Hail and adoration unto Thee O' Source of All Enlightenment. I pray Thee impart to me Thy Illumination."

Lower arms to position two, saying:

"And enlighten my mind that I may perceive more clearly all things in which I endeavor."

Lower arms to position three, saying:

"And illuminate my soul, imparting Thy essence of Purity."

Lower arms to positions four and five, saying:

"I reveal my Inner Self to Thee and ask that all be cleansed and purified within."

Offerings

The following is one of the ancient ways in which offerings were made to the Goddess of the Moon. If you would like to perform this timeless offering, then proceed as described.

First, an offering of any white woodland-type flower was placed before the statue of the Goddess. The classic statue was the image of a beautiful woman carrying a bow and quiver of arrows with a dog at her feet. Upon her forehead, she wore a headband with a Waxing Crescent Moon upon it. Next, a wreath of these flowers was made and placed upon her head, like a crown.

Then, the invocation was given (English translation of the original Italian):

"Beautiful Goddess of the bow, beautiful Goddess of the arrows, and of all dogs and hunting. You who awakens in the stars of heaven, when the sun sinks in slumber.

You with the Moon upon your brow, who prefers the chase by Night, to hunting in the Day, with your Nymphs to the sound of the Horn.

You are the Huntress, and the most Powerful.

I pray that you will think of me, yet even for a moment, for I worship you!"

Following this, the worshipper remains in silent prayer and praise for a few moments. After that, nine white stones or shells were placed before the statue, forming a Crescent Moon. The points of the crescent were placed towards the feet of the statue. Under the middle stone of shell was placed a symbol representing any desire or aid that was requested. In later times, a written request was often used.

Three torches were placed around the statue, forming a triangle (two behind off to each side, and the third one in front). Incense of the moon was often placed within the semi-circle made by the stone or shell pattern. A typical Moon incense was comprised of either Wormwood and Camphor, or Cedar, Sandalwood, and Juniper. To complete the magickal influences, the worshiper left the area immediately and never spoke to anyone concerning one's own actions.

Offerings to spirits, Lare, or even the gods consisted of the harvested grains or fruits. A special offering was made from equal parts of wine, milk, and melted honey. This mixture was called "nectar" and was highly prized as an offering. Such offerings can be placed in a tray or bowl that is set before a shrine or statue.

Following the conclusion of a ritual, such as the Full Moon, traditionally, offerings were made to the gods above and below. Pieces of the ritual meal of cakes were tossed up to the Moon to honor the celestial beings. The remaining wine was poured onto the ground to honor the gods in the Underworld.

The Gesture of Power

The "Gesture of Power," which appears in this chapter, can be used as a tool for evocation and for "charging" objects. It can also be used to open and close a ritually cast circle. Read through the instructions carefully so that you understand this technique completely before performing it (see illustration).

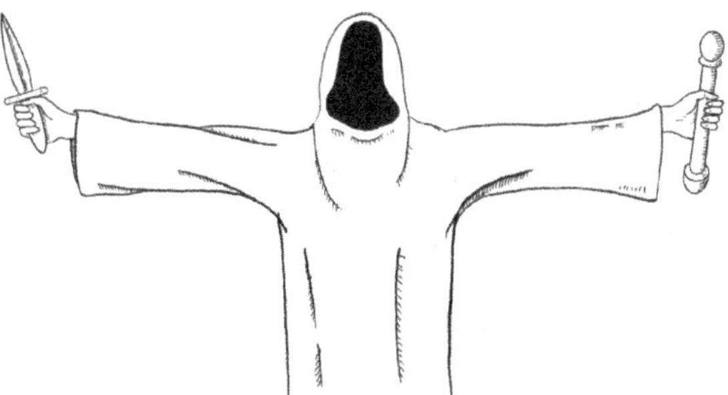

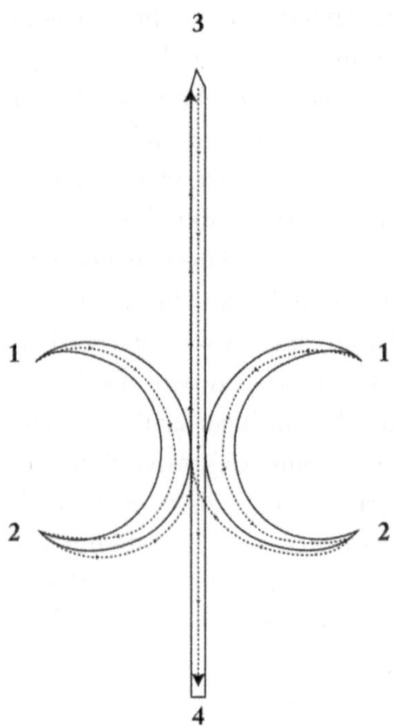

Hold the wand in your left hand and the dagger in your right. Extend both arms out to your sides. Then, bring both tools inward to position one. Next, move the tools down in a circular manner to position two. Each tool will be tracing a separate crescent. Bring both together crossed like an X up to position three. Finally, concentrating strongly, bring the tools down to position four, imagining that you are drawing down power. Position four must bring the tools to touch upon the object being charged, or the area to which the evocation is being directed.

To open a circle that is presently established, go to your point of exit and cross the wand and blade, assuming position three. Move them down to position four, then to two, which will uncross the tools. Move to position one in a circular motion, then assume the arms-outstretched posture. This will unseal your circle.

To close again, simply perform the original procedure of positions one through four at the opening that you created. Each time you perform the gesture, you will be tracing out the symbol as pictured in the illustration. Look at the symbol and practice following the outline of it.

Do not move outside of the image as you pass through the positions. With practice, I think you will find this technique quite useful. You may wish to enhance this technique by visualizing the symbol glowing as you trace it in the air. For charging, you may wish to then condense the image (mentally) into a glowing sphere, then transfer it into the object being charged as the tools are brought down upon it.

The Nanta Bag

The Nanta Bag is a very old tool appearing in various forms as it is traced back through the ages. The form in which we have it today comes to us from fifteenth century Italy. The purpose of the Nanta Bag is twofold. First, it is designed to keep its wearer in harmony with the forces of Nature. Second, it serves as a carrier for the Tools of the Art, so that a Witch can perform their magick anywhere or any time. The original followers of Aradia carried them as they traveled from village to village and, soon, they became a symbol of being a priest or priestess of the Old Religion.

Within these bags were miniature representations of the ritual tools, along with elemental symbols and objects of personal power. Typically, the bag would contain a thimble (chalice), a needle or pin (ritual blade), a coin (pentacle), and a twig (wand). Also included would be a stone (Earth), a feather (Air), a flint stone (Fire) or match (today), and a shell (Water) or vial of liquid. Finally, the bag would contain a symbol for the God and Goddess, along with objects of personal meaning. If one whose power they respected gave someone a small token, then this also would be added to the Nanta Bag.

The principle of "contagion" magick was the foundation for empowering the bag. Basically, this means that objects absorb power and have an energy field around them. When one object is placed into contact with another, then these objects are joined and influence each other. The Nanta Bag, in turn, has a contagion influence upon the person who carries it (in direct proportion to the items it contains). The following is a basic example of a functional Nanta Bag:

- A small stone, smooth and rounded
- A small feather, blue or very light in color

- A small portion of ash (wood or coal)
- A small vessel of pure water
- A small coin with a five-pointed star etched upon it
- A small twig (fruit or nutwood)
- A pin with a black head (or needle)
- A thimble
- A portion of incense
- Two small white candles
- A piece of marking chalk
- A measure of cord (nine feet)
- A small, finger-sized bowl (cup or dish)
- A symbol of the God (an acorn, small pinecone, piece of horn, etc)
- A symbol of the Goddess (a seashell, string of beads, nutshell)
- A personal power object (a lucky piece, a crystal, etc.)
- A portion of salt
- A small vessel of anointing oil

Collect these items and make a bag of leather or cloth large enough to contain them. You may wish to add some healing herbs or other desired items. The first four items are to be gathered in a manner that brings you into contact with the element represented. In conclusion, take the completed bag and consecrate it in the manner of the altar tools, charging by the elements and Gesture of Power (see: The Gesture of Power). Then, say over the completed bag:

"O' Great Nanta Bag,
be thou a natural focus
and a bridge to Power.
I am linked to thee
and thou art linked to Nature.
We are One from Three.
We are the Triangle manifest.
In the names of the Goddess and God,
so be it."

Chapter Five

Signs and Symbols

Signs and symbols have always been an integral part of human expression, especially within the framework of religion and spirituality. Symbols speak to us on a level more intimately connected with the subconscious mind. The advantage of using symbols in a ritual or magickal context is that they convey entire concepts or images at a glance. The older and more used a symbol is, the more power it transfers to the viewer. This is due to the momentum that has carried it through the centuries.

The signs and symbols contained within this section are those of modern Witchcraft. They appear to be a blend of Pagan, occult, and Masonic designs. It seems likely that the origins of all these symbols emanate from the Etruscan and Roman Mystery Traditions, which were somewhat influenced by the Greek Mysteries (and perhaps those of Chaldea). Some of these symbols have become universal to Western Occultism and Witchcraft throughout Europe, and, therefore, it is untenable for any tradition to argue a personal cultural claim to them.

In order to invoke the power of a symbol, the viewer must pause and clear the mind of internal dialogue. To do this, simply close your eyes and slowly breathe in and out (deeply filling the lungs) three times. After the third breath, slowly open your eyes and gaze upon the symbol. Look at each element of the symbol and consider its meaning. For example, look at the Goddess symbol (two crescents back-to-back) you will see a Waxing Crescent on the left and a Waning Crescent on the right. Think about what *waning* means ("decline" or "withering") to you. Try and see it in terms of nature, as opposed to your own personal life experience. Then, do the same with the

Waxing Crescent and consider what *waxing* means to you. Next, think about the Moon and its changing forms in the night sky, and think about how our primitive ancestors (who did not know what the Moon was) must have perceived this mysterious light. Finally, imagine the Moon Goddess as the embodiment of all of these things, and view the symbol as a declaration of Divine Consciousness manifesting as feminine mutability (encompassing the repeating cycle of growth and decline). Through this process, your own consciousness becomes attuned to the symbol. You can then manifest the powers of growth or decline into your magickal or ritual work through mental projection. This is covered in later chapters.

The study of symbols and correspondences is essential to the art of magick. Therefore, any symbol should be examined in context to the culture or system that produced it. Eclectic symbols shift and change meaning and are, therefore, more difficult to employ effectively, especially within a coven of Witches with different personal backgrounds. In such a case, the magickal effects can be sluggish or only slightly effective. Following formal initiation, the symbolism of the Tradition's own *collective consciousness* is conveyed to the initiate, after which any and all symbols can be employed with success.

On the chart below is a collection of symbols pertaining to the more religious elements of Italian Witchcraft. The "Source of All Things" symbol represents the unknowable source itself (top triangle) emanating the knowable personifications of Goddess (left triangle) and God (right triangle). The black and white sphere symbolizes the duality within the Divinity—the light and dark aspects.

The Goddess symbol, as we've seen, is the waxing and waning powers reflected in the Moon. The God symbol represents the Sun with antlers, which reflects his earthly and celestial natures. The "Elements of Creation" symbol depicts the ancient teaching that manifestation is a result of combining and directing the elemental forces. The Elements of Earth, Air, Fire, and Water are drawn and stabilized through the presence of the fifth element, which is called Spirit.

The Source of All Things	The Goddess	The God	The Elements of Creation (Spirit, Earth, Air, Fire, & Water
The Power	Power of the Goddess	Power of the God	Eight-Fold Path
Power of the Union of the God and Goddess	The Goddess Manifest (The Moon Cross)	Tanus (light)	The Spirit of Aradia (The Teachings)

The "Power" symbol is associated with the "Source of All Things" symbol, and represents the action of connecting and drawing the un-manifest source blended with the manifest personifications of Goddess and God. The "Power of the Goddess" symbol represents the emanation of the Moon Goddess in her totality, in effect a "Drawing Down" of the lunar nature of the Goddess. The "Power of the God" symbol represents the same concept viewed as drawing upon the solar and earthly nature of the God.

The "Eight-Fold Path" symbol is more complex than most of the other symbols. In essence, it depicts the "Wheel of the Sun" (the spokes) moving in harmony with the seasons of the Moon (the spheres). This symbol also represents the eight seasonal rites of the Witches' year. In Italian Witchcraft, the eight ritual seasons are known as the *treguenda,* which is what some systems call the *sabbats.* The eight seasons fall into two related categories. One is the year itself, which is comprised of the Goddess season (spring and summer) and the God season (fall and winter). The other is divided into the eight celebrations, which alternate an alignment with the Goddess and the God. This is covered in detail within Chapter Thirteen: "The Rituals."

The "Power of the Union of God and Goddess" symbol represents the combination of the personifications of Goddess and God with the essence of the source itself. This is Divinity manifest within the unmanifest. It is totality comprehensible to humankind and is a very potent symbol to work with. The "Goddess Manifest" symbol reflects the four aspects of the Goddess: Enchantress, Maiden, Mother, and Crone. It also symbolizes the powers of light and darkness, as well as the waxing and waning nature of the Goddess.

The "Tanus" symbol represents the "star god," or higher nature of the godform (celestial). This symbol reflects his waxing and fertile powers. The leaves represent his celestial crown, and the spheres symbolize his fertility (being stylized genitalia). The "Spirit of Aradia" symbol represents the divine flame, pure without the manifest polarities of feminine and masculine. Over time, the symbol has also come to signify the "Teachings of Aradia" (in essence, the tenets of Italian Witchcraft).

The chart below contains some of the spirits and entities with Italian Witchcraft. Arcan is a spirit that teaches esoteric knowledge. Lucinus is a spirit of enlightenment who reveals hidden truths that are covered with false or distorted veneers. Selahna is a spirit that transforms moonlight into a magickal essence. Mensus is a spirit that can draw upon the energy of the Moon's phases each month. The Guardian symbols of North, East, South, and West are stylized postures that are used for evocation in various rituals. The idea of Guardians at the cardinal directions is an ancient concept. In essence, the Guardians serve to protect access to and from the worlds of mortal kind. These are the portals that open into the Otherworld and reside "between the worlds" (covered in detail in Chapters Nine and Ten: "The Moon Tree" and "Magickal and Ritual Gestures").

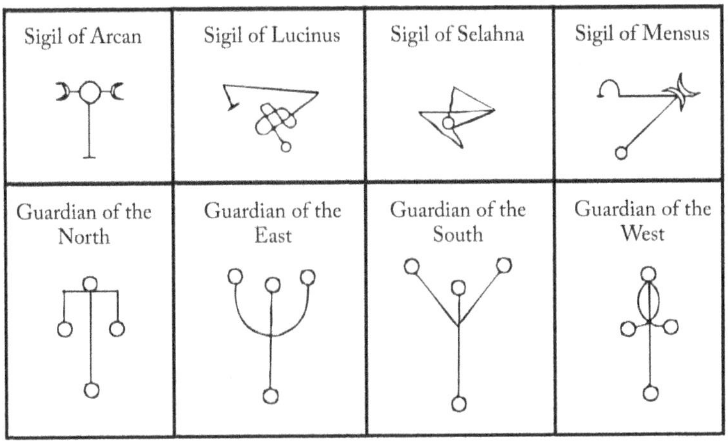

Sigil of Arcan	Sigil of Lucinus	Sigil of Selahna	Sigil of Mensus
Guardian of the North	Guardian of the East	Guardian of the South	Guardian of the West

The next chart contains a mixture of symbols that represent various concepts in Italian Witchcraft. The "Feminine Sexual Power" symbol depicts the female genital area. This is the gateway of manifestation (birth/rebirth) through which souls enter the word of mortal kind. It is also a symbol of magickal fluids, magickal magnetism, and metaphysical processes.

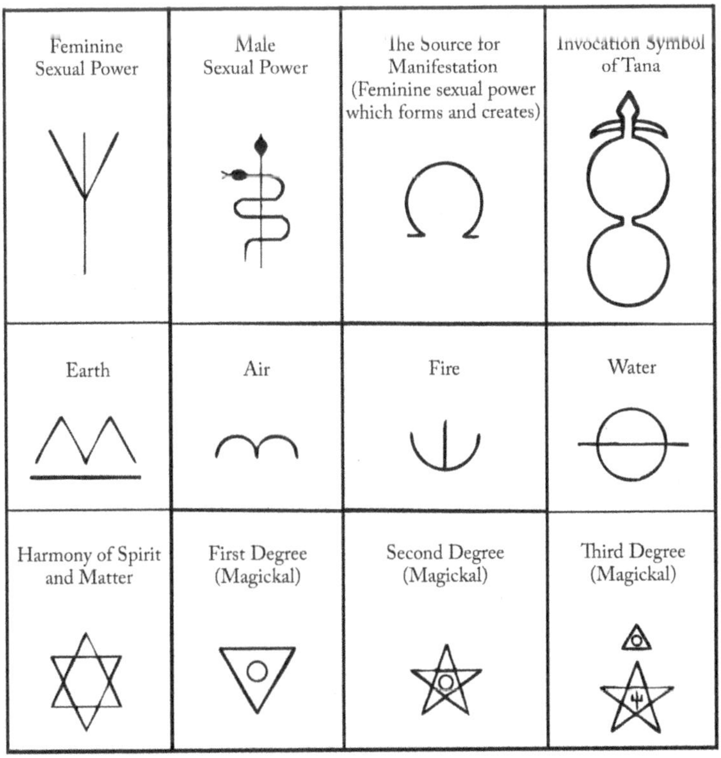

Feminine Sexual Power	Male Sexual Power	The Source for Manifestation (Feminine sexual power which forms and creates)	Invocation Symbol of Tana
Earth	Air	Fire	Water
Harmony of Spirit and Matter	First Degree (Magickal)	Second Degree (Magickal)	Third Degree (Magickal)

The "Male Sexual Power" symbol depicts the male erection and the inner "serpent" essence that is ejaculated into the womb-gate of the female vessel. In this regard, it is the magickal venom of the serpent, or, more accurately, a magickal elixir. The "Source for Manifestation" represents the magickal cauldron, which is the womb of magick. It is pictured as opened downward, which symbolizes the directional manifestation into the Material World, the down pouring of the alchemical process.

The "Invocational Symbol of Tana" represents the celestial nature of the Goddess in her highest personification as Tana, the star goddess. The spheres represent the world above and the world below, over which she reigns. The symbol mounted on the upper sphere represents Tana as the giver and receiver of life, the vessel from which we enter into life and exit into death within the repeating cycle.

The symbols of Earth, Air, Fire, and Water represent the metaphysical properties of the creative forces of the Universe. Earth symbolizes foundation. Air symbolizes transmission. Fire symbolizes transformation. Water symbolizes movement. The "Harmony of Spirit and Matter" symbol depicts the balance of the spiritual with the material. This can be likened to the idea that the soul joins with a material body, which creates a balance of form and light.

The set of degree symbols indicate the magickal aspects of the initiate system. The "First Degree" symbol represents the material focus (inverted triangle) of the initiate who is seeking enlightenment (the sphere) within. This is the period of study, training, and practice. The "Second Degree" symbol represents the attainment of elemental balance embracing the light within. The "Third Degree" symbol represents enlightenment through connection to the Higher Realms (upright triangle with sphere) and the attainment of elemental balance, coupled with the ability to evoke and invoke the divine polarities of Goddess and God. This is connected with the ancient concept of the divine marriage of human to deity.

The concept of intimate relationships with non-material beings appears in various elements of Italian Witchcraft. One of the oldest is that of the covenant between Witch and Faery. The Italian Witch charm known as the *cimaruta* features a vervain blossom, which is sacred to the Faery race. The appearance of the vervain on the cimaruta is a sign of the peace and trust that exists between Witch and Faery.

The cimaruta charm displays the symbols that depict the key and central alignments within Italian Witchcraft. The classic cimaruta charm bears images of a rooster, a dagger, a serpent coiled on a Crescent Moon, a key, and the vervain blossom. The rooster, as herald of the Sun, symbolizes enlightenment. The dagger is the moonbeam, the sacred arrow of Diana, and represents transformation. The Moon symbolizes mystical vision, and the serpent symbolizes the goddess Proserpina. The key is the symbol of Hecate and also represents one who opens the ways. As previously noted, the vervain blossom represents the kindred race of the Faery and the Witches' covenant with these Otherworld beings. According to oral tradition, Witches wore the cimaruta as sign of recognition between them. Later, the charm slipped into popular folk traditions and became a good luck charm, or a charm intended to ward off evil. In Naples, it was once the tradition to place a cimaruta charm on the crib of a newborn. The presence of this charm was believed to protect the baby from misfortune and the Evil Eye.

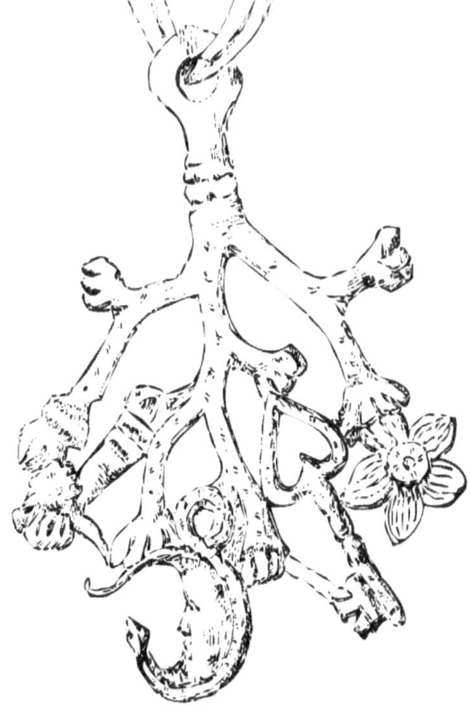

Another popular symbol found in Italian Witchcraft is the *cornuto* ("horn") charm. Although it looks like a horn, it is actually the depiction of a goat's penis, which symbolizes potency and fertility. The goat has long been associated with Witchcraft and is one of the Horned God images used to represent an aspect of the God of Witchcraft.

Among the variety of protective charms and amulets, we find various items of folk magick tradition, such as:

- A spool of red wool yarn
- Red wool bag of coarse salt
- Two keys (crossed) with a cutting from the agave plant
- Garlic cloves
- Horseshoe (with one broken end) tied with a red wool ribbon

Another popular protection is to tie a red wool cord around the handle of a pair of scissors. The scissors are then placed under the mattress at the foot of the bed with the tips of the scissors (spread open) facing the end. This is believed to prevent spirits and astral entities from harming the sleeper/dreamer. Two very popular gestures in Italian Witchcraft are the *mano fica* ("fig hand") and the *mano cornuto* ("horn hand"). The *mano fica* (*figa*) is performed by making a fist and inserting the thumb between the index and middle fingers so that it jets out. The *mano cornuto* is performed by folding the two center fingers and jetting out the little finger and index finger.

Both of these gestures are used to "send away" or banish influences in one's presence. In popular folk customs, the meanings differ. This is very common among non-initiates who do not know the original and traditional meanings and intentions. Such misunderstandings reflect the differences between initiate traditions and common folk traditions, the latter being available to the average person on the street.

The Witches' Alphabet

The alphabet appearing in this section is called the Theban script. According to occult tradition, the Theban alphabet originated in the Ancient Greek city of Thebes. The script bears a strong resemblance to the letter style of the Etruscan alphabet, which, like the Theban, is missing the English equivalent of the letters U, J, and W.

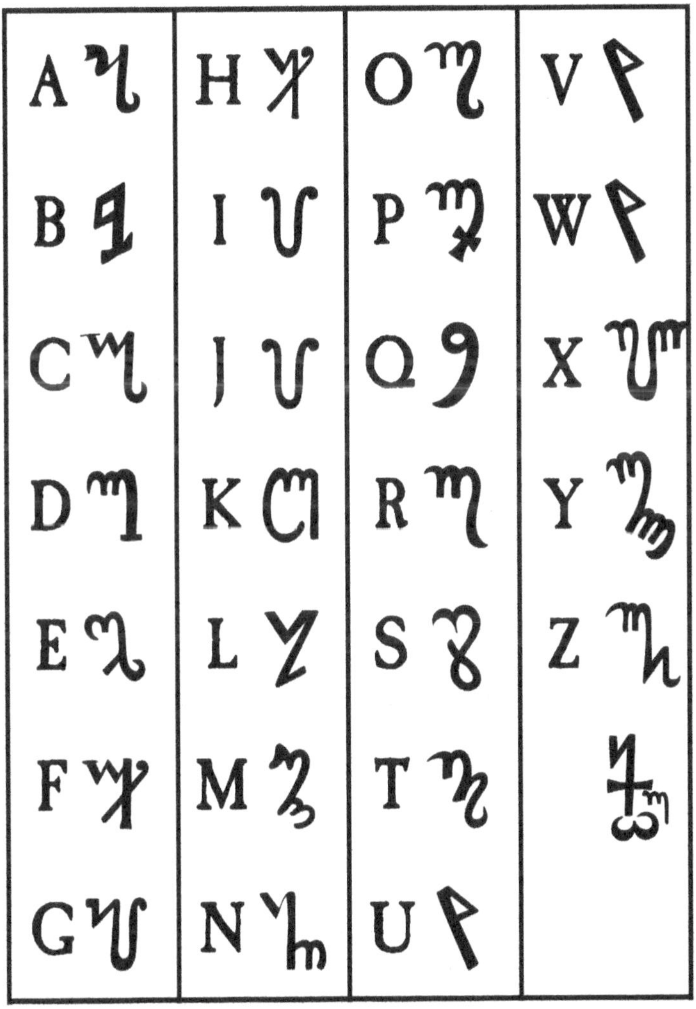

A	H	O	V
B	I	P	W
C	J	Q	X
D	K	R	Y
E	L	S	Z
F	M	T	
G	N	U	

The earliest known public reference to the Theban script appears in Cornelius Agrippa's sixteenth century masterpiece titled *Three Books of Occult Philosophy.* In 1508, Agrippa spent some time in Naples, Italy, and lived in the area of Milan for three years from 1512–1515. Here, he studied the works of Marsilio Ficino and Pico de la Mirandola, who translated the great Hermetic texts of Ancient Greek and Egyptian occultism. Since the Theban script originated in the Aegean/Mediterranean, it seems probable that Agrippa encountered it while studying in Italy.

Among the oldest signs and symbols in Italian Witchcraft is the human hand itself. In accord with hand symbolism is the appearance of the number five as a potent force for manifesting personal desire. The human hand is capable of greater creative tasks than that of the so-called "lower animals" and was, therefore, considered to possess a higher nature. This nature extended into the Spirit World, where the hand could also possess certain talents, influences, and abilities. One of the foundational ideas for palmistry is the teaching that the hand has a connection to things of the Otherworld.

Among the beliefs associated with the hand is its ability to protect and to manipulate. This concept resulted in the construction of hand amulets and charms, as well as the symbolic depiction of the hand as connected to a complete magickal system. Historian Ruth Martin, in her book *Witchcraft and the Inquisition in Venice 1550–1650,* presents some authentic elements of the use of the hand in Italian Witchcraft.

Martin notes the use of the hand in conjunction with the hearthside. This involved placing the palm and fingers against the wall by the chimney. Each finger represented a spirit that could be conjured by the Witch. The chimney served as a doorway for spirits to pass between the worlds. The name of each spirit was conjured as each finger was pressed in turn against the wall.

Martin also mentions the use of the cauldron chain. This involved touching each link one at a time in separate groups of five, for a total of twenty-five links. Spirits of the dead were summoned in order to raise power for the Witch. These were spirits of the dead who had died an unjust or horrible death. The groups of spirits consisted of five hung to death, five dismembered, five tortured, five died in prison, and five slain by knife. This relates to a belief that certain departed spirits could not pass into the next life and fell under the care and protection of Hecate the Goddess of Witchcraft.[10]

The hand appears in specific gestures designed to convey symbolic communication. Just as in everyday life, hand gestures are used to indicate such concepts as "be silent," "stop," or "wait a minute." However, hand gestures are also used for symbolic ritual communication. Here, they operate on a spiritual or Otherworldly level, as opposed to a mundane form of communication. The idea, as noted earlier, is that the hand has power in the Non-Material World in similar ways that it has in the Material World.

Over the centuries, a variety of hand gestures have been created for ritual and magickal use. Some incorporate numerical value, such as the number three symbolizing manifestation or a triple nature of any kind. Others form suggestive meanings through the configuration of the hand, which is posed in a symbolic display. An aspect related to this concept is the forming of "hand shadows" on the wall using a source of light behind the hand, while forming the fingers to reflect a known image. This can be used magically to pass the "spirit" of the image into an object in order to "charge" or empower it. One could, for example, cast the shadow of a cat into an amulet or talisman intended to bestow a stated nature of the cat to the wearer of the item.

For ritual purposes, the fingers of the hand can be displayed to indicate the sending of magickal energy, its reception, or its blocking. Hand gestures often direct energy being invoked or evoked in a ritual setting. They are also used to call upon the aid of other practitioners in raising or drawing magickal energy during a ritual performance.

10 Ruth Martin, *Witchcraft and the Inquisition in Venice* 1550–1650 (Basil Blackwell, 1989).

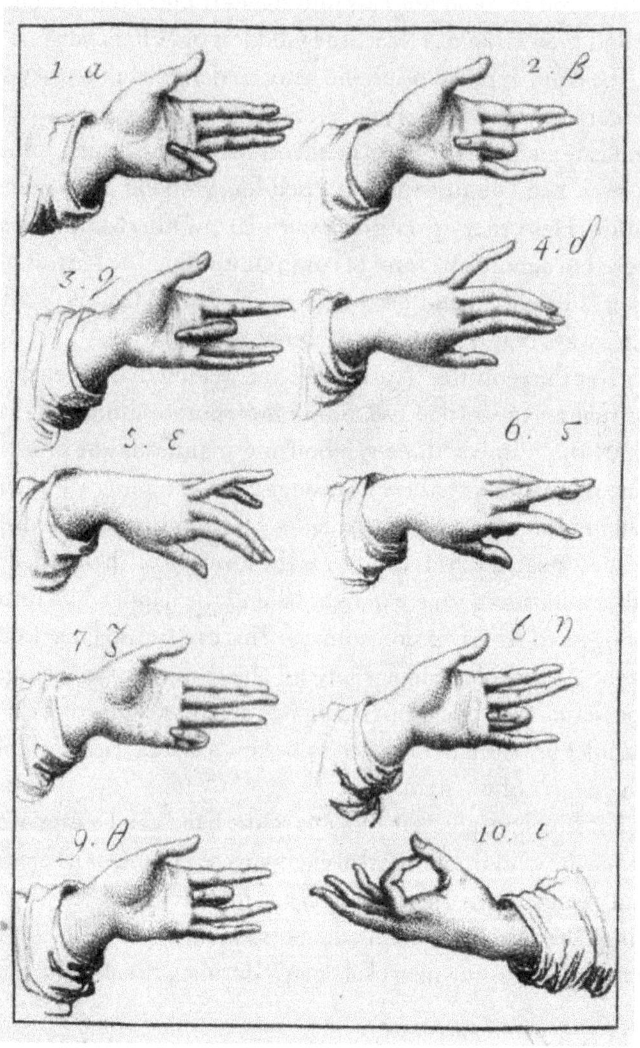
1. α
2. β
3. γ
4. δ
5. ε
6. ς
7. ζ
6. η
9. θ
10. ι

Chapter Six

Raising and Drawing Power

The attraction, accumulation, and direction of power is essential in the magickal arts. Presented here are several of the most common forms of raising and drawing energy for magickal purposes. Also presented here are the centers of power within the human body. For the purposes of this topic, the traditional Italian system is presented along with the common system used in most modern Witchcraft traditions. This will help you to know and understand both.

It is the way of things that systems evolve over the course of time. While traditions can and do survive, they tend to also take on elements and influences related to the culture in which they reside. Witchcraft traditions are preserved, but, even with vigilance, it is difficult to remain pure. The best way to ensure survival through each generation is to allow the changes required to make the tradition viable for each generation, while, at the same, nurturing a love of the tradition itself.

The Ritual and Magickal Circle

References to ritual or magickal circles appear in writings on Witchcraft that date back to the pre-Christian era in Ancient Greek and Roman literature. In one tale, the Witch Medea marks out a circle with a beech twig, sets an altar, and walks around it three times. Various woodcuts and engravings over the centuries also depict Witches operating within a circle traced upon the ground.

Ritual and magickal circles essentially serve two needs. The first is to keep things outside, and the second is to keep things inside. The former is for protection, and the latter is to allow energy to collect and build in strength. In this chapter, we will deal with the subject of retention. Essentially, a circle is constructed by drawing elemental energy, forming it, and fixing it in place. This act is called "casting a circle." Once a circle is cast, it becomes a sphere that contains energy within itself.

The elemental properties of Earth, Air, Fire, and Water maintain the sphere. These elemental forces also absorb the energy of the ritual or magickal work performed within the circle. Once released, with the dissolving of the circle, the elemental forces carry the *charged intent* of the ritual or magick back into the Otherworld. Earth gives it form, Air provides transmission, Fire allows for transformation from mundane to mystical, and Water gives it movement and motion.

There are different ways in which energy can be raised within a circle. Methods such as dancing, chanting, and drumming can be incorporated along with trance inducement to create a generation of magickal energy. Once raised and concentrated, the intent of the ritual or magickal work is stated, then mentally depicted as a symbol, which is then directed into the energy field through visualization.

In the case of rituals and magickal works that draw upon the power of deities or forces, their symbols are used as a means of directing the forces drawn to the circle. Within the circle, upon the altar, the spirit flame burns as the presence of divine or spiritual forces.

Once a circle is dissolved, the accumulated energy will flow away with the elemental forces as they return to their Realms. Traditionally, the condensed energy field is released and directed towards its target, hovers at the top of the sphere until the circle is dissolved, and then it launches itself away. So, in effect, the intent is carried away by the withdrawal of elemental forces, along with the actual launch of the "formed thought" that was magically created as the intent.

It is important to note that everything in the ritual setting absorbs the residual energy of any magickal work, intent, or force. Therefore, it is essential that this energy be released from the Material Plane so that it does not remain to contaminate anyone or anything that comes into contact with the setting. This requires that a ritual or magickal circle is dissolved through counterclockwise movements during the ritual of dissolving. This is covered in later chapters.

The Centers of Power within the Body

In the Old Religion, it is taught that the body has three personal power centers. These are placed at the forehead, heart, and genital region. In essence, they represent the connection of mind, spirit, and body to the Planes of Manifestation.

It is an ancient teaching that three things are required in order for manifestation to take place. These are time, space, and energy. All three must be present in order for manifestation to take place.

On a magickal level, the three centers of the body link the Witch to the three worlds: Overworld, Middleworld, and Otherworld/Underworld. They also bring together the Astral, Elemental, and Material Realms into a meeting place whenever the Witch desires to invoke them. The three centers are labeled: psychic, emotional, and energy. In order, they are linked to the forehead, heart, and genital organs.

As a spiritual teaching, the three zones represent the three inner selves: the higher nature, the indwelling spirit, and the personality being. The first is that part of the soul that dwells in a higher dimension separate from material existence. The second zone represents the light of the soul encased in material form where it experiences the Mortal Realm. The third zone represents the personality or worldly nature of the soul that manifests as a result of material manifestation. It is the only part of the soul that perishes with the death of the body.

Modern System of Power Zones

In Western Occultism, it is taught that there are seven zones within the human body that mark various centers of power. They are organized into seven areas that begin at the genital region and continue up to above the top of the head.

The first center is the *energy zone,* which is also called the "fire center" or "serpent center" (in Eastern mysticism, it is where the *kundalini* power resides). The serpent energy operates within the genital region to channel energy through the body system. This is the *seat of power,* where concentrated life energies and psychic energies dwell. It is, essentially, a center of transmission.

The second center is known as the *personal center* and is located just beneath the navel. This center is both receptive, as well as transmissive and deals with astral energies. It is one of several gates through which the astral body of the individual can exit from the physical flesh. Great amounts of energy can be drawn in and sent out from this area, which is used extensively in shamanic practices.

The third center is the *power center,* which is located at the solar plexus. This center is also transmissive and receptive, dealing with life energies. Through this center, both physical and astral bodies are nourished (the physical body by sunlight and moonlight, and the spirit body by Astral Light).

The fourth center is called the *emotional center* and is located at the heart area. This center is primarily receptive, but is transmissive as well. The emotional center deals with human feelings and ethics. This center enables us to sense another person on an emotional level.

The fifth center is the *vibrational center,* which is located at the throat. It is transmissive and deals with causing actions and reactions. It is the most physical of the non-physical centers and generates sound vibrations.

The sixth center is the *psychic center,* which is located on the center of the forehead, just above the eyebrows. It is basically receptive, but functions in a transmissive manner as well. This center is also called the "Third Eye," or the "purity center." It is a very active psychic center and another exit point for the astral body.

The seventh center is the *divine center,* which is located above the top of the head (actually residing in the aura). It is receptive, as well as transmissive , and deals with "deity-consciousness." This is our link to the higher self and the interfacing point with that which created us (the Divine Source of All Things).

On a physical level, these centers all function together to maintain the body and its organ system. The energy center governs the reproductive organs. The personal center governs general health and specifically the liver, pancreas, and spleen. The power center governs the adrenal glands. The emotional center governs the thymus gland. The vibrational center governs the thyroid gland. The psychic center governs the pineal gland. The divine center influences the pineal gland.

Goddess and God Currents

There are two currents of energy flowing through these centers within the body known as the *God and Goddess currents.* They are opposite masculine and feminine currents and, in an occult sense, are referred to as electric (masculine) and magnetic (feminine). These currents issue forth from the energy center in the genital region, then cross at the emotional center in the area of the heart. After this, they flow upward, then cross again at the psychic center in the forehead and flow downward again in an endless cycle.

The Goddess and God currents directly influence our sexuality and gender preference through the vibrational *frequency* of their energy patterns, which, in turn, define our inner nature. In cultures influenced by the guilt and shame concepts inherent in Judaic-Christian religious beliefs, we find that usually only one of these currents is fully functional. According to the teachings, when one current is dominant, it manifests in the establishment of a governing pattern that directs whether a person is either heterosexual or homosexual. Both currents operating in balance aligns one with the bisexual state. It is interesting to note that the medical symbol of the caduceus, symbolizing perfect health, is itself a symbol of the God and Goddess currents flowing in balance along the spine.

When viewing the patterns, we note that the currents are rooted at the base of the spine. They connect and join on the forehead where they fully manifest in their completed circuit before returning to the base of the spine.

In Ancient Egypt, we find the headdress, which features a serpent mounted on the forehead piece. This was symbolic of fertility and vitality, as well as personal power. The serpent is mounted at the "third eye" zone (in the area of the pineal gland). In sex magick, this area is linked to the nipples and genital region, which, when stimulated together, arouse the magickal serpent energy that rise from the base of the spine and up into the third eye.

The serpent headdress appears on various deities and is also worn by some of the pharaohs. It is likely that sexual prowess, or the legend of it, was intimately connected with the personage of the pharaoh. The serpent has long been a symbol of sexual energy or power.

Drawing Down the Moon

This technique is designed to draw upon lunar energy, or astral energy, with which to empower a spell or work of magick. It can also be used for psychic development and meditation. In the Strega practice, *Drawing Down the Moon* is not the same thing as invoking the Goddess. When we invoke the Goddess upon the *Sacerdotessa* ("High Priestess"), we refer to it as *Calling Down the Goddess.* The first act is connecting with the Moon, while the second act is connecting with the Goddess. The Moon and the Goddess are not the same thing, though, admittedly, they are difficult to separate.

Technique One: Drawing Down the Moon

Sit quietly and visualize the Full Moon above you. Mentally Bring the Moon down to each of your body centers, visualizing each one glowing with the Moon's light. Concentrate on each center for at least a minute before moving on to the next.

Technique Two: Contacting Power

Sit comfortably, close your eyes, and imagine a white sphere of light about six inches above your head. Imagine it flowing down through your head, neck, shoulders, chest, arms, and so on. Let this energy flow through every inch of you. Let it completely saturate the inside and cover the outside. Imagine that your entire being is glowing. At this point, you are in touch with power and may proceed with healing or other works of magick.

Technique Three: Grounding Exercise

There are times when it is necessary to *drain off* excess energy from ritual or magickal work and to regain a sense of balance. Sit directly upon the bare earth with your legs folded in front of you and palms of the hands pressed down upon the ground. Imagine your arms to be hollow (like two hoses) and mentally pour the excess/unwanted energy out into the soil. Slow, deep breathing is helpful in this technique. Once you feel the energy is drained, then quickly get up and leave the area. It is best not to return there for a few hours. The earth will neutralize the energy, and the area will be as it was before you employed it.

Technique Four: Raising the Energy Sphere

This is a basic exercise for raising personal power. This will be the foundation for works of healing, charging, and magick. To raise a sphere of power, place your hands in front of you about six inches apart (palms facing) and begin to move them slowly back and forth (like playing an accordion). Experience the sensations of warmth, pressure, and magnetism.

Once a sphere of power has been established, you can pass a mental sigil into it or project a thought-form, thereby giving the sphere its purpose. Then, mentally visualize the sphere entering the object that you wish to charge.

To increase this energy, use your concentration and imagination. You can visualize a glowing force of power. Do not allow your hands to touch while performing this exercise. Once you have accomplished this method, then begin putting your hands around various objects and feeling their energy fields. Soon, you will discover many other uses for this basic ability.

Technique Five: Energy Cleansing

This is a simple technique for cleansing and repairing the aura that surrounds the body. First, raise your sphere of energy. Next, slowly glide your hands along the form of the body being treated. Avoid touching the person. Keep your hands about four or five inches away.

Starting at the head, completely cover it with graceful sweeps of the hands, moving downward. When you complete this area, then shake your hands toward the ground (as though you were shaking off water).

Continue down the body a section at a time. You may have another person assist you if you desire. Move along the natural curves as you proceed. Remember to "shake off" after finishing a section, as this helps to remove astral debris. After completing the general sweep of the body, run your hands along the aura, sensing for "gaps" in the structure. If you sense any, then raise a sphere and "patch" it into the gap. Let your intuition guide you as you go along.

Part of the training of a Witch is to learn how to draw power through ritual, which involves working with elemental spirits, the Grigori, and the Goddess and God as well. In future chapters, this aspect will be explored.

Chapter Seven

The Art of Magick

The classic definition of magick is the manifestation of desire through personal willpower. More accurately, magick is the manifestation and directed focus of states of consciousness. In this chapter, we will sort magick into the following four categories, which we shall independently examine: natural magick, personal magick, spirit magick, and deity magick.

Even though each level of magick is unique, they are often combined in such arts as spellcasting and ritual magick. When viewing a work of magick, it is important to understand that everything within its structure is designed to influence the state of consciousness of the practitioner.

Natural Magick

Natural magick blends the commonplace into a focused act of manifesting personal will or desire. This can be anything from crystals or herbs, to oils, potions, and natural phenomenon. On a very basic level, let's take a look at something you may never have thought of as magick. When getting ready for a date, or perhaps a job interview, people select certain clothes (incorporating color and design) that they feel make them more desirable. They may add a pleasant scent to their bodies with perfume or cologne. Makeup, hair, and personal grooming complete the ritual. Usually, a change takes place in the consciousness of an individual during the process. They have created the personality and attitude with which to carry out the desired influence. When someone comments on the outfit, scent, or overall look, the spell is then set into action.

In a very similar manner, the creation of a ritual circle also establishes a change in consciousness. As the ritual area is marked, the altar arranged, and candles set, a gradual air of magick is established. Once the celebrants have robed (or disrobed), everyone is "transformed" from their everyday personality into a different persona. Through this process, a change of consciousness has occurred. This transformation can be amplified by the wearing of crystals or other power objects. If the celebrants put themselves fully into the ritual moment and experience, then personal power can be generated, and magick is created naturally.

One aspect of natural magick includes the use of herbs, stones, trees, and other things of nature. From this, we obtain potions, tools, amplifiers, and talismans or amulets. Trees have been used as wands for many generations, and, in Italian Witchcraft, the use of a beech wand has great antiquity. Stones with a naturally worn hole through them have long been associated with Faeries. Talismans, such as a piece of horn, a sprig of rue, and other items, are very traditional in Italian Witchcraft.

At the core of magick in Italian Witchcraft is the belief in an etheric "web" that connects all things. Through this connection, one thing can influence or affect another thing. This web spreads like a mist through the world of mortal kind and to the portal of the Otherworld.

Over the centuries, Witches established signs and symbols used to communicate with various spirits and beings. Such usage has created a momentum of energy that is tied to old traditions. This "momentum of the past" is a living current of energy that flows through time—past, present, and future. Time itself is perceived as a cycle or a sphere and is, therefore, not viewed as linear. This magickal principle allows any point in time or space to be touched and, thereby, influenced.

Part of a Witch's magick is rooted in one's personal rapport with spirits, deities, and other entities. Among the oldest myths and legends, we find tales that link the Witch with Faeries and other magickal beings. In Italian Witchcraft, we also find the Grigori, an ancient race of guardians associated with the stars. In ritual settings, they are evoked at the portals to the Otherworld, which reside in the quarter points of the circle: North, East, South, and West. Here, they keep watch over the rituals and magickal workings.

In ritual and magickal work, the Witch uses the altar as a center of power. Upon the altar is burned the spirit flame of divine light. This is the untamed fire known to our ancestors as divine and reflected in such deities as Vesta. From this primal force, the Witch draws etheric energy to cast ritual and magickal circles, bless tools, and empower items in spellcasting work.

The magickal work of the Witch is one of transformation. This is demonstrated in the depiction of Witches using cauldrons. The cauldron itself is a womb symbol, the vessel of transformation, generation, and regeneration. Whether fire burns beneath the cauldron to produce a magickal brew or flames within the cauldron to transform its contents, the cauldron is magickal vehicle through which the will of the Witch is made manifest.

Personal Magick

Personal magick is the ability to change one's consciousness at will and to collect and focus energy as needed. Usually, this is acquired through much practice and devotion to the art of magick. In some cases, certain individuals may naturally have access to these abilities with little or no effort on their part, and, often, this is due to past life experience.

The basic components of personal magick are: imagination, visualization, will, and expectation. In many books, this is represented by "the magickal triangle." Expectation (for some reason) is usually omitted in the average book on magick. However, it is important to note that, if you do not expect any results, then there probably won't be any. Belief in magick and confidence in your ability to use it is important in the art of magick.

To activate personal power, one must employ the aspects of the Witches' triangle while establishing personal magick. This is often accomplished through acting, drama, or sexual stimulation. In effect, anything that will serve to get you "worked up" or energized is functional. Watch young children at play sometime and you will see a very good example of personal magick. When a child is putting everything they have into being a superhero or warrior, then, in their mind, this becomes a reality. Fortunately, for us adults, children lack the focus and will that is required to manifest their desires. Despite this, they are very good at getting their way, but that's another story.

In Chapter Six: "Raising and Drawing Power," we looked at power centers within the physical body. This is part of personal magick and greatly enhances power and energy. When the personal power centers operate as a result of magickal training, then the astral or spirit body is likewise empowered. This is an advantage on the Inner Planes, because the astral body and your consciousness within it allows personal power and magick to effectively operate within the Astral Realm. This becomes automatic once personal training has established the functional centers.

Spirit Magick

Spirit magick is the attracting and drawing of spirit entities for the purpose of empowering a ritual or work of magick. Traditionally, these are the spirits of the elemental forces of Earth, Air, Fire, and Water. Since these elements comprise all of creation, it is logical to incorporate elemental spirits into any desired manifestation. It is noteworthy that the Italian Witch hunter Francesco Guazzo, in his book *Compendium Maleficarum,* mentions that Witches work with spirits of Earth, Air, Fire, and Water in the rituals.

Spirits from any Realm can be called upon for the purposes of magick. This includes the Elven or Fae spirits, along with various astral entities. It is important that you provide an offering to attract the spirit, as well as providing an environment in which to draw and "house" the spirit. For example, it is not typically appropriate to invoke a fire elemental into a bowl of water or a water elemental into a bowl of soil.

Think about this from a mundane perspective. If you want a fish as a pet, you must provide it with an environment that will allow it to function as a fish. The same is true of any spirit that you draw upon. If you do not do so, then these spirits will quickly disperse.

Respect, trust, and rapport is essential to spirit magick. Make sure this foundation is solid in your practice of the arts of magick.

Deity Magick

Deity magick is the ability to call upon a goddess or a god for assistance. The effectiveness of this is essentially rooted in your spirituality and your rapport with Deity. One very common error people make in this relationship is that of trying to turn the deities into personal servants. Another error is a lack of common courtesy. Many people often begin by requesting something from their deity without any preliminary dialogue. It is important to first call upon the name of the deity and to express your feelings about it or your admiration of it. After this, you may proceed with stating your needs.

Consider this from a mundane aspect. When we phone a friend, we first exchange greetings and concern for each other's wellbeing before we get to the point of the phone call. It is considered rude to bypass the greeting and the "how are you doing" elements. In the case of a deity, it is absolutely foolish. Another error commonly made is to not address your deities for months at a time and then to call upon them in time of need. Just like any relationship, you must keep in-touch during the good times if you expect any help in the bad times. Essentially, this all addresses rapport with deity. Establish an altar and greet your deity each day. Give thanks and show appreciation, be loving, and be loyal.

The Formula of Magick

Now that we have looked at the components of magick, we must now understand how to make it work. To serve as an example, we will use the sending of a letter as an analogy. The purpose of the letter will be to obtain a mail-order catalog. Knowing what the purpose is, we must consider what is required to accomplish the goal. We need a pen and paper, an envelope, a stamp, and three dollars for the catalog. The pen and paper are the ritual tools. The words that are written will be sigils that are understood by both the receiver and us (Celtic runes are useless to address Egyptian deities). The envelope is the vehicle (or element) that will carry our magick. The address is the direction in which the desire or target of the magick abides. The stamp is an offering to the spirits who will assist our spell (the postal workers), and the three dollars is an offering to attract the entities that possess the catalog in hopes that they will respond to our desire.

Having collected all that is required, we must now set it into motion or release it. If we do not do so, then nothing will happen. Therefore, we set the letter bearing the sigils of direction (the address) and the offering (stamp) out on the proper setting (mailbox) so that the spirit (postman) will carry it off for us. Having failed to do any of these properly could easily result in a lack of manifest according to desire.

Always bear in mind that magick is an occult science. It has its own laws and principles. Essentially, magick can be divided into the following categories: earth magick, solar magick, and stellar magick. Each of these can then be divided into subcategories. Traditionally, magick can be thought of as being comprised of "raised magick" and "drawn magick." In other words, power is either raised (or generated) by someone, or drawn from an outside source (whether from Nature or from Otherworld entities).

The Odic Force

In the Ancient Mystery Traditions of Southern Europe, we find a teaching concerning a Universal Agent. During the Middle Ages, this was known as the Great Magickal Arcanum. It was represented in all Mystery Sects by the serpent figure. In Western Occultism, this agent was depicted as twin serpents, each symbolizing a certain aspect of the Force itself. In its active nature, it was called *Od,* and, in its passive nature, it was called *Ob.* When the two forces were said to be in equilibrium, the resulting state was called *Aour.*

Eliphas Levi described Od as magnetism controlled by the will of the operator. Ob, he referred to as a passive clairvoyance called "trance." The synthesis of the life-giving Od and the death-giving Ob he called the *Aour.*[11] Passive Astral Light is symbolized by the

11 Eliphas Levi, *The Great Secret, or Occultism Unveiled* (1868).

mythological the spirit of the python. The Scepter of Hermes or Rod of Aesculapius reconciles the serpents of Od and Ob. Harmony arises from the analogy of these contraries. It is the inner harmony that creates the necessary internal balance for the practice of magick. This same balance establishes health for the mind, body, and spirit. This is one of the reasons why the caduceus was chosen to represent healers.

In ancient times, the Odic Force was symbolized by the serpent (specifically, by the Great Python). This was the symbolism employed at the ancient Oracle of Delphi, which was known earlier as Pytho (where a chthonic Serpent Cult once flourished). According to legend, a great serpent inhabited the chasms deep within the oracle cave. The god Apollo slew the creature and cast it down into the pit over which the oracle seat was suspended.

A priestess sat upon the oracle seat, and legend has it that the fumes from the decaying serpent rose up and imparted to her the power of prophecy. In a metaphysical sense, we can say that heat (Apollo being the Sun God) released the power of the accumulated Odic force (the serpent), which allowed the priestess to discern the patterns forming within the Astral Plane (prophecy).

On the magickal staff of Hermes, we find two serpents, one white and one black, entwined around a staff upon which sits a winged sphere. The staff as a whole depicts the equilibrium of contrary forces culminating in harmony. Od, as the white serpent, represents the active power of magnetism directed by the personal will of the Witch. In other words, the power to make one own our choices, the free will. Ob, as the black serpent, represents the passive power of magnetism directed by patterns already established in the Astral Plane. This can be said to be fate or destiny playing a role in one's life. The winged sphere represents the point between fate and personal will, that which we call Aour. Levi tells us that the secret of employing the Odic Force lies in this: "to rule the fatality of the Ob by intelligence and the power of the Od so as to create the perfect balance of Aour."[12]

The Astral Light, also known as the Great Magickal Agent, can be controlled by two things. First, by fixing the mind upon

12 Levi, *ibid.* Chapter XIV: "Dark Intelligence."

the image of the desire, and second, by projecting energy into the astral material. This is accomplished by generating the Odic Force through emotional investment. Such a disturbance of the ether engages the electro-magnetic properties of the Odic Force, which, in turn, stimulates the Astral Light. Within the malleable substance of the Astral Light, the projected images form into active vessels by personal will and imagination. By moving with the flow of this occult formula, your magick is not deflected. The moving charge of the emotions (electrical) passes along the magnetic field of the Odic Mantle encasing the Earth and, thus, gains access into the Astral Level. Carried within this current is the image focused by the mind, around which the Astral Light will then form.

The Mechanism of Magick

For humans, all magickal operations begin within the mind and are directed outward. The subconscious mind works through corresponding images under the direction of the conscious mind. In this, we find the interplay between the Material World, the Elemental Plane (Earth, Air, Fire, and Water), and the Astral Plane (where thoughts become forms). The subconscious mind is linked directly to the Astral Portal within the Dream Realm. This is why symbolism and visualization are essential in the art of magick.

There are many different aspects of magick and many different ways of employing it. Basically speaking, however, most types of magick will fall into one of two methods: "raised" or "drawn" magick. Raised energy is what can be emanated from the body and/or mind of the person. Drawn energy is what can be attracted from other Realms (usually through ritual methods). This includes workings that involve gods and/or spirits.

Magick may also fall into the realms of "black magick," which is considered to be negative, and "white magick," which is considered to be positive. There is also a third type referred to as "grey magick," which is a blend of the two. In the oldest forms of Italian Witchcraft, no distinction was made, and Witches did what was necessary. Over the centuries, certain sects adopted a philosophy based upon what is now known as the *Three-Fold Law.*

The Three-Fold Law is attuned to Nature and the principle of how energy affects a human. It is an old teaching that the type of energy that we send out will come back upon us three-fold. In other words, affecting us *physically, emotionally,* and *spiritually.* One single act can affect us on these three levels whenever we perform an action. Our body, emotion, and soul are all intertwined. So, there is a need for clear thinking when it comes to employing a work of magick.

Many people believe that magick has no basis in scientific fact. This is not correct, for there are many reasons related to the laws of physics why magick does indeed work. These reasons are connected to energy fields and various currents that exist around our planet. The rotation of the Earth and the gravitational forces of the Sun and the Moon, as well as other celestial bodies, cause various energy currents. The actual spinning of the Earth creates electro-magnetic currents within our bound atmosphere. As the Earth moves around the Sun, stress is created on the Earth by the Sun's gravity. This stress causes vibrational currents in our atmosphere as well.

Positive currents of stress flow from East to West across our planet. There are also seasonal tides, which are based on fluctuations of the electro-magnetic current surrounding the Earth (corresponding to the position of the Sun and the Earth). Positive (electric) tides flow from late March to late September. Negative (magnetic) tides flow from late September to late March. These tides mark the onset of the waxing and waning cycles of the year. The seasonal religious festivals of Witchcraft mark the peak times of each of these currents.

Generally, we can say that magick is really a matter of vibrational cause and effect. Essentially, we disturb the fabric of the bound etheric atmosphere of our planet, and certain things result. It is the art of magick to impregnate the ether with our "formed desires" (thought-forms) and, then, to direct them towards manifestation. The major difference is whether the ripple is sent out or brought down (as in raised or drawn magick). Magick that deals with the invocations of spirits and/or deities incorporates the principle of vibration as a catalyst. The forces behind magick are real, being both natural and supernatural. It is the art of getting these forces to work for you, and not against you, that is the art of magick.

Ritual magick works on the basis of attracting sympathetic energies by means of words (which are vibrations), gestures, and dramatic portrayals (ritual drama plays). The theory here is that the combination of these factors directed by the personal or *group will* (and boosted by the need/desire) attract sympathetic energies. These energies will then cause a ripple in the necessary Plane, resulting in manifestation. Everything that is now a physically-created object was once only a concept.

Let's look at an example of manifesting thoughts. When you hold a book in your hands, you literally hold the author's idea in material form. Various people working for the publisher had to mentally *form the image* that was to become the book. Once visualized, they could then proceed to take the steps necessary to cause their *thought-forms* (the publisher's added vision) to become a physical book. This is, essentially, the formula for magick. The tools and articles used in a ritual setting serve to trigger or stimulate the participants so that the necessary energies can be raised. The tools that are used in a ritual also act as extensions of the ritualist's *willpower* and mental/psychic abilities.

Everything placed into a magickal operation serves to gradually induce a change in consciousness within the person or persons involved in its performance. Candles, robes, chanting, the actual setting up of the altar, and the casting of the circle all contribute to this evolution of consciousness from mundane to magickal. This is also one of the reasons why, for example, many Witches choose Craft names, such as say Ladyhawke. This allows a person to perceive something beyond who and what they are in the mundane world.

Magnetism

When we speak of magnetic energies or forces in an occult context, we are speaking of the metaphysical counterpart of the Physical Plane expression. The initiate-level understanding of the magnetic force is an extremely refined substance that can be controlled and directed by the mind. It can be condensed and stored within inanimate objects. These objects then become magickally charged objects. Experience has shown that liquids of any kind and all metals will readily accept and store an occult magnetic charge. Wood or wood products will accept a charge, but will not store it for long periods of time. Silk is the only known material to date that will not accept or store this type of charge. For this reason, it is used as insulation against occult magnetic charges and magnetic contamination. Thus, it is useful to wrap charged objects in silk, so that the magnetic charge does not leak away from the charged object. It also prevents outside energy from being able to contaminate the object wrapped in silk.

The power to employ occult magnetism can also be termed *fascination* or *enchantment*. Basically, there are two methods of using personal magnetism. One is to impregnate the aura of another person with a thought-form generated by your own mind. The other is to persuade the individual so that their own personal will shapes the thought-form. This may be accomplished by accumulating energy within your own aura for projection, by physically touching the other person, by projecting the magickal vapor through the eyes, or by the tonal quality of your voice.

The vibrational qualities of the voice carry personal magnetism, which stimulates the etheric substance of Astral Light (also known as the *Astral Fabric*). There is a direct link to the spoken word and to the breath. From an occult perspective, the element of Air is the mediating element between electrical and magnetic energy (it is a transmission element). Through slow, deep breathing and emotional arousal, the blood accumulates energy from the odic atmosphere around us. This charged blood passes through the lungs, imparting magnetic energy into the breath. When merged with the personal desire of the individual, a powerful thought-form can be created within this magnetic field. It can be projected out through the eyes by focusing upon a person or an object, holding in the breath, and visualizing a stream of vapor passing out through the eyes, as though you were exhaling out of them. The key to employing elemental energy is strongly linked to controlled breathing, because the breath can be strongly charged with Odic Energy.

Warming the breath (from a deep inhale) carries an electrical charge, and cool breath (blown from a shallow puff of air) carries a magnetic charge. This is apparent when the breath is applied to another person just at the base of the cerebellum. A puff will send a magnetic current into the person's aura, resulting in an electrical response. Usually, this is annoying to the person, and you get a startled reaction, an electrical snap. A slow exhale from deep within the lungs sends an electrical current, resulting in a magnetic response. This is usually an erotic response, the receptive magnetic energy associated with sexual submission.

When employing Odic breath in connection with any life form, an opposite polarity will result; magnetic breath evokes an electrical response, and an electrical breath evokes a magnetic response. When using breath charges upon inanimate objects, the active charge is delivered without a polarity response. An exception to this rule is any inanimate object already bearing a magickal charge or any magnetized object. Essentially, you will want to bear in mind that magnetic energies *draw* and electrical energies *vitalize.* With experimentation, you will also find that magnetic energies can sometimes deflect directed charges, just as electrical energies can sometimes cause inertia.

For healing purposes, you will generally want to use a magnetic breath, so that the electrical response will accelerate the healing process. This is particularly effective with wounds, burns, and other short-term injuries. An electrical breath is best used in the healing of long-term illnesses, only when using other magickal techniques in conjunction. The magnetic response is useful in allowing the illness to be receptive to other types of magickal energy directed towards the patient. Electrical breath will also enhance the effects of medication.

Magickal Energy

When you hold your hands a few inches apart, palms facing, you create an electro-magnetic field between them. This magnetism indicates the presence of polarities—opposite poles that attract one another. The first thing we can say about magickal energy is that it is composed of opposites. The best way to understand these opposites is to think of them as directions of force:

feminine > < masculine
magnetic > < electric
receptive > < active

Though we divide them to talk about them, these opposites within energy can never be separated. One cannot exist without the other. Positive and negative pulls are both necessary for movement. Together, the two create vibration. When opposites are in the correct relationship, the result is balance. When they are not in balance, then they are negative and destructive.

The second thing we can say about energy is that it is balanced. Balance is the natural state of the Universe. However, when energy becomes plural, it is reduced to positive and negative charges and is considered unbalanced. Because they are incomplete forms of the "Universal All," these energies create a separation between the whole and its parts. Separations manifest physically and mentally in specific ways. Here, they must occupy definable territories. You may have noticed this in yourself, perhaps as sadness in the heart area or fear in the pit of your stomach; these are energies occupying a specific space.

When energies are held in by emotion, they can be felt as a weight or a presence. In this context, another word for energy is "ego." Ego separates us from the All. The truth is that we are no more or less than anything around us. Everything is a physical manifestation of energy in its state of positive and negative charges. The effects of magick are worked through the aspect of energy, which are sometimes called Od or Odic Force. It is the vital element that flows through all terrestrial globes and all living beings. By its various influences, this agent attracts some things, but also keeps other things away as well. The human body radiates this energy and can influence and affect people and situations in the general vicinity.

The Odic Force is capable of being consciously developed, energized, and intensified. It is this power, concentrated and directed, which is the basis of personal magick. The will of the person performing a work of such magick concentrates and controls the energy. This concentration of energy is then sent to its goal, either stored in a talisman or sent in a thought-form to the person or thing to be affected. The power of the Odic Force must be used in accordance with the solar and lunar tides, as well as cosmic tides.

When speaking of energy polarity, we are speaking of magickal energy. It is an old teaching that each of us has within us an energy current comprised of masculine and feminine (active and receptive) polarities. When we raise or draw magick, we cannot help but give it dual polarity, because that is our own inner nature. In the Eastern Mystical Traditions, this is known as the *Ida* and *Pingala* currents. As demonstrated earlier in the text, these currents originate at the base of the spine, divide and flow up from the base chakra, cross at the heart chakra, and then flow into the third eye, uniting once again.

If we take the old occult axiom "as above, so below," we can also say that the Creators set within all things this same Ida and Pingala nature (since it would be the Divine Imprint within anything created). The nature of the artist is always within the nature of their art. So, what we're speaking of is the etheric essence of energy. The occult nature of a physical object, or a principle of physics, is not always readily apparent. That is why it is called *occult,* which means "hidden" or "secret."

All the actions of magickal manifestation take place within the Astral Dimension. Time and space, from a magickal perspective, do not exist as commonly understood by the scientific community. Magick has no limited range, per se, because it does not travel in a linear manner. Instead, it permeates the Astral Sphere of our world and behaves (from our perspective) as though it had infinite range, because it manifests without reference to distance. One way to think of this is to think of blowing a puff of air into a balloon. The breath within the balloon is everywhere, touching upon the interior walls of the balloon. You can access the breath on any point along the surface of the sphere of the balloon, because it is already present there. Essentially, we can say that magick travels at the speed of thought (whatever that might be).

Magickal energy is affected by a variety of external forces. Magickal force fields, such as protective pentacles, can slow or deflect these forces. This is not unlike the flow of an electron beam being diverted when it crosses perpendicular to a magnetic field. Greater forces, such as those exerted by Deity or high-level spirits, can also certainly alter the course of one's magick.

Basically, there are only two reasons why one's magick will ever fail: it was performed incorrectly/inappropriately, or a greater force opposes it/diverts it. In the final analysis, magick is based upon the consistent and reliable laws of metaphysics. We may someday discover that magick and quantum mechanics are intimately related. In any case, if you know, understand, and apply the appropriate formula, then your magick will not fail you.

Witchcraft and Magickal Energy

There are many different types and styles of magick involved in the practice of Witchcraft. Some traditions differ in the type used; some use all, and some may combine only a few techniques. Basically, magick may be organized into two categories: operative and ceremonial. The first covers spells, words of power, the use of unguents/potions, etc. The second is concerned with the operation of Craft rituals. The aspects of magick can be thought of in this manner: sympathetic, ritual, raised, drawn, and sex magick.

Ritual is a means of concentrating and attracting those energies that are symbolized through the use of gestures, word phrases, and images (symbols, runes, etc). The magickal theory behind this is that, by acting out certain symbolic gestures with concentration upon their meanings, one can attract sympathetic energies inherent throughout the Universe. These energies can be directed by the use of one's controlled will. This aspect is sometimes called the "Witches' Pyramid," which was discussed earlier in this chapter.

Sex magick is the use of energy raised through sexual union. This is the most condensed and powerful form of energy that can be raised from the human body. Some Craft Traditions employ it in the Third-Degree initiation ceremony. In Eastern Mystical Traditions, it is known as tantra.

The Ancient Egyptians employed it as well. The energy raised in sex magick is sometimes referred as the *kundalini power*, or "serpent power." The serpent headdress of Ancient Egyptian rulers was symbolic of the serpent power having been raised to the third eye, the sign of Divine Union, or *samadhi*. The *kundalini* force is seated at the base of the spine and governs the sexual nature of the individual. In magick, it is drawn up through each of the chakra points to the third eye, employing sexual energy as the energy of propulsion.

The Imagination and Will

Among those who do not practice magick, it is quite common to find an attitude that imagination is purely fantasy. To a practitioner of magick, however, imagination is a vapor that can carry thought-forms into the Astral Levels through the subconscious doorway. On the Physical Plane, a person's thoughts in imagination can manifest as novel, a movie, or a work of art. On the Astral Plane, a person's imagination can manifest as an etheric image. This image can be as real to astral entities as any physical form is to material beings.

Consistently effective magick requires the actions of both the imagination and the personal will. The will, by itself, is an undefined current of energy. The imagination, by itself, lacks vitality. When the two factors are brought together, substantial magickal effects are possible. In practical application, the Witch must first evoke the imagination so that an image of the desired effect is created. Then, the personal will must be used to direct the energy of the imagination. Eastern mystics call the creative power of the imagination *kriya shakti.* They view the imagination as the womb, and the will as the impregnating seed. When joined together, they can produce the magickal child of external manifestation. It must be understood that *will* is not the same thing as *desire.* The personal will is an act of concentration and must be kept separate from desire. The imagination arises from desire and is vitalized by the will. Therefore, the mind must be free of desire when focusing the will upon the image evoked by the imagination. This is why symbols and sigils are favored by the Witch, because they address the goal of manifestation, and not the desired effect itself.

Magickal Links

All things connected with a person contain an energy link with that individual. For example, a person's hair holds the vibrations of their energy pattern and, by the use of sympathetic magick, that person can be influenced by energy directed their way. This could be used for emotional healing of that person, motivation, or whatever it may be. The hair acts as a point of concentration and as a kind of "homing device" for the directed energy. The same is true for unwashed items of clothing and other personal items. By making an image of an individual and placing their personal items within it, one creates a center of focus. Works of magick for the gain of something should be done while the Moon is waxing (new to full) and works to be rid of something or to undo something should be performed when the Moon is waning. The Full Moon is the time of peak power when the forces of Light and Darkness are in total balance. Essentially, any and all works of magick are possible at this time, and portals to the Astral Plane are most open to access during this lunar phase.

Cord magick is a basic magickal tool in Witchcraft. The theory being that, by concentrating a desire upon the cords and using them as a focus, one can raise and condense magickal energy. This energy can be set into the cord itself by knotting the cords at the point of greatest concentrated effort. In other words, you concentrate on your desire and make an exclamation of said desire as you quickly make a knot (pulling it tightly as you confirm your wish). Later, untying the knot will release the desired effect. This can be helpful when working with someone who really bothers you a lot. In advance, you can set the message "leave me alone" into the cord (knot) and untie it (secretly) when the person is really on your nerves. For this scenario, you would simply think about the person so that you raise your emotions on the subject, then begin to loop the cord into a knot. Before pulling the cord tight into a knot, visualize the person's face. Then shout (out loud or within yourself) "Leave me alone!" Visualize the person leaving you alone as you continue for a moment to exert tension on the cord. When you next encounter the person, you are ready to release the spell.

As with all forms of magick, you must be responsible when you perform a work that affects another person. Why you did something is more tied to *karmic debt* than the act itself. For example, if you harm someone in order save another person's life as opposed to harming someone because you seek revenge, there is a difference in the karma that you are creating for yourself. Obviously, you should seek to harm no one in the first place, but this isn't always possible.

The Components of Ritual Magick

There are essentially five so-called ingredients that comprise the art of creating successful works of magick or effective ritual. You can adapt them or arrange them according to your own needs, so long as you employ them all. They are:

1. Personal Will
2. Timing
3. Imagery
4. Direction
5. Balance

Let's look at each one for an understanding of the concept.

Personal Will

This can also be thought of as motivation, temptation, or persuasion. You must be sufficiently moved enough to perform a ritual or work of magick in order to establish enough power to accomplish your goal. If you care little about the results or put only a small amount of energy into your desire, then you are unlikely to see any real results. The stronger the need or desire, then the more likely it is that you will raise the amount of energy required to bring about the change you seek. But desire or need is not enough by itself. Remember that desire must be suppressed, and the will must be focused only upon a detached view of the desired outcome of your spell or magickal rite.

Timing

In the performance of ritual magick, timing can mean success or failure. The best time to cast a spell or create a work of magick is when the target is most receptive. Receptivity is usually assured when the target is passive. People sleep, corporations close overnight, as well as for holidays, etc. One must also take into account the phase of the Moon and the season of the year. Witches always work with Nature—not against Her. Generally speaking, 4am in the target zone is the most effective time to cast a spell of influence over a person or a situation.

Imagery

The success of any work also depends upon images created by the mind. This is where the imagination enters into the formula. Anything that serves to intensify the emotions will contribute to success. Any drawing, statue, photo, scent, article of clothing, sound, or situation which helps to merge you with your desire will greatly add to your success. Imagery is a constant reminder of what you wish to attract or accomplish. It acts as a homing device in its role as a representation of the object, person, or situation for which the spell is intended. Imagery can be shaped and directed, all according to the will of the Witch. This becomes the pattern or formula that leads to realization of desire. Surround yourself with images of your desire and you will resonate the vibrations that will attract the thing you desire.

Direction

Once enough energy has been raised, you must direct it towards your desire. Do not be anxious concerning the results, because anxiety will act to draw the energy back to you before it can take effect. Reflecting back upon the spell tends to ground the energy because it draws the images and concepts back to you. Try to give the matter no more thought, so as not to deplete its effectiveness. Mark a seven-day period off on your calendar and evaluate the situation seven days later. It usually takes about seven days for magick to manifest (one lunar quarter).

Balance

The last aspect of magick one has to take into account is personal balance. This means that one must consider the need for the work of magick and the consequences upon both the spellcaster and the target. If anger motivates your magickal work, then wait a few hours or sleep on it overnight. While anger can be a useful propellant for a spell, it can also cloud the thinking. If possible, make sure you have exhausted the normal means of dealing with something before you move to a magickal solution. Make sure you are feeling well enough to work magick and plan to rest afterwards. Magick requires a portion of your vital essence drawn from your aura. Replenish this with rest, even if you do not feel tired. Health problems begin in the aura long before the body is aware of them.

As noted earlier, there are certain Tides of Power within the *magnetic field* and the ionosphere of the Earth that aid us in all of our works of magick. The stars, Sun, planets, and the Moon radiate their influence upon us through the magnetic sphere of the Earth. In Eastern Occultism, these tides are called the *Tattvic Tides,* and the medium through which they flow is called *Prana.* This is the substance just above Terrestrial Matter, known as "Etheric Matter," of which there are two kinds: *Free Ether* and *Bound Ether*. Free Ether is that field which surrounds the Sun, and through which passes the Earth and other planets within its sphere of influence. Bound Ether is that which surrounds the Earth itself (or any planetary body) and may be called the magnetic sphere.

As the Earth orbits the Sun, revolving on its axis as it does so, centers of stress occur in the magnetic sphere of the Earth. As a result, there is a positive current of energy flowing from East to the West, and a magnetic current passing from North to South during six months of the year (which reverses for the remaining six months). The "positive" currents emanate from the northern center, and the "negative" from the southern center. The Winter Solstice marks the beginning of the positive current that reverses after the Summer Solstice to negative. These currents of energy are marked by the seasonal rites occurring at the Solstices and Equinoxes. The terms "positive" and "negative" refer to electrical and magnetic energies of an etheric nature, as well as to those energies that we might call "waxing" and "waning."

The Equinoxes mark the periods when the daylight and darkness are of equal duration. We call this the balance of the powers of Light and Darkness. The Spring Equinox marks the time of planting. What we plant in the Spring Equinox we shall harvest by the time of the Autumn Equinox. Therefore, we should look to our plans and projects and prepare works of magick intended to put us well on our way in the path we wish to walk. Careful and detailed plans should be laid out and worked towards. The fact that the powers of Light and Darkness are in balance during an Equinox stabilizes our magick and allows us to create magick without encountering an imbalance of one energy or the other.

The Autumn Equinox is a time to assess one's gains or losses as the time of Harvest arrives. What we worked for, or failed to work for, at the time of the Spring Equinox has now come to fullness. It is a time now for choosing the seeds we wish to plant, or replant, and to create magickal spells which will be the new sprouting seeds come spring. Self-examination is essential at the time of the Autumn Equinox. This provides us an opportunity to identify what we need to cast off in order to advance in our spirituality. These things should be identified, sigilized, burned in the cauldron, and buried in the earth. In this way, the season of decline will help ebb away what is detrimental to our higher nature.

The solstices mark the longest and shortest periods of sunlight in the year. The Summer Solstice is the longest day of the year, and the Winter Solstice is the shortest. The powers of Light and Darkness are in imbalance. This is marked by the ritual battle of the Oak King and the Holly King. The Summer Solstice is the time to pay particular attention to important matters in one's life. Blessings upon loved ones and spells of protection and nurturing are best done at this time of the season. The fruits and flowers of our labors are now in full array before us. The promise of Nature is seen both in actuality and in potential. This is one of the reasons why the Otherworld is known as the *Summerland* in Witch theology. The Winter Solstice is the time for planning spring magick. In the autumn, we assessed and discarded. The Winter calls to us now to plan for new projects and to correct the mistakes we have made. Spells of peace, forgiveness of self and others, and restoration are in good order during the Winter Solstice.

Chapter Eight

Aradia, Woman of Power

In many religions, we find a central figure that is often referred to as a founder. Some examples are Buddha and Jesus. In Italian Witchcraft, there is no "founder figure," per se, because Witchcraft is an evolutionary system stretching back to pre-History. However, in the literature on Witchcraft, we do find a key individual that is credited with the revival of the Old Religion of Witchcraft. She is known by the name Aradia and, even to this day, she remains a mystery in many ways.

Many people are already familiar with the legend of Aradia, as told by Charles Leland in his nineteenth century book titled *Aradia: Gospel of the Witches.* Unfortunately, the tale supplied to Leland is a distortion of the original legend. Despite the many misrepresentations in Leland's book, the portrait of Aradia as a rebellious leader is an accurate portrayal. To better understand this, we must turn our attention to the original legend of Aradia, as preserved in oral tradition.

According to the oldest stories, Aradia was born in the city of Volterra, Italy, during the early half of the fourteenth century. A legendary date exists for her birth, which is August 13, 1313. Skeptics dismiss this date as an unwarranted fabrication. Others understand it as symbolic within a secret society, for August 13 was the sacred festival day of the goddess Diana, and thirteen was the mystical number associated with the Moon (thus, thirteen twice, 1313). The legendary date may not be so far off-base, however, when we consider that there is some evidence that Aradia did exist and was alive during the fourteenth century.

According to the original legend, Aradia brought about a revival of the Witch Cult in Italy during the mid-fourteenth century. She was reportedly taught the Old Ways by her aunt and later returned this Ancient Pagan heritage to the oppressed peasants of Italy. But what evidence do we have to support a revival?

The Italian Inquisitor, Bernardo Rategno, documented in his *Tractatus de Strigibus* that a "rapid expansion" of the "witches sect" had begun 150 years prior to his own time.[13] Rategno had studied many transcripts from the trials of the Inquisition concerning Witchcraft. He carefully traced back through the years and pinpointed the time of the onset of the Witchcraft trials, noting their sharp increase over the following years. Through this means, Rategno was able to fix the time of the revival somewhere in the mid-to-late 1300s. If Aradia had actually been born in 1313, as the legend states, then she would have been old enough to have taught and influenced others by the mid-fourteenth century. This would also have allowed for groups to form which later carried on her teachings.

Skeptics point out scholar Norman Cohn's contention that Rategno's chronology is not confirmed by other Italian documents, but they avoid mentioning that Rategno's claim is not actually disproved or contradicted. There is simply an absence of supporting documentation for what Rategno felt he discovered. This does not, of course, mean that no such revival ever took place. In the final analysis, we have only the view of a man whose research indicated to him what appeared to be a revival pertaining to the Witches sect.

When we consider the idea of a "revival,' there are two things that come to mind. The first is that the use of the term "revival" indicates a previous status, meaning a belief in the existence of the Witches' sect prior to the fourteenth century. The second factor is that, in order to have a revival, there must be a catalyst. It is here that the story of Aradia becomes important.

There are currently no public records concerning Aradia and no references to her by name in any literature until Leland's account of her in 1890. In 1962, T.C. Lethbridge (former director for Cambridge University Museum of Archaeology & Ethnology)

13 Bernardo Rategno, *Tractatus de Strigibus* (1508).

published a book titled *Witches,* which does refer to Aradia in several chapters. He writes:

> *We can then, I think, assume that Leland's Vangelo and Dr. Murray's trial evidence are more or less contemporary and that it is reasonable to use the two together to form a picture of the witch cult at about A.D. 1400…Aradia was sent to earth to teach this art to Mankind. That is, she was, in the opinion of her devotees a personage, known in Hindu Religion as an Avatar, who taught them how to harness magic power. Aradia, at some far-off time, may have been as much an historical person as Christ, Krishna or Buddha…*[14]

This is one of the few references written by a non-Witch or non-Pagan to pose the possibility of Aradia having been a real person in history. There is also quasi-acknowledgement regarding a historical possibility in an article by anthropologist Sabina Magliocco:

> *What if some women, inspired by utopian legends of the Society of Diana/ Herodias, decided to try to replicate such a society in medieval Europe? Though we have no proof such a society ever existed, it is not inconceivable that a few inspired individuals might have decided to dramatize, once or repeatedly, the gatherings described in legends. The use of the term giuoco ("game") by Sibillia and Pierina suggests the playful, prankish character of ostension. A "game" based on legends of Diana/ Herodias and the fairies would probably have been secret and limited to the friends and associates of the creative instigators, who might well have been folk healers. One or more women might even have played the role of Diana or Herodias, presiding over the gathering and giving advice. Feasting, drinking and dancing might have taken place, and the women may have exchanged advice on matters of healing and divination. The "game" might even have had a healing intent, as was the case for many comparable circum- Mediterranean rituals, and may*

14 T.C. Lethbridge, *Witches* (Citadel Press, 1962) 13.

have involved trance-dancing. This is one possible explanation for the remarkably consistent reports of Sibillia and Pierina, tried within a few years of each other. The existence of ostension in connection to these legends could also mean that Grimassi's claim that Aradia was a real person may, in fact, not be entirely out of the question; a healer who was part of the society might have chosen to play the part of, or even take on the name of, Erodiade.[15]

It is interesting to note a passage by Carlo Ginzburg (Professor of Italian Renaissance Studies at the University of California in Los Angeles) in his book titled *Ecstasies: Deciphering the Witches' Sabbath*. Here, another possible link to a historical Aradia may be found; Ginzburg writes of a Pagan sect known as the "Calusari." During the Middle Ages (as late as the sixteenth and seventeenth centuries), the Calusari worshipped a "Mythical Empress," who they sometimes called "Arada" or "Irodeasa" (and also used the term "mistress of the Faeries" for her).[16] Could this sect have still been practicing a form of worship initiated by Aradia over one hundred years ago? According to the original legend of Aradia, she left Italy at some point in her mission and traveled out of Italy. Serbia, the home of the Calusari, lies a short distance across the Adriatic Sea from Central Italy, and travel by ship was not uncommon in that era.

According to oral tradition, Aradia was an outlaw-figure sought by agents of the Church. When Aradia left Italy, it was unsafe to relocate in France because the Papacy was still established there at that time and the Church was still seeking Aradia. Equally dangerous was a move to Northern Europe, because Witches were being burned or hanged in that region. Italy did not begin the execution of Witches until after the time of Aradia. All of this makes an eastern exodus to the region of Serbia the only logical action for Aradia.

15 Sabina Magliocco, "Who Was Aradia? The History and Development of a Legend." in *The Pomegranate: The Journal of Pagan Studies,* no. 18, Feb. 2002.

16 Carlo Ginzburg, *Ecstasies: Deciphering the Witches' Sabbath,* Raymond Rosenthal, tr. (Penguin Books, 1992) 189.

Unfortunately, no academically acceptable evidence is available regarding the historical Aradia, and the truth of her existence may never come to light. However, it is noteworthy that, just as in the case of Aradia, no historical documentation exists to prove the personage of Jesus Christ. Both Aradia and Jesus leave us with little more than a few references to the persecution of the sect and the existence of a gospel. However, as we know, all legends have their basis in some event.

Leland's public account of Aradia includes a legend about the "beautiful Pilgrim," which is possibly a remembrance of Aradia that was preserved among Tuscan Peasants for generations. In part, this legend says:

> *Then having obtained a pilgrim's dress, she traveled far and wide, teaching and preaching the religion of old times, the religion of Diana, the Queen of the Fairies and of the moon, the goddess of the poor and the oppressed. And the fame of her wisdom and beauty went forth over all the land, and people worshipped her, calling her La Bella Pellegrina (the beautiful pilgrim).*[17]

Alexander Murray presents an interesting Faery connection in his book *Who's Who in Mythology.* Murray, while addressing the subject of the Roman god Faunus and the goddess Fauna, (Fatuus and Fatua) states: "*The offspring of Fatua and Fatuus were the Fatui, who were considered to be prophetic deities of the fields... which we call Fays –that is, beings with the power of witchcraft and prophecy...* "[18]

In Italian Witchcraft, the name Fauna (or Fana) is another name for Diana, just as Faunus is another name for Dianus. Leland refers to the goddess Diana as the Queen of Faeries (Fae) and Murray names Fatua/Fauna as the Mother of Fae. Leland's book on Aradia contains several stories connecting Faeries to Diana, Aradia, and to Witchcraft

17 Charles Godfrey Leland, "La Bella Pellegrina (The Beautiful Pilgrim)," *Aradia: Gospel of the Witches* (David Nutt, 1899) 68.

18 Alexander Murray. *Who's Who in Mythology.* (Crescent Books, 1988) 140.

in general. He also mentions that *La Bella Pellegrina* was converted to Moon worship and taught others the Old Religion of Diana.

In the original story of Aradia, we find a woman rebelling against her parents and their Catholicism. In the fourteenth century, this was not a tolerable situation. According to the legend, Aradia often went for long walks through the Alban Hill region near Lake Nemi. It was here that she one day experienced a vision that shaped the course of her life. In the manner of many mystics, Aradia experienced a spontaneous moment of spiritual enlightenment. It is said that she heard a "voice" that told her that she was chosen to fulfill a quest. It was revealed that Aradia must challenge the order of things and provide hope to those who were enslaved by the wealthy noble class. This life-altering event set Aradia on a course that few women of that era would ever dare dream possible.

According to legend, Aradia came to be known as the *Holy Strega,* a spiritual teacher and wise woman. During her time, Aradia's natural healing abilities and knowledge of herbal potions were legendary. She collected a small band of followers from the outlaw camps in the Alban Hills and traveled the countryside, teaching the Old Religion of pre-Christian Europe. During her brief time as a Holy Woman among the peasant people, Aradia came to be regarded as the *daughter* of the goddess Diana. Following her later disappearance, many people worshipped her as a goddess figure.

In the final instructions to her followers, Aradia asked to be remembered through a sacred meal of wine and cakes, and she bid her followers to always keep to the Old Ways. Aradia told them to gather together when the Moon was full and to worship the Great Goddess. She told them that they must be free when they come together and that, as a sign of their freedom, they were to be naked in their rites and were to celebrate in joy and make love with one another. The freedom that Aradia spoke of was the freedom of the mind, body, and spirit. She urged her followers to reject the Judaic-Christian morality that served to control them and to practice in the *Ways of Old.*

In fourteenth-century Italy, Aradia taught hope and personal empowerment to an oppressed peasant population. She taught them freedom and openness in a time when the Church taught them shame and guilt. She gave peasants hope and self-worth in an age that offered them only slavery and servitude. Aradia taught them how to discover their roots and to remember who they were so they could start to live the lives of the people they were meant to be. She returned their ancestral heritage and pride to them, teaching them that they were not simply labor for the fancy of the wealthy. The message of Aradia is much the same today, and her teachings offer the same path to liberation and personal empowerment.

The Gifts of Aradia

In the fourteenth century, Aradia taught that the traditional powers of a Witch would belong to any who followed in the ways of the Old Religion. Aradia called these powers "gifts," because she stressed the point that these powers were the benefits of adhering to the Old Ways and not the reason for *becoming* a Witch. These are the powers:

- To bring success in love
- To bless and consecrate
- To speak with spirits
- To know of hidden things
- To call forth spirits
- To know the Voice of the Wind
- To possess the knowledge of transformation
- To possess the knowledge of divination
- To know and understand secret signs
- To cure disease
- To bring forth beauty
- To have influence over wild beasts
- To know the secrets of the hands

Let us look briefly at each of these gifts as they pertain to Witchcraft. To *bring success in love* refers to an ancient link with the goddess Venus, who was originally a Goddess of Cultivated Gardens. So, in this sense, we find a connection to the Witch as an herbalist, a maker of potions. But, additionally, Witches served also as the wise women of their period, and counseling still remained one of the Witches' art.

The ability *to bless and consecrate* brings to mind the ancient role of Medea as a priestess to the goddess Hecate. Creating a "sacred space" with the setting of an altar and the casting of a ritual circle all incorporate blessing and consecrating. These acts appear in various ancient tales of the Witch known as Medea.

The aptitude t*o speak with spirits* has long been associated with Witches and their Art. The goddess Hecate, who gathers wayward souls at the crossroads, has long been portrayed as a Goddess of Witches and Witchcraft. The idea of communicating with the dead also appears in the Witches' festival that falls on November Eve, which, in some Italian traditions, is known as "Shadowfest." The Catholic Church displaced this Pagan season with the celebration known as "All Souls' Day" or "All Hollow's Eve."

The gift *to know of hidden things* refers to the psychic nature of the Witch and the knowledge gained from their familiar spirits. It also refers to a belief popular in the Middle Ages that Witches could find hidden treasures. One belief held that a Witch could bind a spirit to a stone with a hole through its center, and that this spirit could be directed to reveal hidden treasures.

The power *to call forth spirits* refers to invocations and evocations used by the Witch. It also refers to the use of familiar spirits that work with Witches. Other types of spirits can be called forth as well, and the Italian Witch Hunter named Francesco Guazzo notes that Witches have dealings with spirits of Earth, Air, Fire, and Water.

The faculty *to know the Voice of the Wind* refers to communicating with the forces of Nature and hearing spirit voices in the air. It also refers to being taught "in spirit," as opposed to formal training. There are some things that have to be learned through rapport and results. Additionally, the voices can also be those of one's ancestors.

The gift to *possess the knowledge of transformation* refers to the magickal powers of the Witch. It was once believed that Witches cold change physical form and become a bird, a mouse, or an owl. However, the gift actually addresses the use of magick to shape and reshape. This is symbolized by the Witches' cauldron, which has long been a symbol of transformation.

The skill *to possess the knowledge of divination* refers to a seer or fortune-teller. In Ancient Roman times, such a person was known as a "saga." This word is the root source for the modern term of *sage,* meaning "a wise person."

The ability *to know and understand secret signs* refers to the initiate-level knowledge, what can be called "occult knowledge," that resides within a Witchcraft tradition. It also refers to the ancient art of reading omens and other signs in the environment.

The gift *to cure disease* refers to various forms of knowledge, such as herbal, as well as to the use of magickal energy and healing techniques taught or directed by beings of the Otherworld.

The power *to bring forth beauty* refers to the art of glamour, which is cohesive manifestation of an illusion. It also refers to the Witches perception of the things in Nature and one's way of revealing what is missed with mundane eyes.

The aptitude *to have influence over wild beasts* refers to a type of rapport in which the wild creatures recognize the "untamed" within the Witch, who is, therefore, not viewed as alien or "out-of-place." The vibration of the Witch is not predatory, but instead resonates like the energy of fields and forests, which allows wild creatures to see the Witch as safe.

The faculty *to know the secrets of the hands* refers to the art of palmistry, but also to the knowledge of ritual gestures using different formations of the fingers.

Chapter Nine

The Moon Tree

There is an ancient glyph that appears in the Old Religion, and it is known as the "Moon tree." Variations of the Moon tree symbol can be found in Ancient Etruscan, Assyrian, Greek, and Roman art. This is a testimony to the antiquity of the Moon tree and its commonality among the ancient peoples. The Moon tree is perhaps the earliest form of tree veneration and is most certainly associated with ancestral spirits. One ancient view held that the souls of the dead were drawn into the Moon, and its light grew with them until it was full. Then, the souls were released back to the Mortal World, which caused the light of the Moon to decrease.

Trees have long been viewed as symbolic bridges to other worlds. In European folklore, doorways to the fairy kingdom sometimes appear in the tales. In some mythologies, a tree becomes the vehicle for enlightenment, as in the case of the god Woden, who hung on a tree for several days. This theme is recalled in the Tarot card of the Hanged Man. Sometimes, trees bear a forbidden fruit or in some way contain the key to a higher consciousness (as in the myth of the Garden of Eden). The association with the Moon in tree lore is quite ancient and is connected to the Moon deity itself, as well as to the themes of forbidden fruit and enlightenment.

There is a very ancient association between the tree and the serpent which has its roots in the fertility cults of our ancestors. In ancient times, a snake cult existed in Benevento, Italy, which was centered around a walnut tree. The Witch charm known as the *cimaruta* reflects the veneration of the plant kingdom, as the charm itself is designed as a sprig of rue. On the rue hangs a serpent coiled around a Crescent Moon, which depicts it as guardian of the secret fruit of the sacred tree. The *cimaruta* depicts the Goddess of the Moon in her three aspects: Hecate, Diana, and Proserpina.

The earliest symbolic representation of the Moon deity was a stone that appears in ancient art as a rudimentary pillar. Early legends tell of a stone having fallen from the sky as though it had come from the gods themselves. It is interesting to find that both the symbol and the legend appear in early Greek, Assyrian, and Etruscan/Roman legends. In Chaldea, the Moon Goddess known as Magna Dea was worshipped in the form of a black stone obelisk, as was the Arabian goddess Al-Uzza.

Goblet d'Alviella, in his book *Migration of Symbols,* shows a series of drawings in which the Moon stone is carved (maintaining the general form) into the goddess image of Diana of Ephesus.[19] It is interesting to note that the Ancient Ephesians claimed the statue of Diana had fallen from the sky. It is likely that this story has preserved the ancient legend of the Moon stone itself. It appears that the original stone was carved, over a period of time, into a human image.

In addition to the pillar of stone, a wooden pillar (or tree) frequently appears in ancient art as a symbol of the Moon. The Moon tree symbol is quite ancient and appears over and over again in religious art. At times, the Moon tree imagery is that of actual tree and, other times, it may appear as a truncated pole or a stylized pillar. In some ancient myths, the Moon tree was cut down and carved into a boat for a slain god or a coffin, as in the myth of Osiris. This becomes of particular interest when we consider the Italian Witchcraft myth of the Goddess who journeys to the Underworld, traveling in her Moon boat upon the Sacred River of Descent.

In art forms, the Moon tree is often shown bearing thirteen blossoms or thirteen torches (for there are always thirteen moons in a year, being either Full Moons or New Moons). In Assyrian art, it sometimes appears bearing ribbons, similar to the European

19 Goblet d'Alviella, *Migration of Symbols* (Archibald Constable & Co., 1894).

maypole. Images have been found that depict the Moon tree enclosed in a shrine of trellis work, recalling the fact that the Moon Goddess was first worshipped in a grotto or a grove of trees (which was the case in Ancient Italy). The arch represents the grotto, the sacred gateway into the Otherworld. The center pole is the Moon tree, and the trellis represents the inner connections that weave all things together.

An Ancient Italian carving discovered at the site of the Barberini Palace in Rome pictures the Moon hidden in a secret place within an altar; the symbolic tree and pillar of stone is still included in the image. This particular drawing was taken from the book *Ancient Pagan and Modern Christian Symbolism* by Thomas Inman.[20]

According to oral tradition, near the site of the Temple of Diana, within the sanctuary of Lake Nemi in Italy, two upright pillars of wood were erected, which supported a cross beam of wood (forming a "doorway") on the northeast shore of the lake. The ritualists would kneel and wait for the Full Moon to rise until it appeared (from their angle of sight) to "sit" upon the crossbeam. At this point, they would rise and pass through the doorway structure in a symbolic act of passing into the Lunar Realm. This structure was often referred to as the *Moon Portal.* Lanterns or oil lamps were hung from the ends of the crossbeam and, when the Moon "sat" upon the center of the beam, a triangle of light could be seen. This was the mystical sign of access to the Astral or Lunar Dimension and was sometimes referred to as the magickal sign of the enterer. To this day, Italian Witches enter and exit the ritual circle at the northeast point and still employ a version of this ancient Moon Portal.

20 Thomas Inman, *Ancient Pagan and Modern Christian Symbolism* (J. W. Bouton, 1875).

The inner teachings of The Old Religion deal with the esoteric meaning of the Moon tree. In this aspect, it is seen to represent the Sacred Mysteries themselves and, in a practical sense, the structure of the Old Ways. Legend states that the Moon tree bears a single white fruit that is the sacred food of Enlightenment. In the outer Mythos, the tree is located in the center of the Sacred Grove of Diana at Nemi and is guarded by the Hooded One. The Hooded one is a powerful warrior who is not easily vanquished. Within the inner mythos, the tree resides in the Otherworld and is guarded by a serpent coiled around the Fruit of Enlightenment.

Symbolically, the Moon tree represents our system of beliefs, and the fruit of the tree is the Enlightenment that arises from its teachings. The guardian of the grove represents the conscious mind that keeps us from embracing the mystical vision by always questioning and discounting "supernatural" experiences and the inner voice that often leads us to revelations. It is through the practice of magick and the experience of mystical encounter that one forms the mentality necessary to defeat the guardian. Once the guardian can be defeated, then the fruit of the Moon tree is within reach. To taste of its essence is to receive initiation from the Source itself.

The Moon Tree Serpent

In Italian Witchcraft, the serpent is a healer from the Underworld Realm, which is reflected in the image of the caduceus that features two serpents wrapped around a pole. An earlier version of the caduceus appears in Italian Witchcraft and is known as the "Moon tree serpent."

Upon examination, we find the combination of the upright pole and a circle. The pole represents the axis of the Universe, and the circle symbolizes the Divine Receptacle. The pole is the Moon tree, the stabilizing force and the pillar of the night sky. In the Mystery Tradition, the staff and the spindle are symbols of the devotees of the Moon tree. The latter connects the fates who weave the destiny or mortal lives.

In Italian Witchcraft, the serpent symbolizes the goddess Proserpina, who is an Underworld deity. It appears on the cimaruta charm, coiled around the Crescent Moon, which is suspended from one of the branches of the rue sprig. Here, we see the integration of the Moon tree symbolism, creating a composite image of the Moon, the tree, and the serpent. Next to this image on the cimaruta, we find the key, which is followed by the vervain blossom. The key is a central symbol for Hecate, whose other symbols are the serpent and the torch. The key unlocks the gateway that seals the inner mysteries from the sight of the uninitiated. The torch represents the light of the Moon, which, like the serpent, appears from beneath the earth (bringing light into darkness).

The vervain represents the fruit that hangs upon the Moon tree. Here, too, resides the Moon seed, which represents the inner renewal of the Moon as it journeys each month throughout the year. The serpent is also the guardian of the seed, for, in ancient times, they were left in peace among the stores of grain to protect it against rodents. The seed will, in its time, enter beneath the soil and bring renewal, just as the Moon will in its own cycle.

In the region of Benevento, a place famous for Witches' gatherings, we find an ancient snake cult. In his book *The Barbarian Conversion,* scholar Richard Fletcher writes:

> *The Lombard settlers in the Benevento region had adopted a snake-cult which they encountered there. The cult is attested in classical sources and probably dates back to a remote antiquity. Like the altars in Spain it had evidently survived the legislation banning Pagan worship which had been issued by the Theodosian emperors in the late fourth century (the Beneventan region may have had powerful patrons among the still largely Pagan senatorial aristocracy of the day). The snake cult continued to flourish. Even so late as the time of the Lombard king Grimoald (662–71), the brother-in-law of Wilfrid's friend King Perctarit, the Lombards of Benevento, "although washed in the waters of holy baptism nevertheless held to earlier pagan worship and bowed their heads to the image of a viper."*[21]

21 Richard Fletcher, T*he Barbarian Conversion: From Paganism to Christianity* (H. Holt & Co., 1998) 241.

In the book *The History of Magic* by Joseph Ennemoser, we read:

> *The Neapolitan Streghe assembled under a nut-tree in Benevento; the people call it the Benevento wedding. Exactly on this spot stood the sacred tree of the Longobards; and thus witchcraft depends clearly on ancient pagan worship. The witch-mountains of Italy are, the Barco de Ferrarra, the Paterno di Bologna, Spirato della Mirandolo, Tossale di Bergamo.*[22]

Another interesting passage is found in the book *Travels in Europe for the Use of Travelers on the Continent and Likewise in the Island of Sicily*, to which is added an account of the remains of Italy:

> *A variety of fabulous tales are told, by its inhabitants, respecting a walnut-tree, reported to have been for ages the altar of witchcraft. Benevento is accused of having worshipped idols long after the promulgation of Christianity; and the chief object of this idolatry seems to have been a winged serpent of gold with two heads; to which serpent a wood near the town was consecrated, and to a walnut tree in the wood the idol was attached. It likewise appears, from the history of the middle ages, that so late as the year 667, Romualdus, Duke of Benevento, although professing Christianity, kept a winged serpent of gold with two heads in a private recess in his palace; where he and some of his court worshipped this pagan deity. His consort, however, revealed the circumstance to the Bishop of Benevento, who not only enjoined and persuaded her to deliver up the idol to him, but at the same time severely reproved the Duke for his irreligious conduct; and, at length, after encountering much anger and opposition, the Bishop succeeded in transforming the idol into a golden chalice. Tacitus seems to think the worship of idols of this description originated with the Germans; but more probably the adoration paid at Benevento to the winged*

22 Joseph Ennemoser, *The History of Magic*, William Howitt, tr. (H. G. Bohn, 1854).

> *serpent was a remnant of the worship of Isis. We know that the serpent (the emblem of prudence and foresight) was held sacred by the Egyptians; and we see, by the paintings of serpents on the walls of Pompeii, that long before the Germans overran Italy, serpents were considered as a charm against the witchery of an evil eye, equally dreaded by the ancient and the modern Campanians.*[23]

The Moon Fountain and the River of Descent

The ancient tales tell of the sacred tree at Nemi, which rises up from the stream of the nymph Egeria. Egeria is associated with Lake Nemi, as the stream flows into waters of the lake. Here, we find Egeria as a "Lady of Lake" figure. In the Mystery Tradition at Nemi, we find some very interesting similarities between the sword of King Arthur and the staff of the king at the Sanctuary of Diana at Lake Nemi. Only a person bearing certain strengths could draw the sword from the stone or break the branch from the oak tree at Nemi. To do so, in either case, bestowed kingship. The sacred oak represented the Sun God and was under the protection of the guardian of the grove.

The wellbeing of the King of the Woods was attributed, in part, to his relationship with Egeria. According to Scholar James George Frazer, Egeria's stream bubbled up from the roots of the sacred oak at Nemi.[24] Oak was the wood used to heat the forge from which swords were produced; oak produces higher temperatures than most other woods. Therefore, the spirit of the Oak God was passed to the flames and, thus, to the sword carried by the King of the Woods. This mythos may well underlie the Celtic legend of King Arthur and the Sword of Excalibur. Arthur's magickal sword was rooted in the stone from which he drew it and was returned to him by the Lady of the Lake after it had been broken in a foolish challenge of

23 Mariana Starke, *Travels in Europe for the Use of Travellers on the Continent and Likewise in the Island of Sicily* (A. & W. Galignani and Co, 1836) 367.

24 James George Frazer, *The Golden Bough: A Study in Magic and Religion* (Macmillan & Co., 1900).

combat. The branch broken from the oak at Nemi was a challenge of combat to the guardian of the grove. It was part of the tree rooted in the earth, filled with the water bubbling up from Egeria's stream. It is not difficult to see the Sword of Excalibur rising from the lake and the oak branch ascending from the sacred tree within the stream of Egeria as the one and the same image.

Water is never separated from the Moon in ancient mythology. In the oldest tales, the Moon is called the "Fountain of the Living Waters." The fountain is sealed by a rock that is shaped like the Moon disc. At the Spring Equinox, a solar beam pierces a hole in the center of the rock, which allows the water to flow out. It is then that the Earth is healed from its decline into fall and winter, as the fountains opens, the rainbow appears, and the dew again begins to form upon the surface of the land.

At the fountain sits the Moon Maiden, who is beautiful and bewitching. Within the fountain dwells the light of the Moon. In the ancient tale, the Solar Stag-God appears and is attracted to the beauty of the Lady of the Fountain. The stag sees its reflection in the pool of water and becomes enchanted through the vision of his antlers encircling the reflection of the Full Moon. Under the spell of the Moon, the stag is then drawn deep into the forest and his antlers become entangled in the branches of the nocturnal forest (as the sunlight itself seems caught in the treetops). It is then that the hounds of Diana take down the stag, symbolizing that the God must be returned back into Nature, just as the seed must fall into the earth. This mythos later became distorted in the tale of Actaeon and Diana. Actaeon encounters Diana bathing and, seeing her naked, is punished by Diana, who transforms him into a stag. Actaeon's hunting hounds then attack and slay him. However, this is a contrived tale from the patriarchal period and does not concern us.

As the water flows from the Moon fountain, it becomes a stream, which then turns into a river. The river flows across the Mortal Realm and then pours down into the Underworld as it meets the Western Horizon. This occurs at the Autumn Equinox, and the waters will well up again from the Underworld in the spring, where, once again, we find the Fountain of the Moon.

In the mythos, the Goddess enters her Moon boat and journeys to the Underworld to retrieve the Slain God. In the Underworld, the Goddess is impregnated, and, from her womb, the God is born again at the Winter Solstice. The myths of the Old Religion are multi-layered and preserve the teachings passed down through countless centuries. Some of them overlap and tell a similar tale in a different way. These reflect different levels of perception and understanding, leaving many footprints in the sands of time.

The Aegean/Mediterranean tales of the Underworld depict it as being similar to the Realm of Mortal Kind regarding terrain and geographical features. In the oldest tales, the Underworld has its own stars, Moon, and Sun. A vast river flows into the Underworld, diving into different branches. One branch is known as the "River Lethe." Souls that drink from the waters of Lethe are freed of their troubles and worries and lose the memories of their former mortal life. The absence of memory causes a desire to re-enter bodily life, and the soul is then returned to the World of the Living.

Some of the oldest tales tell us that souls await rebirth within a tree and that the Moon tree spans the three known worlds: the Overworld, the Middleworld, and the Underworld. The tree serves as a bridge: its roots are in the Underworld, its trunk in the Middleworld, and its branches in the starry heavens of the Overworld.

The Moon Cup

The Moon, as the source of the waters, is typically symbolized as a cup, pitcher, bucket, pail, jug, kettle, or cauldron. In the oldest tales, the crescent of the New Moon symbolizes a mystical cup belonging to the Faeries. In various tales, this cup is stolen, and then retrieved, in an endless cycle. On May Eve and Yule, the cup is stolen during a festival celebration. This occurs at the meeting of the Sun and Moon during the monthly period where they cross on the three dark nights when the Faeries have the Moon cup hidden and concealed. However, the bright solar people seize the cup on the third evening, which is marked by the appearance of the New Crescent Moon (following the dark period when the Moon goes unseen). For the Moon wanes to a thread, disappears for three dark nights, and is then reborn in the West as the New Moon.

In other myths and legends, the mystical symbolism is centered on a cauldron. The cauldron is usually in the Underworld or is hidden in a cave. Sometimes, it is concealed in the dungeon of a castle. One classic example is the cauldron of Ceres or Ceridwen, which has a ring of thirteen pearls around the rim and whose fire is kindled by the breath of nine maidens. Within the cauldron brews a concoction of herbs, which create an elixir that bestows enlightenment. Three drops were reportedly given to new members during their ritual of initiation.

The thirteen pearls represent the thirteen Full Moons of the year, and the nine maidens represent the gestation period of human birth. Tradition states that a circle was traced around the cauldron on the ground and divided into twelve sections to represent the signs of the Zodiac. Into each compartment was placed an herb magically linked to the Zodiac sign. An invocation was sung four times, representing the four cardinal points (the chief stations of the Sun), then the herbs were placed into the cauldron.

The dark brew that fills the cauldron to its rim symbolizes the Dark or Unseen Moon. After three nights, when the crescent appears, this symbolizes the white foam that appears when the brew is ready for use. The brewing of the cauldron represents the churning of the Black Moon waters at conjunction with the Sun to produce the foam of the New Moon. The Sun is the fire beneath the cauldron, just as the Sun is "below" the Earth when the Moon is completely dark.

The symbolism of the Moon cup and the dark brew appears later in the folk tradition of scrying or reading tea leaves (the herbal connection). For example, the teacup becomes the Moon cup by which fortunes are told. Traditionally, the cup is turned around three times before the leaves can be interpreted. This symbolizes the role of the Dark Moon, which spans three nights. Just as the "Old Black Moon" requires three nights before she reveals her light, the divination cup must also turn three times in order to reveal what is hidden.

The Fruit of Enlightenment

Ancient writings tell us that the mystical sibyls of Rome interpreted the sound of the wind in the leaves of trees, which was regarded as messages from the gods. A teaching exists in old Witchcraft traditions that one can be taught by the Voice of the Wind. Such an idea may have evolved into the concept of divine muses, who inspire humankind. It is interesting to note that both the muses and the sibyls were associated with the god Apollo, the brother of the goddess Diana. In ancient myth and legend, Apollo is intimately connected to trees and transformation.

An old superstition conveys the belief that wind foretells various things. On the first day of January, the direction of the wind is noted as an indication of what the coming year holds. A southern wind foretells heat and fertility, a western wind promises abundant milk and fish, a northern wind predicts cold and storms, and an eastern wind assures abundant fruit on the trees.

In ancient myths and legends, the fruit of certain trees holds mystical meaning and power. Among these trees are the fig, apple, pomegranate, lemon, and the date palm. All of these are found in old lore, including the date palm, which was used as food for the dead. The apple and the pomegranate feature prominently in myths and legends associated with the Otherworld or Underworld.

The apple and pomegranate, in particular, are fruits associated with rites of passage, and they have control over the power of time itself. In some myths and legends, the apple allows safe passage to and from the Realm of the Faery. The pomegranate compels one to be bound to certain cycles, as in the tale of Persephone, who must spend a third of the year in the Underworld. There is also a connection between menstruation and the pomegranate. Menstruation is, in essence, a binding to cycles.

In the Three Great Mysteries (Birth, Life, and Death), we find the repeating cycles of the soul reincarnated into the Material Realm. The purpose of such incarnations is to educate and, thereby, enlighten the soul, which can then be liberated from rebirth once enlightenment is obtained. It is here in this mystical theme that we encounter the Fruit of Enlightenment.

There is an interesting passage from a folklore source that provides a glimpse into the first stirrings of enlightenment:

> *With enlightenment there comes to the agriculturalist an awakened consciousness of his own power and its limitations, and a more rational realization of the possibilities of his own resources. He no longer charges up to diabolical agencies the failures which are clearly attributable to his own lack of foresight or to his neglect. Hope of the harvest no longer centers in anticipated special divine favors, or in the ministrations of priests and saints.*[25]

This passage points to self-awareness and the recognition of internal power within the individual, as opposed to surrendering to external forces.

Self-awareness and reliance upon the self is the first step in the quest of enlightenment. Ironically, with enlightenment comes the realization that there is no separation between the self and the source from which it originated. In other words, everything is connected to everything else, and the concept of self is actually an illusion. In essence, "individuality" is a collapsing of the collective consciousness into singular manifestations that appear to be separate for relatively brief moments in time and space. This can be pictured as a wave breaking and turning into particles of foam. The ocean pulls the water back out into the whole, which then becomes a wave again, and so the cycle repeats. The prevailing "reality" is the ocean (the whole) and not the particles of foam (the individuality).

In the myths of quest, we find the hero-figure traveling to another Realm. This is often symbolized as seeking a magickal tool or vessel that is hidden in a cavern or a castle dungeon. These places represent the Otherworld or Underworld. It is the journey and the return that transform the hero into someone who can understand and wield the thing they desire to obtain. Consciousness must be transformed; the self must reunite with the source and restore the connection.

---

25 Lewis Dayton Burdick, *Magic and Husbandry: The Folk-lore of Agriculture; Rites, Ceremonies, Customs, and Beliefs* (Otseningo Publishing Co., 1905).

In old Witch lore, the quest leads to the Moon tree, where the hero or heroine discovers the single, white fruit that hangs from an inner branch. This is the Fruit of Enlightenment, which must be tasted where it is picked. It cannot be brought out and given to another. However, what it gives to the hero or heroine, they can bring to others in the form of teachings. Ultimately, the teachings allow the student to encounter the Moon tree and taste its fruit directly.

When the Fruit of Enlightenment is encountered, a snake is seen to be coiled around it as the fruit hangs on the tree. To be bitten by the serpent is an act of initiation, and the venom is the catalyst to internal transformation. To overcome the fear of the serpent's bite and the fear of death (loss of individuality) is the only way to take the fruit from the tree. This, and the quest itself, is perhaps best summed up in the following text written by Joseph Campbell:

> *We have not even to risk the adventure alone. For the heroes of all time have gone before us. The labyrinth is thoroughly known. We have only to follow the thread of the heroe path. And where we had thought to find an abomination we shall find a god. And where we had thought to slay another we shall slay ourselves. Where we had thought to travel outward we shall come to the center of our own existence. Where we had thought to be alone we shall be with all the world.*[26]

26 Joseph Campbell, *The Hero with a Thousand Faces* (Pantheon Books, 1949).

Chapter Ten

Magickal and Ritual Gestures

Before humans developed a formal language, they no doubt used gestures as a means of communication. Even today, we use gestures to communicate or to enhance verbal communication. Italians in particular use their hands when speaking, which adds a great deal of energy to the conversation. In everyday life, we see and use gestures all the time. Some of them are inviting and some are offensive, but gestures can communicate a great deal without a word ever being spoken. Although when we think of gesture we think primarily of the hands, a ritual gesture can involve the arms and even the posture of the person performing the rite.

Ancient magickal and mystical societies created systems by which ritual communication could be performed void of any spoken word. This is, in essence, the meaning behind the old phrase "a picture is worth a thousand words." In the Strega Tradition, a system of ritual and magickal gestures (along with postures) was established for this purpose.

Among the gestures used in Italian Witchcraft, we find the signs of recognition, of which there are two types. One type was used to identify the Witch to another person of the Old Religion. This required a gesture and a counter-gesture of recognition. Other gestures were created for ritual use and served to identify the Witch as they stood before the Grigori. In this case, the sign or gesture signified the Witch as one who had rightful (and responsible) access to the Inner Planes, wherein magick and ritual intent take place.

Another type of gesture appears in ritual as a form of communication, and this can be used between the ritualists or as a means of attracting, collecting, and directing energy. In this case, the gestures are considered to be acts of power, although they can also be catalysts to altered states of consciousness. In this light, the gestures help stir the emotions or aids in shifting the mental focus.

Ritual gestures help the participants of the ritual to focus on mystical and magickal concepts that are symbolized by the person displaying them. The concept is communicated instantly, and the participants response instantly. On a mundane level, one example is the gesture of placing the raised index finger against the lips. This is the sign that requests silence. It is as effective in ritual as it is in daily life. The response is always immediate when such a symbolic gesture is displayed. The sign for silence in ritual is reflected in the posture of the Egyptian god Harpocrates and also appears in occult organizations of the nineteenth century.

The evocation of silence in a ritual generates an air of mystery and a sense of something impending. It is, in this regard, the moment of procreation in which all things are possible. This is the essence of magick itself. It is, for this reason, why ritual begins with the gesture of silence, which invokes the mysteries.

Another preparatory symbol is the clasping of hands. This gesture begins with then hands joined, and then the right hand rocks back and forth in a type of grinding motion (the heel of the right hand sliding back and forth across the lower left palm in a horizontal motion). This gesture is performed prior to speaking an invocation or any words of power.

To intensify an evocation or invocation, the posture of horns can be used. This is performed by placing the inner edges of the hands against the temples, with the thumbs protruding outward to form horns. This is also known in some occult societies as "rousing the temples," which is a play on words.

In Italian Witchcraft, the left hand is the hand of receiving, for the left is considered to be receptive. Therefore, whenever something is handed to a person, they accept it with their left hand. This is the spiritual message of receiving, as opposed to taking.

The right hand is considered to be active. It is used to direct energy and for blessing something when only one hand is involved.

In ritual, the right hand is often placed over something when a blessing is directed.

The hands are also used together in ritual for a variety of purposes. The sign of stabilizing is often used once the circle is cast. The hands glide over and across the inner edge of the ritual circle area, from North to South, sealing the circle in the manner of spreading the energy out evenly.

A very simple ritual gesture is the sign of halting, which is used to stop an energy flow or block an energy flow. This allows the ritualist the opportunity to re-direct the current. The sign is also used against spirit entities that enter uninvited or unwanted. Note that it is always the right hand that is used and never the left (because left receives).

As noted earlier, in addition to hand gestures, there is a ritual tradition of body posture gestures that establish occult principles that empower ritual energy. This is because they invoke and evoke the active principle of what they symbolize or represent. One example is the classic posture of the Magician in traditional Tarot symbolism.

The Tarot symbolism reveals a great deal concerning the nature of the ritualist. The Rider Tarot deck is a good one to focus upon, because it was printed prior to the individual adaptations introduced into Tarot decks during the late 1970s and early 1980s. Therefore, it still contains much of the hidden symbolism, which was overlooked in later versions (or possibly even unknown to the new generation). Above all, the Magician is a card of transformation. It is the first character encountered by the Fool in one's journey through the Major Arcana. The Magician transforms the Fool so that he may be prepared to approach the High Priestess in the next card of the deck. Let's examine this symbolism.

The Magician is standing beneath an arbor of roses. Roses represent desire, and, because of their relationship to Venus, they specifically symbolize desires of the heart. The roses tell us that the powers the Magician draws from on high are modified by personal passion or desire. Therefore, we can discern the Magician's consciousness by those things that they bring into their life.

Hovering just over the Magician's head is the symbol for eternity. It is also the number eight resting on its side and is symbolic of Hermes or Mercury, the God of Communication. This tells us that the Magician is connected to the momentum of the past, the Akashic Records, and all that has been. They stand in the Current of Time. The Magician's dark hair represents ignorance stemming from the human condition. The headband symbolizes a limit to this ignorance achieved by the knowledge accumulated by the Magician.

The Magician holds a wand that is raised in the right hand, while the left hand points down to the earth. This symbolizes the higher nature invoked into the lower nature. This is the acquisition of true will (knowledge of, or connection to, the Divine Plan). It is also a reflection of the principle "as above, so below." The wand is a phallic symbol, representing generative energy—the procreative force. Its base animal nature has been purified for spiritual purposes, and this is reflected in the fact that the wand is colored white.

White is also the color of the Magician's robe and is symbolic of inner purification. Around the robe is a serpent biting its own tail and, thus, serving as a belt around the robe of the Magician. The serpent represents wisdom, and the Ob and Odic Forces of polarity balance. Thus, the purified inner nature of the Magician is the equilibrium encircled by the serpent power. The red outer cloak is symbolic of desire and passion, even of the animal nature. It is depicted without a belt, which symbolizes that the Magician is not bound by their passions and desires and can wear or remove them as they please. This is both the gift and the burden of free will.

The Magician stands before the four classic ritual tools of Western Occultism. These represent the Four Elements of Creation. The Magician becomes the fifth element of Spirit, overseeing the creative forces of the Elements. They also represent the Four Worlds of Occultism: Physical, Mental, Spiritual, and Divine. In an occult sense, these tools also represent the four admonitions of the Magician: to know (chalice), to will (blade), to dare (wand), to be silent (pentacle).

The final Tarot symbolism lies at the feet of the Magician. Here is depicted a beautiful garden of roses and lilies. The roses are wild roses, which have five petals. They represent desire as reflected by the five physical senses: taste, touch, sight, hearing, and smell. Lilies have six petals, which is the symbolic number of the Macrocosm.

There are four lilies representing the four worlds that comprise the Totality. The garden itself at the feet of the Magician represents the subconscious mind, as well as self-consciousness. The symbols of desire here symbolize the subconscious response to self-conscious direction. Desire is the catalyst to manifestation and, yet, it must be suppressed during the magickal act and be transformed into subconscious imagery. This is one of the keys to magick. It is also the principle of sigil magick.

The Magician card teaches us that personal power originates from conscious control of the forces and things that lie within the subconscious and self-conscious levels. The posture of the Magician illustrates that the energy comes to us from above. It is drawn, modified by acts of attention, and then directed by the will of the Magician. The Magician becomes the channel through which the forces of a higher nature flow into the Physical Plane. The balance for the Magician is to know that they are no longer the Fool, but also to know that one is not yet equal to that consciousness that we call the High Priestess.

Continuing with the role of symbolism, we come now to the ritual gesture of "Calling Down the Goddess." This is used in a ritual designed to prepare the consciousness of the High Priestess to become a vessel through which the divine feminine can be focused between the Planes. In essence, the gesture symbolizes the principle of manifestation through the Sacerdote's (High Priest) gesturing of the Triangle of Manifestation, which he creates by joining his hands together. The Sacredotessa (High Priestess) assumes the Posture of the Goddess, which forms the divine chalice of cauldron. In some modern traditions, such as Wicca, we find the use of tools, instead of the human body. We also find the displacement of sensuality with rituals tools that are manipulated in such a way as to symbolize sexual union. In this example, the wand or dagger represents the phallus, and the chalice represents the female genitalia.

In the rite of "Calling Down the Goddess," the Sacerdote kneels in front of the Sacerdotessa. He uses the tip of the wand to lightly trace a triangle across the body of the Sacerdotessa. The triangle is marked by the nipples and genitalia area, which form an inverted triangle. This is traced from right nipple to left, then down to genitals, and then back up to the right nipple. The Sacerdotessa raises arms to form cauldron or chalice imagery.

The Sacredote then raises his hands so that, through the opening, it appears from his perspective to be over her head. He then lowers the triangle to appear at her forehead, then continues to the heart and genital region.

As the Sacerdote is performing the gestures, the Sacerdotessa visualizes the Full Moon overhead. She then visualizes it lowering down into her body, pausing at the forehead, heart, and genitals. She feels her own consciousness being gently displaced by that of the goddess as the visualizations continue (they actually share consciousness).

Another set of ritual postures to present is that of the *Goddess Posture* and the *God Posture.* The Goddess posture symbolizes the X pattern that we find in prehistoric art, where it is featured with female imagery. Her crescent symbolizes her lunar nature, while the ample breasts and body stance represent the Birthing Earth Goddess

The God Posture symbolizes the bound sheaf of the harvest and is very similar in style to the image of Osiris, the Egyptian God. The erect phallus is the symbol of the rising stalk of grain, as well as the general symbol of fertility. His horns reflect his earlier aspect of the Lord of the Woods (prior to the development of agriculture).

Chapter Eleven

Italian Folk Magick

In this section, we will explore Italian folk magick. It is important to note that, although elements of it appear in Italian Witchcraft, the two are not the same tradition. To better understand all of this, we will now look at the evolution of traditions in Italy. This is something touched upon previously, but it is worth revisiting here as well.

The magickal beliefs of a people are rooted in the "enchanted world view" of their ancestors. The ancestors developed their view from a direct experience of the world and from their understanding of how invisible beings influence material existence. From this arose the belief in a variety of spirits and deities.

The next phase of development was certainly akin to a shamanic religion or magickal system. This primitive form of interfacing with non-material beings and Realms was the foundation of future religion. This was further enhanced by the interaction of humans with what they perceived to be spirits and deities. Over the following centuries, this evolved into a structure system or tradition.

The Etruscans are said to be the heirs of Neolithic religion in Italy, and the study of Etruscan beliefs and practices is fruitful. We know that archaic Roman religion was based upon Etruscan religion, so a study of the early phases of Roman religion is also beneficial to our understanding.

Among the oldest tales of Witches, we find the writings of Homer, Horace, Ovid, and Lucan. Collectively, they provide a portrait of beliefs about Ancient Witches and Witchcraft. What stands out most is the repeated pattern of the cauldron, wand, Moon, magick, ritual, a triformis goddess, and a chthonic connection to spirits of the dead.

In ancient writings, the Witch Medea possesses regenerative cauldron that can restore life to the dead. She uses a wand, calls the forces of Nature, spirits, and deities, and traces a ritual circle on the ground. Other Witches, such as Canidia, work with a triformis goddess: Hecate, Diana, Proserpina, and sign incantations that can Draw Down the Moon and stars from the night sky.

The Ancient Greek and Roman writings on Witchcraft provide what surely seems to be an organized system of magick and worship. However, with the collapse of the Roman Empire, Europe enters the Early Middle Ages, in which the art of writing is passed on only to a select few, usually people associated with the Church and its efforts to exert power and influence.

With the collapse of cities and their supporting structures, the people inhabiting the rural areas were isolated from "sophisticated" society and its benefits. Reliance upon the folk healers, Witches, and magicians became increasingly more necessary. It was here that the Old Ways of Witchcraft merged with the country people.

When a Witch gave a cure, potion, or a charm, the country person was already familiar with the root or herb. For the country person, these things were relatively easy to procure. The Witch provided something new in the form of an accompanying charm, rhyme, or incantation. This led the country person to believe that all one had to do was obtain that herb and speak certain words in order to cause something to occur. The country people were not aware of what the Witch secretly contributed in terms of magick. This magick included how the herb was charged and how the connection to a source of energy for the spell was established. They knew only the material assembly and verbal delivery, but not the empowering elements. This is how folk magick traditions were created.

In some cases, the momentum of the past was great enough that some power flowed automatically into the latter part of the spell (its components and the spoken charm). In other cases, random chance made people believe in the effectiveness of the spell. In further cases, the person's belief in the spell helped obtain the desired results. However, even in cases like these, the effects of the spell were not assured, and the results were not consistent.

With the rise of Christianity and the decline of open Paganism, people began to turn to Christian elements for a source of power. This resulted in the incorporation of such things as the communion wafer, holy water, the rosary, and saint worship into the folk magick tradition. Over the course of time, the Catholic-based magickal traditions overshadowed the former Pagan ones.

The Old Religion of Stregheria slipped into the shadows and was preserved by handfuls of family Witchcraft traditions and isolated Witches operating behind a Catholic veneer in order to not draw attention. The magickal arts of Stregheria were arrogated by the Catholic-based folk system, which resulted in a new form of sorcery. In order to distinguish between white magick and black magick, the Old Pagan sorcery of Stregoneria was equated with demonic forces. From this arose the Church's view that Witchcraft was evil. From this foundation, the Church and its agents went on to concoct a view of Witchcraft as satanic, which is the popularized depiction from the Middle Ages, through the Renaissance period.

Folk Magick Distortions

In Italian folk magick traditions, we find a variety of charms, amulets, and talismans. Among the common people of Italy, many of these charms are believed to ward off evil. Despite the obvious Pagan elements easily recognized in the appearance of these items, they are commonly viewed as non-Pagan. This dismissal of the Pagan aspects of folk magick is central to the Catholic-based magickal tradition. Italian practitioners of the folk magick view themselves as Catholics and *not* as Pagan or Witches.

The classic charm known as the *Italian horn* is another example of the dismissal of Pagan elements in folk magick. The so-called "horn" is actually not a horn at all, but is instead shaped to represent the penis of a goat. The charm was originally intended to bestow virility and increase fertility. In common folk traditions, the "horn" is worn for good fortune.

Among the characters or figures of Italian lore, we find the Witch Befana and her consort Befano. Among the common people, Befana is a gift-giver figure, similar to Santa Claus in the United States. However, she is actually traceable to an ancient goddess associated with chthonic themes related to the harvest and the Underworld.

As late as the nineteenth century, it was the annual custom to burn a Befana figure, which represented the end of one year and the beginning of the next. The celebration consisted of making a large wooden Befana puppet holding a spindle and distaff. Inside the figure, grapes, dried figs, chestnuts, pears, apples, and carobs with grapa and cognac were placed.

The Befana figure was placed upon a conical pyre six to seven meters high. Chopped wood was placed around the bottom. Next, brambles and straw were stuffed around the frame, and sacks of chestnuts were poured on the structure. As the fire burned, the chestnuts would explode, sending a shower of sparks from the burning structure. Individuals who were skilled in pyromancy (divination by fire) observed the sparks as signs of good or ill for the coming year.

The remaining ashes from the fire are gathered the next day and placed into sacks. The ashes are later scattered over the fields that are plowed for spring planting. It is here that we see the remnants of the Pagan rites. It should be noted that the inner tradition, which is lost to the common people, was to burn the Befano figure who was consort to Befana. Befano is depicted in costume as a hunchback, a distortion of his earlier form as a horned beast.

The ancient sacrifice was originally a stag that symbolized the Lord of the Forest. As humans developed into an agricultural society, the animal sacrifice turned to a plant sacrifice. This figure became the Harvest Lord, consort to the Goddess of Nature.

Among the common people of Italy, the Old Gods gave way to the Cult of Saints. The veneration that was once reserved for the Old Ones was transferred to various patron saints. Some of these incorporated the former Pagan nature, powers, and attributes. Even among some Witch families, the saints became safe veneers through which the worship of the ancestral deities could continue without the danger of discovery.

The Saints of Folk Magick Tradition

- **Saint Barbara:** In folkloric tradition, Saint Barbara is the equivalent of the Goddess of War. She is the protector and champion when called upon for aid or service.
- **Saint Martha:** Saint Martha is the equivalent of the Goddess of Crossroads Magick. She is called upon to bind enemies and influence others to bend to one's will.
- **Saint Agatha:** Saint Agatha is the equivalent of the chthonic goddess and is associated with graves and the dead. She also possesses power over fire and is also known as the "cat saint."
- **Saint Lucy:** Saint Lucy, or Lucia, is the equivalent of the Goddess of Moon Magick. She was venerated by the Benandanti, who believed she bestowed upon them the ability to see in darkness. Lucy dispels the forces of darkness and brings forth the light.
- **Saint Mary Magdalene:** Saint Mary Magdalene is the equivalent of the Goddess of Love. She is called upon to attract a lover.
- **Saint Genevieve:** Saint Genevieve is the equivalent of the fates and is called upon to make changes in one's life.
- **Saint Francis:** Saint Francis is the equivalent of the Lord of the Woods figure. He is called upon for working with Nature and its creatures.
- **Saint Anthony:** Saint Anthony is the equivalent of the healing gods and is called upon to aid against infectious disease.
- **Saint Dunstan:** Saint Dunstan is the equivalent of the magickal blacksmith and is called upon to build, repair, and strengthen (mentally, spiritually, and physically).
- **Saint Vitus:** Saint Vitus is the equivalent of the God of Divine Intoxication and Trance. He is called upon for shamanic work.
- **Saint Athanasius:** Saint Athanasius is the equivalent of gods who reveal and preserve teachings and is called upon for Hermetic knowledge and wisdom.
- **Saint Cosmas and Saint Damian:** These saints are associated with "All Souls' Day" (November 1) and are called upon for ancestral work and dealings with the departed.

The Archangels

In folk magick tradition, the archangels represent the elemental forces and are also Guardians of the four directional quarters.

- **Uriel** (Earth Element)
- **Raphael** (Air Element)
- **Michael** (Fire Element)
- **Gabriel** (Water Element)

Traditional Spells and Enchantments

To Silence Gossip

Items needed:

- Incense
- Incense dish for burning
- A spindle
- A distaff

For use against people who chatter evil against us (*le persone chi ciarlano sui nostro conto*), take incense with the two fingers and the thumb (*con tre dita*) and put it on the threshold of the door and at the window, put a distaff and a spindle with the weight (*penzoloni*) hanging down, and then set fire to the incense, saying:

"Incense, Incense,
may you burn well,
and as you burn, so may burn
the tongues who speak ill of me.
When you have burned away,
then will I take from the window
the distaff and spindle.
These will I burn,
and as they burn, so too may burn,

those evil tongues; may they never return
to their gossip until the distaff
and spindle turn as once before.
May neither turn again!
And so may the vile, unworthy tongues
never speak ill of me again."

For Young Women to See their Future Husbands

Items needed:

- A spring of myrtle (for each girl) that has been carried between the breasts all day
- A piece of tissue paper (to wrap the myrtle in)
- A dish to burn charcoal in
- A piece of charcoal
- Nine hairs (plucked from each girl)
- A fingernail clipping and toenail clipping (from each girl)
- Some dried myrtle leaves
- Some frankincense

This spell *must* be performed by virgins and *must* be done in complete silence.

On the evening of November 25, no more than seven (but not less than three) young women must go into a room that is private and will not be disturbed. As the clock strikes eleven, each maiden removes the sprig of myrtle. This is wrapped in tissue paper, which is then folded.

The charcoal is lit and, when it is hot, the nine strands of hair, the nails clippings, some dried myrtle, and frankincense are burned. As the smoke rises, the sprig of myrtle is passed through it (myrtle is sacred to Venus).

Once this is done, everyone goes to bed just as the clock strikes midnight. The spring of myrtle is placed directly under the head. The maidens will see their future husbands in a dream.

A Spell for Gambling

Items needed:

- Ancestral shrine
- Three playing card aces: spades, clubs, and diamonds
- Three candles

At midnight, light the candles in front of the ancestral shrine. Then say the following:

"Lasii, Lasii, Lasii!
Ye who are gracious
There is a favor
Which I need greatly,
And of ye spirits,
Spirits and Lasii,
Here in a cellar
Now I am kneeling,
And I commend myself
Unto your graces,
That ye will grant me
This special favor!

Lasii, Lasii, Lasii!
Here, I present myself,
Bearing three candles,
Three candles lighted,
Three cards—the ace of spades,
And that of clubs,
And that of diamonds.
I fling them in the air
That you may see them
Plainly before you,

Here just at midnight
In air I throw them;
If you grant me a favor,
Cause me to find
The ace of clubs plainly.
If 'tis the ace of spades
'Tis a sign that you will not
Grant me the favor;
But if you make me find
The ace of diamonds,
Then 'tis a sign
That my wish will be granted."

If the request was granted, then carry the ace of diamonds with you when you gamble.

A Blessing Spell (Lemon)

Items needed:

- One unripe lemon
- A variety of pins with multi-colored heads
- A glass bottle (optional)

If you wish to bestow a variety of blessings upon a person, pick a green lemon and let it dry until it is black. Then, insert many different colored pins into the black skin and say what blessings you wish upon the person. Push them all the way down until only the colored heads are showing.

The lemon can be kept as is, or can be kept for up to three days. In the latter case, the pins are extracted, and the lemon is dropped into a body of water. The pins can be kept in a bottle in the home to secure the continued blessings.

A Cursing Spell (Lemon)

Items needed:

- One unripe lemon
- Pins with black-colored heads

If you wish someone ill in an act of revenge, then pick a lemon while it is still green. Insert many black-colored pins (only black), and push the pins all the way down until only the head of the pins is showing. Say what you wish to happen to the person you are cursing. If possible, place the lemon in or near the home of that person. As the lemon dries, it will turn black, and the intent of the curse will likewise increase ("go black").

An Oracle Spell (Lemon)

Items needed:

- One unripe lemon
- One fish spine (sufficient size and strength to support weight of the lemon)
- A colored cord (color should represent the intention of the spell)
- Playing cards

To use as an oracle, pick a green lemon and allow it to dry until it is black. Then, pierce the skin and insert a fish spine into the lemon. It must be deep enough to hold the lemon while it is suspended. A colored cord is then tied to the fish spine, and the lemon is suspended as a pendulum.

Questions are asked, and the movement of the pendulum speaks the meaning. Back and forth (East to West) means no, back and forth (North to South) means yes. Playing cards can be set in a cross pattern (the four directions) and the pendulum can be used to reveal a person you suspect. Use the court cards, male and female. Name them after different people you know. When the pendulum moves towards one card, this means that this is the person in question.

Hex-Breaking

Items needed:

- A bottle of oil
- A glass of water
- A piece of charcoal
- Three pinches of salt

1. Take a small container of oil and make with it thrice the sign of the Crescent Moon on the forehead, saying:

   "In the name of the sky, the stars, and the Moon, this trouble leaves me in exchange for good fortune and prosperity."

2. Then, with the same bottle or vial, make three crescents with the right hand over the glass of water, exactly from side to side, also making the *corna* or *jettatura* with the forefinger and pinky of the left hand extended, and the middle and ring-finger closed, or held by the thumb. These extended fingers rest on the edge of the tumbler.

   While doing this, repeat (three times):

   "Befana! Befana! Befana!
   Whoever caused this trouble,
   bear it away from me!"

3. Then, very carefully drop three drops of oil across the surface of the water. If they combine at once, it is a good sign; but, if the three drops remain apart, it is a bad or negative sign.
4. Pour the oil and water mixture out onto the ground (outside). Refill the glass of water and hold it with your left hand. Next, mark the forehead again with three crescents, repeating the Befana invocation three times as before.

   "Befana! Befana! Befana!

Whoever caused this trouble,
bear it away from me!"

5. Now, with the right hand, make the gesture of the *mano in fica,* then pour three drops of oil across the surface of the water (with the right hand).
6. If the oil does not combine, then the spell is not broken. To completely break the spell, do the following. Drop the salt into the water and oil mixture. Next, drop the hot charcoal into the glass. Then, say these words:

"Blessed fire that burns immensely,
You who gives warmth to all,
I pray you to burn away this evil spell
And mark the one who sent it to me."

7. Pour out the contents outside on the ground. The spell is thereby broken, and the ill intent goes back to the person that sent it.

Spell-Reversing (Incense on Coals)

This is used to ascertain who has bewitched anyone or to remove an evil spell.

Take a *scaldino* (a receptacle of glazed crockery like a basket in form) with charcoal glowing hot, then take incense and cummin and put them on the coals. Then, with a large knife in the left hand, the *scaldino* being held in the right, go into all the rooms of the house, focusing above and below the bed, pronouncing the benediction the whole time. And with this knife, stir the contents.

As the cummin and incense burn, repeat:

"I do not stir the incense,
but I break loose the body, the soul,
and all the feelings
of the person who wished misfortune
to me and my home."

When all the incense is burned, put into the *scaldino* a leaf of yellow paper (always yellow), and two nails tied in the shape of an X. If you do not know who has done the harm, throw the incense and coals into a running stream or into a river. But, if you suspect any person, have the *scaldino* and nails carried into their house and hide it under the roof where it cannot be found. Do not forget to include the crossed nails. Then, the guilty person will be compelled, or impelled, to undo the harm or spell; they will have no rest 'till this be done.

Chapter Twelve

The Ritual Tools

Humans have always been users of tools, from the days of stones and clubs to the current age of push-button destruction. In this chapter, we will examine the purpose and the evolution of ceremonial/magickal tools in humankind's quest to gain a balance with Nature. The earliest of Strega's tools was the wand, which was closely followed by the shell or gourd (depending upon the region). Over the course of centuries, other tools appeared and, today, we possess the wand, cup, sword, and pentacle. In some magickal lodges, these tools are shown with the following correspondences: Wand of Intuition, Cup of Sympathy, Sword of Reason, and Pentacle of Valor.

Many people have noticed the resemblance of the Witches' tools to the armor and weapons of a knight. There is a definite connection, and any true Witch must (to some degree) be a Spiritual Warrior. This is equally true of anyone who walks a magickal path in life. In a metaphysical sense, the sword is necessary to maintain a stable mind and to "cut through" deception and delusion. The chalice or cup serves as a reminder of compassion as one grows in personal power. The wand focuses the intuitive mind so that one can discern and realize what one perceives. The Shield (Pentacle) of Valor is often left out in most texts of this nature, but it should be stated that one must carry their valor before them to serve as a protection against fear (the great enemy). A person of magick must hold true to their own set of values and codes of conduct, for one can only be as strong as their most vulnerable weakness. As we continue, we will take a look at each tool, its background, and its preparation as a magickal tool.

Part One: The Primary Tools

The Pentacle

The pentacle (or pantacle) is the ritual platter symbolizing the elemental force of Earth. It is used as a focal point for spells and rituals, in which it serves as a connection to the Material World.

The pentacle is the interface point for magick between the worlds. Whatever is placed on the pentacle or directed to it joins with the astral and material energies. Through this principle, a ring can be charged with magickal astral energies attracted from the Elemental or Astral Realms. The reverse is also true, and desires from the Material Realm can be transmitted from the pentacle into the Elemental or Astral Realms.

In Italian Witchcraft, the pentacle is made from a natural substance taken from the earth. Stone or clay is the most common material for the pentacle. The pentacle is aligned to the North Quarter, which is assigned the attribute of the Earth element.

One mystical connection to the pentacle is found in the lore of the gemstone. Here, we find the ancient belief that the Underworld was illuminated by gems, which served as light in the Realm of the Dead. The inner teaching reflects this idea that this is the spiritual or astral substance of light and its connection to both worlds (the living and the dead). Therefore, the pentacle emanates energy which, within the Hidden Realms, is perceived as light. Light can attract or banish, depending upon the intent of those who come within its sphere of influence.

The Wand

The wand is a ritual tool symbolizing the element of Air. This connection is tied to its nature as the branch of a tree. In early times, it was observed that the branches of trees brought forth life. From season-to-season, they issued buds, leaves, flowers, and fruits. Trees were venerated as sacred beings who gave life and provided food and shelter. These beings were rooted in the earth and reached upward into the sky. They were bridges between the Underworld and the Overworld.

In reverence to the tree, strict procedures were adopted for the taking of a branch to use as a wand or staff. First, offerings had to be made to the spirit (or numen) of the tree. These were usually "first fruits" of the harvest or "nectar," which was made up of wine, honey, and milk. The wood was taken from the bend in the branch, out to the fork. This represented the human arm from the elbow to the tip of the middle finger. The reason for this was due to the resemblance between a human arm and hand to the extending branch of a tree. Therefore, over the course of time, a measure was established. Wands were to measure from the inside of the elbow to the tip of the middle finger. Staffs were to measure the height of the person plus the measure of their wand (so that the staff was taller than the person, i.e. more powerful).

Once formed and prepared, the wand became a tool of Nature's inner magick. The wand is a tool which is used to request, rather than demand, and it is gentle with its power. This request possesses great influence, for its source is the Divine itself. It is used for calling upon the gods and Nature Spirits. It is a symbol of the element of Air and is associated with the East. Magically, it is often used for healing, divination, and astral workings.

The Ritual Wand Procedure

Choose a tree of the fruit-bearing variety, as these are best. If you wish, however, you may use oak or willow (even rosewood is fine). These woods have magickal associations with ancient cults, and many people prefer them for that reason. Wood that bears fruit is actually superior for a wand of general use.

Before sunrise, go before the tree and give an offering. Tell the spirit within the tree what you wish to do and why. Wait a few moments, then proceed (unless you feel that the spirit has rejected your request). If you are going to take the branch, then do so quickly. Wrap it up in cloth and return home. Trim the wood smooth, removing the bark, and shape the tip so that it resembles a phallus. Allow the wood to dry for nine days before carving or painting symbols upon it.

On the night of the Full Moon, place the symbols of the art upon it. Present it to the East Quarter and declare it to be a wand of magick and a power over the element of Air. At midnight (or 9pm, if necessary), go out beneath the Full Moon and hold the wand up towards it, saying:

"My Lady, Mistress of Night and of Magick,
You who rules the star-filled heavens,
bless and empower this wand,
that all may see, and know Thy Greatness.
Wherefore, do I consecrate and dedicate this wand
to you, Great Mistress of Magick."

After completing this, set a bowl out beneath the Moon. Place equal portions of the following herbs into the bowl: pennyroyal, rosemary, hyssop, and acacia. Pour boiled water into the bowl, and steep the herbs for three minutes. Strain the mixture through cheesecloth, and then add this liquid potion to a half-filled bowl of fresh spring water. To the spring water, add nine drops of almond extract. Then, drop three moonflowers (or white jasmine flowers) into the bowl. Pause a moment and look up at the Moon. Raise the wand up to her, then lower it into the bowl. Bathe the wand in the liquid briefly, then remove and dry it. It is now ready to use.

The Spirit Blade

One of the most common tools associated with the practice of the Witchcraft is the ritual dagger. In Italian Witchcraft, it is known as the "spirit blade," as it has power over non-material. Because the forge fire brought about the knife, it was associated with the element of Fire in which it was created. Unlike the wand, the blade is a tool of force.

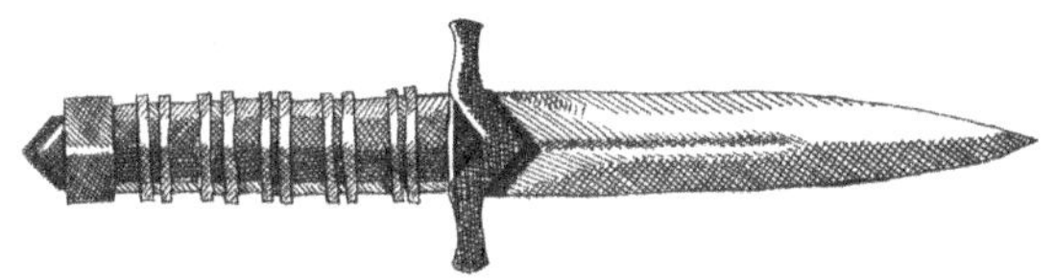

Preparation of the Blade

Three nights before the Moon is full (the third night being the Full Moon), dig a small hole in the earth which is as deep as your hand is long. Then, take equal portions (about a handful) of the ground herbs: rue, vervain, and fennel. Add them to the soil dug from the hole and mix this all together. Then, replace the soil into the hole. Leave this until the night of the Full Moon.

On the night of the Full Moon, boil some water (about 8 oz.), to which you will add three pinches of salt. Then, go out to the hole you filled and pour the boiled water out (slowly) upon it. After this, trace out a triangle that will enclose the area you filled in. Then, place nine drops of liquid camphor directly upon the center of the hole. At this point, grasp the dagger in both hands, with the blade pointing down, and raise your arms up to the Moon, saying:

> *"Night, trusted keeper of secrets deep, and stars who, together with the Moon, follow on from the fires of the daylight, and you, Goddess of the Three Faces, who know all designs and aid the incantations and the Craft of the Witches, and Earth, who furnish Witches with powerful herbs, and Breezes, Winds,*

Mountains, Rivers, and Lakes, and by all the gods of the grove and all the gods of the night, be present to aid me!"

Then, push the blade down into the soil (directly center in the hole) up to the handle base. Next, Draw Power Down from the Moon (as follows):

Kneel before the Moon, hands upon the thighs, and say:

"At will, I make swift streams retire
To their fountains, whilst their banks admire;
Sea toss and smooth; clear clouds and clouds reform.
With spells and charms the misty powers fetch
Lift solid rocks, oaks from their seizures stretch
Whole woods sway, the lofty mountains shake,
Earth for to groan, and shades from graves awake,
And Thee, O Moon, I draw…"

(As you begin the last verse, raise your left hand and "cup" the Moon).

Then, quickly close your hand in a grasping manner, seemingly closing the Moon within your hand. Do not look up at this point, but bring your closed hand down (as if drawing or pulling) and grasp the knife handle. Next, place your right hand firmly over your left and concentrate upon the knife, imagining it glowing with power. After a few minutes, remove the knife from the soil and clean it off with a white cloth.

The final step is to magically charge the blade. To charge the ritual dagger for use, it must first be heated over an open flame for a couple of minutes. This awakens the memory of the creative force of fire within the blade. Once the blade is hot, say these words:

"Blade of steel, your charge shall be, to banish all I bid of Thee!"

Then, immediately plunge the blade into herbal potion (poured into a bowl) in order to seal the memory. Afterwards, dry off the blade and set it aside.

To complete the process, you will need to magnetize the blade. Take a medium size magnet (or loadstone) and rub it from the hilt to the tip of the blade, firmly and moderately, nine times on each side of the blade. Then, rub it again nine times on the first side of the blade, for a total of twenty-seven times. For an extra charge, repeat this three times, for a total of eighty-one times. Be sure to always go in the same direction with the magnet. As you stroke the magnet along the blade, periodically say these words:

"Blade of steel, your charge shall be, to attract all things I bid of Thee!"

The knife is then ready for the symbols to be placed upon the handle. All that remains is to charge the knife with the four elements and to dedicate it to the service of the goddess.

The Chalice

The chalice is a vessel tool associated with liquids and, as such, is linked to the element of water. It is a receptive tool and is related to the cauldron-in-womb symbolism. Traditionally, the chalice holds the sacred wine, which is the essence of the Goddess in Witchcraft rituals. In addition, the chalice is used to pour libations upon the Earth as offerings to the chthonic forces and to ancestral spirits.

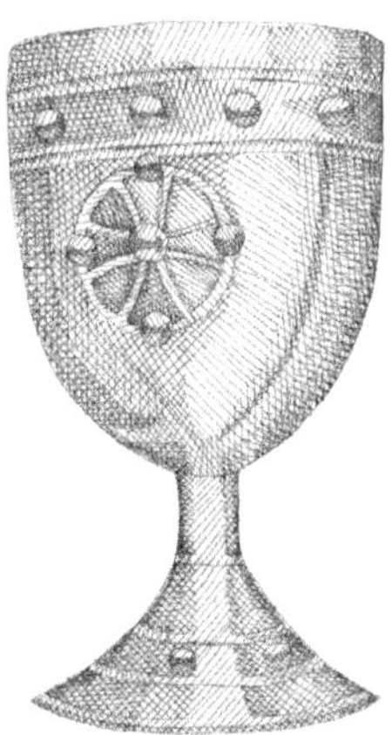

In Modern Italian Witchcraft, the chalice is made of silver, the traditional metal of the Moon. However, the peasant Witches of past centuries most likely did not possess silver tools. Therefore, you can choose any material you find suitable, although a silver chalice is preferred.

The Spirit Bowl

In Italian Witchcraft, we find the use of a blue flame in rituals and works of magick. This is often referred to as the *spirit flame.* According to oral tradition, this was used at the Temple of Diana in Ancient Italy, which stood on the eastern shore of Lake Nemi. The flame represented the presence of Divinity and it floated on the surface of flammable liquid, just as the Moon's light reflected upon the waters of the lake.

Today, the spirit bowl is placed upon the center of the altar. An alcohol-based liquid (such as Strega liqueur) is poured into it and lighted. This is done to a series of gestures and verbal incantations that aid to empower the Flame. Once established, the Flame is considered to be the living presence of Divinity within the ritual setting. Traditionally, a woman tends the altar and renews the liquid, so that the flame will not die out during the rites.

Ancient Origins of the Bowl

One of the oldest ritual tools in Witchcraft is the shell or bowl. Originally, large shells were used to contain seawater for blessings and for various works of magick. The Moon has long been associated with the tides of the ocean. It is for this reason seawater was considered to contain the essence of the Moon's power.

In ancient times, shells were placed upon stone altars with the open end facing upwards. Large shells were of particular value. Seawater was poured into a ceramic or wooden bowl, and a small white shell was placed in the center of the bowl. This represented the Moon, and so the worship of the Moon could be carried out even when the Moon was not visible in the night sky.

In another type of symbolism, the bowl represented the Womb of the Great Goddess, and the shell within it symbolized the "Child of Promise." The Child was the promise of prophecy and the mediator between humans and gods. With the shell in place, the priestesses were assured of the divinatory powers of the Moon bowl. A series of small white shells were also placed around the base of the bowl, forming a crescent shape around it. As the stones were placed left to right, the name of the goddess being invoked was chanted. At the conclusion of the rite, the shells were removed one at a time from right to left.

The Secondary Tools

The secondary tools of Stregheria are all folk magick tools and are associated with the hearth and home. They are, therefore, tools of the Matriarch and symbolize her power. It must be remembered that Italian women were (and still are) very powerful forces in the family. The association of domestic tools with women in the Strega tradition is not an insult, but rather a remembrance of when women ruled.

The Broom

The broom was not associated with Italian Witches as a symbol until around the latter half of the eighteenth century. Strega were always portrayed as riding to the *treguenda* (sabbat) on the backs of goats, unlike Witches of Northern Europe, who were portrayed as flying on broomsticks. There is a similarity in this mythos in as much as the goats provided flight in the same manner as the broomsticks.

As a ritual tool, the broom can be used for protection and banishment, and also serves as a symbol of the Goddess when turned brush-side up. As a tool of protection, the broom is laid across a doorway or entryway of any sort. When a ritual "doorway" is opened in a ceremonial circle, the broom can be set across the opening while members exit and re-enter the circle. Ritual blades can also be used for this same purpose.

In banishment, the broom can be used to sweep salt (scattered around the affected area) out through the front door or entry area. The sprinkling of salt to remove negative energy is a very ancient practice. It can also be used to "thrash the air" in any setting to purify the area. Typically, this involved censing the place with incense smoke, then swinging the broom through the smoke.

The broom can also be set fiber-side-up near a ritual gathering sight to represent the presence of the Goddess. This represented the fertile and sexual power of the Goddess, a symbolic representation of female genitalia (unshaven).

Traditionally, a new broom was given to the bride on her wedding day as a symbol of her own power within the home and family. In ancient times, this was meant to honor her for nurturing and supporting the family structure. The entire family was dependent upon her and, through this, she was given a great deal of respect and authority.

Scissors

Another domestic tool wielded by the women of the home was a simple pair of scissors. In the folk magick of the Strega, scissors are used to break spells and sever magickal or astral connections. This is accomplished by acts of cutting, slashing, or actually dropping the scissors. Cutting up a picture can sever the connection with that person, as can cutting up a piece of their clothing.

Olive oil drops can be placed upon the surface of a bowl of water to represent whatever needs banishment. The scissors can then be jabbed into the drops while visualizing the problem. A person believed to be under a spell can be freed by sneaking up behind them and dropping the scissors to the floor. I suppose that this is similar to curing "hiccups" by scaring the person.

A charm in the image of a pair of scissors can also be worn for protection, or hung in a window, or over a doorway. The same is also true of a horseshoe, key, or a piece of horn. These, of course, are folk magick beliefs.

The Cauldron

The cauldron is used primarily for offerings within a ritual setting. This can be either an offering to deities or spirits. Typically, the cauldron is set at the appropriate directional quarter of the ritual circle, which symbolizes the powers or forces whose influence is sought.

Offerings to the spirits of Earth would be performed at the North Quarter. Spirits of Air receive offerings at the East Quarter, spirits of Fire to the South, and spirits of Water to the West. Most deities are given offerings at the North, but, occasionally, this may be performed at either the East or West. In such a case, it would involve aspects of deity associated with either the Sun or Moon, since those are the quarters of rising and setting.

The cauldron is viewed as the regenerative womb of the Goddess. Because of this, offerings can be placed in front of the cauldron, and wishes written on parchment can be placed inside with some seeds. This is symbolic of impregnation, and the desire is to give birth to your wish. This is of particular importance at the Spring Equinox, which is the time of planting.

The Mortar and Pestle

During the time of the Middle Ages, the Strega began to use the common mortar and pestle as ritual tools. These served as the ritual cup or bowl and the wand. Because these were tools common to most homes, no suspicion of Witchcraft would fall upon anyone found with such implements.

The mortar and pestle naturally represents the feminine and masculine polarities. When combined with a platter and a knife (common tools), the Witch (in days of old) could safely keep tools of the Craft in the home.

As a magickal tool, the mortar and pestle can be used in spells of joining or combining, as well as in works of magick intended to refine or transform. For simple spells, objects or photos can be joined together and placed in the mortar. The pestle is then set on top of this (the object or photo is sandwiched between the pestle and the inside of the mortar). Place a candle of a color to symbolize your desire and leave this burning in front of the mortar. Focus your intention. This is best performed under the phase of the Moon that suits the nature of your intent.

Chapter Thirteen

The Rituals

The rituals of the Old Religion are rooted in pre-Christian Pagan rites associated with fertility and the seasons of nature. But even older roots exist and are connected with ancestral veneration. This will be further explored as the chapter continues.

In Italian Witchcraft, we find the word *tregenda* or *treguenda* used to indicate the assembly of Witches (commonly known as the *sabbat*). It is derived from (or related to) the Italian word *tregua,* which means "a respite." This is an interesting term when we ask the question—a respite from what? The answer may come from the celebratory or festival nature of the Witches' assemblies, as described in early writings. In this light, we can view the *tregenda* as a break from the mundane work and cares of everyday life.

When viewing the sabbat as depicted during the period of the Inquisition, it is important to understand that we are looking at an evolved concept. The ideas and depictions of the sabbat evolved and grew in layers that transformed into something quite different from its original structure and purpose. In order to discover the original model, we must look to what has been called "The Society of Diana."

Historian Franco Mormando notes, on the Society of Diana, while commenting on the Witches' Sabbat:

> *This notion of the assembly is yet another universal item in "the classic formulation of the Witch Phenomenon." Like much else in the baggage of the European witch, it has its roots in pagan mythology, specifically in the un-Christian but non-diabolical "Society of Diana," an innocuous, festive ride and*

> *gathering of woman under the tutelage of the pagan goddess of the moon and the hunt . Turned into a demonized witch phenomenon by the theologians and canonists of Christian Europe, the assembly was by the end of the fifteenth century to be known (with tinges of anti-Semitisim) as the witches' "Sabbath." With the passing years, it slowly acquired ever more heinous, orgiastic characteristics. During Bernardino's lifetime, the gathering was called by various names; the preacher himself, in one of his 1424 sermons to the Florentines, refers to it by the Italian term tregenda.*[27]

As to what Bernardino of Siena imagined as occurring during the *tregenda,* we cannot be completely sure, since the notion of the "sabbath" was still in its development phase. While the friar's 1424 sermon does not describe this convocation of Witches, his later treatise on Witchcraft and superstition, "*De Idolatriae Cultu*" (1430-1436), contains a reference to the *tregenda,* though the word itself does not appear in the text. This Latin work nonetheless gives us some idea of his conception of the regular Witches assemblies, which eventually evolved into the "sabbath."

Scholar Walter Stevens writes:

> *About 1354, the Dominican preacher Jacopo Passavanti was writing in Italian (in Lo specchio della versa penitenza, or The Mirror of True Repentance) that "some people say they see dead people and talk to them, and that they go by night with witches [colle streghe] to their tregenda." Many such people are simple impostors, he says: they take advantage of others' bereavement for financial gain or out of sheer malice. Nonetheless, some people do sincerely think that they see dead people. This is impossible, says Passavanti (presumably because these soul are in hell or purgatory and are not allowed out). But people*

27 Franco Mormando, *The Preacher's Demons* (U of Chicago Press, 1999) 66.

> *are seeing something that is real. The Devil can take on the semblance of dead people and falsely impersonate them...*[28]

Despite the stereotypical inclusion of the Devil and the dismissal of Pagan elements as deceptions perpetrated by Satan, the reference to dealings with the dead is a significant sign of surviving Pagan elements in Italian Witchcraft. Among the most ancient literature on Witchcraft, we find Witches involved with the crossroads, which was a favored place of Witches and Magicians of all kinds.

It was an ancient belief that spirits of the dead gathered at the crossroads, which was itself considered to be a passageway between the Worlds of the Living and the Dead. The goddess Hecate has long been associated with the crossroads, Witchcraft, and spirits of the dead. The souls that gathered at the crossroads were those that had not crossed over into the World Beyond. Beliefs varied as to why souls remained, but the most popular belief held that injustice and violence prevented the soul from leaving the World of the Living. In this regard, Hecate became the caretaker of these souls.

In Ancient Aegean/Mediterranean lore, Hecate is also known as Trivia (Goddess of the Crossroads) and Enodia (Goddess of the Road). She was known as the Goddess of Gateways, Doorways, and Portals. Ancient writers on Roman Witchcraft portrayed her as a triformis goddess: Hecate, Diana, Proserpina. This triple nature is reflected in a popular symbol of unknown date and origin.

28 Walter Stevens, *Demon Lovers—Witchcraft, Sex, and the Crisis of Belief* (U of Chicago Press, 2002) 132.

The Lare spirits (or gods) were also associated with the crossroads and with ancestral veneration. This suggests a connection to dealings with the spirits of the dead. Added to this is the appearance of a serpent with the Lare in ancient art; the serpent is chthonic in nature. The Lare were also linked to the seasons and their celebration. In this regard, we can link the Lare to the sabbats in an archaic view of the roots of the tregenda.

In Ancient Rome, we find the *Mos Maiorum,* which refers to the custom of the ancestors or the inherited experience of the race. These were the Old Ways of past generations and they defined the spiritual fiber and character of the tribe or community. The honoring and the veneration of ancestral teachings were at the core of Roman civilization. This is also true of Italian Witchcraft.

An interesting connection to the theme of communication with the dead in Italian Witchcraft appears in the legends of the sibyls. In the Aeneid, Vergil presents the Cumaean sibyl as conducting Aeneas into the Underworld. She lives in a cave near Lake Avernus, which was believed to be the entrance to the Underworld. Avernus is located in the region of Campania near Naples. Ancient writers depict the sibyl as an oracle woman, prophetess, and spirit medium. The sibyl wrote her messages and teachings on leaves, which she set on at the entrance to her cave. She was, in many ways, a mystical Witch-figure.

One of the key stories connected to the sibyl is the tale of the Golden Bough. The sibyl provides Aeneas with a sacred branch by which he can enter the Underworld and return again to the World of the Living. The theme of a sacred branch granting access to Mystical Realms is widespread throughout Europe. In the north, it appears as the Silver Bough, which is associated with Faeries. It is in such tales that we find the connection to the Moon tree of Italian Witchcraft.

Among the oldest and lasting tales of Italian Witchcraft is the sacred tree at Benevento. According to legend, Witches from all over Italy gathered at this tree to celebrate the *tregenda* or "Witches' Sabbat." The site featured a walnut tree that was sacred to Proserpina (herself part of the triformis goddess: Hecate-Diana-Proserpina). From her name, Proserpina, we can draw out the connection to serpents. Benevento was once the site of serpent worship in ancient times.

In the seventh century, the Bishop of Benevento suppressed snake veneration at the walnut tree site, this featured a golden serpent placed by the tree with an animal hide slung over one of the branches. In the course of time, the bishop had the tree cut down and he ordered the golden serpent melted and made into a golden chalice.

Pipernus, in his treatise on the "magic walnut tree of Benevento" (written in 1647), links the worship of Diana to the Benevento tree. Drawing from the treatise, folklorist Charles Leland writes:

> *Finally we come to the fact that from the testimony and traditions recorded in the manuscripts of an old witch trial, and from information gathered by many holy Inquisitors, that it was believed in the fraternity of sorcerers that not only from the times of the Lombards, but even from those of the ancient Samnites, there had ever been at Benevento an immense walnut-tree which was in leaf all the year (the same tale was told of old Druidical and German oaks), the nuts of which were of a pyramidal form, "qua tragularibus lincis emittebat.*[29]

Leland adds: *"Pipernus gives us a long array of causes why the nut-tree was dreaded by Christians, and loved by witches, the only sensible one of which is that it was of yore, because of its dense shade, sacred to Proserpine, Night, and the Infernal Gods."*[30]

In looking back at the roots of Italian Witchcraft, we note that nighttime, and particularly nights when the Moon is full, was the preferred time for gathering. In this setting, the Moon and the stars were intimately connected to Witchcraft. It is here that we find the old belief that the souls of the dead abide in the Lunar Realm while they await rebirth. For this reason, the Full Moon ritual, in part, is a time to remember and commune with those who have gone before us.

The association of the Moon with a goddess is extremely ancient, and the connection to a triformis goddess comprised of Hecate-

29 Charles Godfrey Leland, *Etruscan Roman Remains: in Popular Tradition* (T. Fisher Unwin, 1892) 190.

30 *Ibid.*

Diana-Proserpine appears in Ancient Roman writings. Over the course of time, the goddess name Diana became almost singularly identified with Italian Witchcraft. It is important to note that "Diana" is actually a title more than it is a name. It is formed on the adjective *dius* (luminous); the neuter *dium* designates "the luminous sky." Therefore, Diana means "the luminous one."

Because Witches gathered at night and belonged to a secret society, they were known as the "Hidden Children" of the Goddess. They found in the light of the Moon an essence of magick and mysticism. Here, a softer enlightenment existed in contrast to the religions that flourished in the light of day. It was also here in the dark sacred night that Witches communed with spirits of the Otherworld, such as the Elven or Faery race.

Otherworld contact held great importance because the link between the mystical operations connected with the Plant Kingdom. This is one of the reasons why trees were held to be sacred and why Witches were herbalists. When we look at the Full Moon ritual, we can see the importance of the seed, ritual cakes made from the grain, and the intimate connection to spirits of the Otherworld who impart mystical knowledge and power.

A Solitary Full Moon Ritual

1. Cast circle in the usual manner.
2. Stand before the altar and look up at the Moon or a symbol of the Moon, saying:

   "I come on this sacred night of the Lady, beneath the Full Moon to adore Her symbol, which She has placed among the stars. And to give due worship unto the Great Goddess, for this is the appointed time that the Holy Strega bid me observe. As it was in the time of the beginning, so is it now, so shall it be."

3. Hold your palms out in front of you, facing away, and form a triangle with your hands by touching the index the fingers and thumbs together (the gesture of manifestation). Enclose

the Moon or its symbol in the opening of the triangle you have formed with your hands, then recite:

"Hail and adoration unto You O' Great Diana. Hail Goddess of the Moon, and of the Night. You have been since before the beginning, You who caused all things to appear, Giver and Sustainer of Life, Adoration unto You."

4. Perform the Rite of Union (see page x) as you gaze upon the Moon: standing or kneeling before the *Light* (or symbol), raise hands as in position one, saying:

    "Hail and adoration unto Thee O' Source of All Enlightenment. I pray Thee impart to me Thy Illumination."

5. Lower arms to position two, saying:

    "And enlighten my mind that I may perceive more clearly, all things in which I endeavor."

6. Lower arms to position three, saying:

    "And illuminate my soul, imparting Thy essence of Purity."

7. Lower arms to positions four and five, saying:

    "I reveal my Inner Self to Thee and ask that all be cleansed and purified within."

8. Place offerings to the Goddess at the West Quarter. Kneel before the offerings and recite:

    "O' Great Diana, think yet even for a moment, upon this worshipper who kneels in Your name. Beneath the Sun do people toil, and go about, and attend to all worldly affairs. But beneath the Moon, Your children dream and awaken, and draw their power. Therefore, bless me O' Great Diana, and

impart to me Your mystic Light, in which I find my powers. Bless me, O' Great Diana."

9. Look up at the Full Moon and recite:

"O' Ancient Wanderer of the Dark Heavens,
Mystery of the Mysteries,
emanate Your sacred essence upon me
as I wait below at this appointed time.
Enlighten my inner mind and spirit,
as do you lighten the darkness of night."

10. Sit quietly within the circle, and recite the *Veglia:*

"Once, long ago, all Witches worshipped in the open fields and upon the ancient sites. And our chants were carried upon the winds. Our prayers were received upon the smoke of our incense by the Old Ones. But in time, we were enslaved by the worshippers of a jealous god, and our villages were given over to cruel Lords. The Old Ways were forbidden, and we were forced to accept the ways of our oppressors.

Now, it is a time of gathering in the shadows. We have suffered persecution for our beliefs, and many of you. I am one of the hidden children of the Goddess. From generation unto generation has the knowledge been passed and the Old Ways been kept by those who kindle the flame. In remembrance, I come this evening beneath the Full Moon, to honor the past, secure the future, and receive the essence of the Old Ones."

11. Place something made from grain upon a plate. Next to this, set a chalice of wine. Bless them by tracing a crescent over them and then recite:

"Blessings upon this meal, which is as my own body. For without such sustenance, I would perish from this world. Blessings upon the grain, which as seed went into the earth where deep secrets hide. And there did dance with the elements, and

spring forth as flowered plant, concealing secrets strange. When you were in the ear of grain, spirits of the field came to cast their light upon you, and aid you in your growth. Thus through you shall I be touched by that same Race, and the mysteries hidden within you, I shall obtain even unto the last of these grains."

Trace a crescent over the wine with your spirit blade and recite:

"By virtue of this sacred blade, be this wine the vital essence of the Great Goddess."

Trace a crescent over the cakes, and recite:

"By virtue of this sacred blade, be these cakes the vital substance of the Great God."

12. Lift up the plate and the chalice, look up at the Moon, and recite:

"Through these cakes and by this wine, Diana and Dianus bless me, and give me inner strength and vision. May I come to know that within me which is of the gods. May this blessing be so, in the names of Diana and Dianus."

(Eat a portion of the meal and drink some of the wine. Leave some for libations at the close of the ritual)

13. Raise your chalice in a toast to Aradia and, in her memory, recite the Charge:

"Whenever you have need of anything, once in the month when the moon is full, then shall you come together at some deserted place, or where there are woods, and give worship to She who is Queen of all Witches. Come all together inside a circle, and secrets that are as yet unknown shall be revealed.

And your mind must be free and also your spirit, and as a sign that you are truly free, you shall be naked in your rites. And you shall rejoice, and sing; making music and love. For this is the essence of spirit, and the knowledge of joy.

Be true to your own beliefs, and keep to the Ways, beyond all obstacles. For ours is the key to the mysteries and the cycle of rebirth, which opens the way to the Womb of Enlightenment.

I am the spirit of Witches all, and this is joy and peace and harmony. In life does the Queen of all Witches reveal the knowledge of Spirit. And from death does the Queen deliver you to peace and renewal.

When I shall have departed from this world, in memory of me make cakes of grain, wine and honey. These shall you shape like the Moon, and then partake of wine and cakes, all in my memory. For I have been sent to you by the Spirits of Old, and I have come that you might be delivered from all slavery. I am the daughter of the Sun and the Moon, and even though I have been born into this world, my Race is of the stars.

Give offerings all to She who is our Mother. For She is the beauty of the Green Wood, and the light of the Moon among the stars, and the mystery which gives life, and always calls us to come together in Her name. Let Her worship be the ways within your heart, for all acts of love and pleasure gain favor with the Goddess.

But to all who seek her, know that your seeking and desire will reward you not, until you realize the secret. Because if that which you seek is not found within your inner self, you will never find it from without. For she has been with you since you entered into the ways, and she is that which awaits at your journey's end."

14. Sit now before the altar, facing North. Look up and at the Moon and visualize it as the Goddess appearing to you in a sphere of light. Kiss the palm of your left hand and extend it up to her. Then, recite:

"O' Great Diana, Queen of all Witches, hear my adoration. Hear my voice as I speak Your praises. Receive my words as they rise heavenward, when the Full Moon brightly shining fills the

heavens with Your beauty. See me for I come before You, and reach my hand up to You. As the Full Moon shines upon me, give me all Your blessings.

O' Great Goddess of the Moon, Goddess of the Mysteries of the Moon, teach me secrets yet revealed, ancient rites of invocation that the Holy Strega spoke of, for I believe the Strega's story; when she spoke of Your timeless glory, when she said to entreat You, and when seeking for knowledge to seek and find you above all others.

Give me power, O' Most Secret Lady, to bind my enemies. Receive me as Your child, receive me though I am earthbound. When my body lies resting nightly, speak to my inner spirit, teach me all Your Holy Mysteries. I believe Your ancient promise that all who seek Your Holy Presence will receive of Your wisdom.

Behold, O' Ancient Goddess, I have come beneath the Full Moon at this appointed time. Now the Full Moon shines upon me. Hear me and recall Your ancient promise. Let Your Glory shine about me. Bless me, O' Gracious Queen of Heaven. In your name, so be it done."

15. Three works of magick may be performed before circle is closed, if desired. Ritual tools may be blessed by touching them to each of the four elements represented upon the altar.
16. Close celebration and banish the circle. Offer libations to the Earth and the Moon. The celebration is complete.

In contrast to the Full Moon ritual, the eight tregenda or sabbat rites of the year are primarily solar in nature. However, it should be noted that the rituals actually reflect the relationship between the Goddess and the God of the Seasonal Year. It is in this that we understand the Goddess as the whole and the God as the part of the whole. In other words, she is the infinite, and he is the finite.

In the mythos of Witchcraft, the goddess never dies. It is the God who dies and crosses into the Otherworld. The Goddess descends into the Otherworld to retrieve him, and this comprises the classic myths and legends of Witchcraft. In essence, such tales depict the

God as the Harvest Lord who surrenders his life essence, which is symbolized by grain. The goddess is a vessel for his birth and is also the womb to which he returns for rebirth.

The Spring and Autumn Equinoxes are doorways to and from the Otherworld. Spring leads to the World of the Living, and Autumn opens to the Realm beyond Mortal Life. The tregenda rites that fall in-between mark pivotal moments in the connective mythos of the Wheel of the Year.

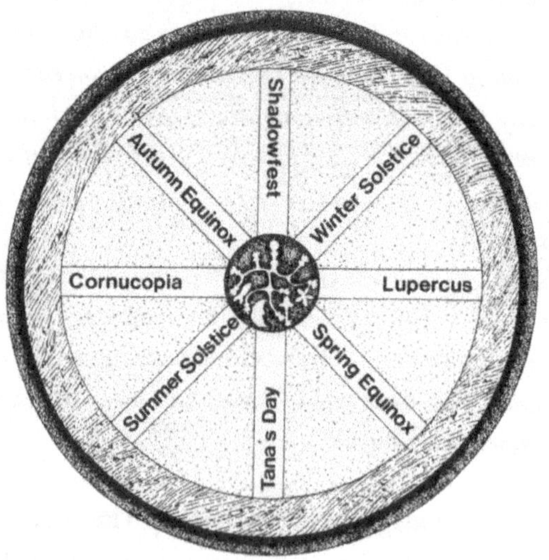

Overview of the Tregenda

- **Shadowfest:** The festival of shadows, held on the Eve of November. This season begins the Wheel of the Year, which is conceived in the dark womb of the Goddess. In the mythos, the Goddess and God are in the Underworld, and, through their union, a child is conceived who will grow to become the Lord of Light.
- **Winter Solstice:** The festival of rebirth, held on the day of the solstice. This season signals the return of light. In the mythos, this is the time of the Sun God's birth.
- **Lupercus:** The festival of purification; it is held on the eve of February. This is the season of purification and the preparation for the coming season of growth and abundance. It is the shedding

of contamination and limitation. In the mythos, the Lord of Light is now in his adolescence.

- **Spring Equinox:** The festival of life's renewal, held on the day of the equinox. This is the season of preparing and planting fields. In the mythos, the Goddess has returned to the Mortal World from the Underworld. She is renewed in Maiden form.
- **Diana's Day:** The festival of fertility, held on the Eve of May. This is the season of fertile essence, which renews the life of Nature. In the mythos, this is the period of courtship between the Goddess and the God.
- **Summer Solstice:** The festival of celebrating growth is held on the day of the solstice. This is the season of generation and gain. In the mythos, this is the wedding of the Goddess and God that will lead to the pregnancy of Nature (from which the harvest shall come).
- **Cornucopia:** The festival of abundance is held on August eve. This is the season of abundance. In the mythos, this is maturity of the Goddess and God, whose union has brought forth the fullness of Nature. It is the time of the anticipation of a ripe harvest.
- **Autumn Equinox:** The harvest festival, held on the day of the equinox. This is the season of harvesting the abundance of Nature. In the mythos, the Harvest Lord is slain and his seed falls back into the earth for the continued renewal of life.

Shadowfest
(La Festa dell' Ombra)

Items required (in addition to standard altar items):

- One vial of essence oil (god-scent)
- Two red candles for altar
- Four black candles for quarter points
- One human skull symbol, placed at the West Quarter
- Winter treguenda incense
- Root of a rue plant
- A small white candle
- Dried leaves (oak leaves or pine needles)

- Personal offering to the God
- Cauldron

The Rite:

1. Cast the circle in the usual manner.
2. Go before the altar and say:

"I come on this sacred night when the veil between the worlds turns to mist. I join now in spirit with those who have gone before. As it was in the time of the beginning, so is it now, so shall it be."

3. Place skull at the West Quarter. Stand before it in the Slain God Posture and say:

"O' ancient gods of my ancestors, bless this sacred setting, that I who worship in your ways may be protected from the coming powers."

Stand at the West Quarter and read the Myth of the Descent of the Goddess out loud:

"Diana, my Lady and Goddess, would solve all mysteries even the mystery of Death. And so, she journeyed to the Underworld in her boat, upon the Sacred River of Descent. Then it came to pass that she entered before the first of the seven gates to the Underworld. And the Guardian challenged her, demanding one of her garments for passage, for nothing may be received except that something be given in return.

And at each of the gates the goddess was required to pay the price of passage, for the Guardians spoke to her: "Strip off your garments, and set aside your jewels, for nothing may you bring with you into this our realm."

So, Diana surrendered her jewels and her clothing to the Guardians, and was bound as all living must be who seek to enter the Realm of Death and the Mighty Ones. At the first gate, she gave over her scepter, at the second her crown, at the third her necklace, at the fourth her ring, at the fifth her girdle, at the sixth her sandals, and at the seventh her gown.

Diana stood naked and was presented before Dis, and such was her beauty that he himself knelt as she entered. He laid his crown and his sword at her feet saying: "Blessed are your feet which have brought you upon this path."

Then he arose and said to Diana: "Stay with me I pray, and receive my touch upon your heart."

Diana replied to Dis: "But I love you not, for why do you cause all the things that I love, and take delight in, to wither and die?"

"My Lady," replied Dis "it is age and fate against which you speak. Thus, I am helpless, for age causes all things to whither, but when all die at the end of their time, I give them rest, peace and strength. For a time, they dwell within the Moon's light, and with the spirits of the Moon; then may they return to the realm of the living. But you are so lovely, and I ask you to return not, but abide with me here."

But she answered: "No, for I do not love you."

Then, Dis said "If you refuse to embrace me, then you must kneel to death's scourge."

The goddess answered him: "If it is to be, then it is fate, and better served!" So, Diana knelt in submission before the hand of death, and he scourged her with so tender a hand that she cried out "I know your pain, and the pain of love."

Dis raised her to her feet and said "Blessed are you, my Queen and my Lady."

Then he gave to her the five kisses of initiation, saying: "Only thus may you attain to knowledge and to joy." And he taught her all of his mysteries, and he gave her the necklace which is the circle of rebirth. And she taught him her mysteries of the sacred cup which is the cauldron of rebirth.

They loved and joined in union with each other, and for a time Diana dwelled in the Realm of Dis. For there are three mysteries in the life of man which are: Birth, Life, and Death (and love controls them all.) To fulfill love, you must return again at the same time and place as those whom you loved before. And you must meet, recognize, remember, and love them anew. But to be reborn you must die and be made ready for a new body. And to die you must be reborn, but without love you may not be born among your own.

But the Goddess is inclined to favor love, and joy and happiness. She guards and cherishes her hidden children in this life and the next. In death she reveals the way to her communion, and in life she teaches them the magick of the mystery of the Circle (which is set between the worlds of men and of the gods)."

4. At the West Quarter, set a burning white candle. Pause for a moment, then extinguish it, saying:

   "Diana dwells now in the Realm of the Dread Lord of the Shadows. The world grows cold and lifeless. But I do not sorrow in this harsh season, for all is as it must be. Therefore, I draw close to the Dark Lord and embrace Him. I find comfort in the knowledge of His Essence. May my path be blessed in the name of the God."

5. At the North Quarter, lay the spirit blade and wand. Then, assume the God Posture, facing the tools (South). Recite the following:

   "The reign of the Goddess surrenders in love to the reign of the God."

6. Then, pick up the ritual tools, kiss them, and place them down at the North Quarter again. Sit facing the skull and recite *The Charge of the God:*

   "These are the words of the God: By the fallen temple stone or in a forgotten glen, there shall you gather, all who seek to know my secret mysteries. I am He who guards and He who reveals all of these things.

I am the Lord of earth and sky, of rocky cliffs and forests deep and darkened. I was there when the world was new, and I taught you to hunt and to gather plants for food. Look within yourselves, for I am there. I am that strength upon which you draw in times of need. I am that which conquers fear. I am the hero and the fool. I am your longing to be free, and your need to be bound.

In my love for you, I give up my life. I die but rise up again. I prepare the path upon which you journey, going always on before you. For it is in becoming. Hear the thunder, there am I. See the hawk and the raven soar, there am I. See the great wolf and the stag appear in the forest clearing, there am I. Close your eyes at the end of your days, and there am I, waiting by the temple stone."

Carry the goddess icon from the altar to the West Quarter and place it there.

Recite:

"These are the words of the goddess: The Wheel of the Year has turned, Cycle unto Cycle, Time unto Time. I have journeyed to the Hidden Realm of the Shadows; there to prepare a place for you. The harshness of the season I leave behind me; kindle for yourselves a fire of love within, and I shall remember you, and return to you. For you are the Keepers of the Flame, and to all who kindle the flame, I shall never abandon.

By the changing of the harsh season shall you know that I draw near you again. And I shall return then the greenness of plants and trees; then will you know that I have come."

7. Go to the altar and retrieve the chalice. Place the candle at the West Quarter. Then, set the chalice of wine in front of the Goddess icon. Lift up the chalice and dip the wand in it (tip down).
8. Move the candle in front of the chalice and light it. Go to the North Quarter, pick up the skull, return to the West Quarter, and set the skull down in front of the candle.
9. Pick up the candle in one hand and the skull in the other. Then, recite:

"This is the light that was bore from the season before. I accept now the essence of the God."

10. Snuff out the candle with the skull. Taste a small piece of rue root dipped in the wine.
11. Set the cauldron at the North Quarter. Fill it with the dried leaves and ignite them. Place an offering in front of the cauldron. Look at the cauldron flames and recite:

"Behold the womb of the Goddess of Night, that kindles the Child of the coming year. O' symbol of the Mystery by which we return, I honor your Essence, and the magick that emanates from Union with you."

12. Perform gesture of manifestation to the cauldron and recite:

"O' bring forth the Child of Promise."

13. Retrieve the skull from the West Quarter and, holding it, recite:

"I shall be secure in the protective power of the God. Not shall I be in want, nor shall I suffer for I am in his care. Therefore, I feast and celebrate all in his praise."

14. Celebrate with wine and cakes.
15. Close ritual circle and snuff all candles.

Winter Solstice
(La Festa dell' Inverno)

Items required (in addition to usual ritual items):

- Evergreen wreath
- Small log of oak
- Small "newborn God" candle for the "god flame"
- A cauldron
- Offerings

1. Cast the ritual circle.
2. At the altar, recite:

   "I mark now at this sacred time, the rebirth of the Sun God. It is the Great Mother who gives him birth. It is the Lord of Life born again. From the Union of the Lord and Lady, hidden in the Realm of Shadows, comes forth now the Child of Promise!"

3. Place the God icon at the North Quarter. Perform Rite of Union to the God image and recite:

   "I call forth now into the Portal of the Northern Power. I call to the Ancient God, He who brought forth the beasts of field and forest. I call upon the Ancient God, He who was beloved of the ancient tribes."

4. Assume God Posture and recite:

   "My Lord, I greet You. O' Horned One, horned with the rays of the Sun, by whose blessings and grace shall life always be born again. Behold, I have come before you at this appointed time. Bless me and the days before me. These gifts do I offer you…"

5. Set a vessel at the North Quarter and place an offering within it.
6. Sit in front of the cauldron and recite:

   "O' most ancient provider, Lord of Light and Life, I pray You grow strong that I may pass the Winter in peace and fullness. Emanate Your warmth and Your Love that the cold and harshness of Winter not dwindle Your followers.

   O' Ancient One, hear me! Protect and provide in the harshness of these times. I give You adoration and place myself in Your care. Blessed be all in the God!"

7. Anoint yourself with oil and taste the prepared *ruta* (sprig of

rue), saying:

"Blessed be in his care."

8. Read the *Myth of the Season* out loud:

"Now the time came, in the Hidden Realm of Shadows, that Diana would bear the Child of the Great Dark Lord. And the Lords of the four corners came and beheld the newborn God. So it came to pass that the Great Lords were brought before the throne of the Dark One. And they spoke saying "Do we find You here, O' Dianus?" And the Great One replied "Yes, it is I. Now you have truly seen my two faces. Then Diana spoke to the four Lords, saying "Take my son who is born of Dianus, that he might bring Life to the World. For the World has grown cold and lifeless." So the Lords of the four corners departed to the world of men, bearing the new Lord of the Sun. And the People rejoiced, for the Lord had come that all upon the earth might be saved."

9. Place a candle in the cauldron and light it. Symbolically, give it birth through cauldron. Once born, take the flame to the East Quarter. Present it and proclaim:

"Hail, to the newborn Sun. Hail Dianus, Hail Lupercus, Hail Lord of the Sun."

10. Repeat at each quarter.
11. Take the god-flame from the North and make one full pass around the circle again (holding up the god flame). Upon returning to the North, raise the flame to this quarter. Then, set it on the altar.
12. Recite at altar:

"Let the spirit be joyful and the heart to despair not. For on this sacred day is born He whose Light shall save the World. He has come forth from the Darkness and His Light has been seen in the East. He is Lord of Light and Life."

(Gesture the Horned God sign with your hand towards the god flame)

"Behold the Sacred One, the Child of Promise! He who is born into the World, is slain for the World, and ever rises again!"

13. Now, the sacred evergreen wreath is brought out and placed before the altar. The small oak log is set in the center of the wreath. The god flame is then set on top of it (symbolic of the Lord of Light and the Lord of Vegetation, being as one and the same).
14. Extend palms out above the god flame and recite:

"Behold the God whose life and light dwells within each me. He is the Horned One; Lord of the forest, and the Hooded One; Lord of the Harvest, and The Old One; Lord of the Clans. Therefore, do I honor Him."

15. The ritual is then concluded with the meal of cake and wine. Close circle when finished.

Lupercus
(Festa di Lupercus)

Items required (other than usual ritual items):

- Symbolic wolfskin cloak
- Symbolic deerskin or goatskin strap (for scourge)
- Small fur or skin piece for charging chalice (traditionally, wolf or goat)
- A small candle for personal use
- A Lupercus torch or candle (for presentation)

1. Circle is cast in usual manner.
2. Recite opening for rite:

"I come at this sacred time to give due praise and worship to the Lord of Light. He who was Dianus has risen again and

enters into the world that all the people of the earth might be saved. I mark now, at this appointed time, the waxing splendor of the young god. He who is Lupercus, Lord of Light, Banisher of Darkness, the Great Golden Wolf."

3. Light a candle from the altar and tread the circle from North, returning North again as you recite:

   "Behold the Lord of Light, He who mastered the twelve labors of the Great Lords. He who causes the world to rejoice in his rising. He whose Light brings Salvation to the earth."

4. Go to the East Quarter and begin the tonal invocation to the God as you assume the God posture:

   "Vorte tu apro, Osa datae Lupercus! Orphae il athe daei aldus ayeo kae aeto. Nigla gai avato kiel nada omnae, arae il athe okri maedeta, doma akaes lae il ba!"

5. Take an unlit candle and move to the North, pause, then proceed to the South, saying:

   "O' Ancient One, rayed in splendor and horned with power, embrace me, for without You I shall surely perish. It is now the appointed time, and I offer You this worship. Warm now the sleeping seeds that lie beneath the cool earth, within the womb of the Great Mother. Comfort me and renew my strength! Behold this circle I have prepared; I have lighted the ancient fires and do faithfully serve you. I await Your emanation of warmth."

6. At the South Quarter, light the candle and move to the East, then place an offering to Lupercus.
7. Move to the East and charge the chalice of wine (wrap it in a fur piece and twist it clockwise while visualizing the newly kindled Sun rise in the wine). Hold up the chalice to the East and say:

"Behold the cool drink of Immortality. For herein is the Essence of Life, and the Giving of Life. Let my heart now be joyful as I drink of the Light of Rejuvenation; receiving this into my blood to be fulfilled."

8. Drink the wine.
9. Recite the closing prayer:

"I now give due praise and adoration unto the Lord of Light. For he is the symbol of the Mystery by which I am reborn again. May I always rejoice at His rising, for by this I am joined to the Essence of Rejuvenation and Rebirth. Hail and adoration unto You, O' Lord of Light."

10. Cover yourself with the wolf cloak as you sit before the altar. Extinguish all candles except those on the altar and open a gateway out of the circle.
11. Take the strap in your dominate hand and say:

"I awaken now to the lash of the God. Thus, shall I be purified and rise anew from within."

12. Flip lash over shoulder, striking your back at least three times. The force of the lash is meant to sting only. Traditionally, the breasts, back, and buttocks are struck as well.
13. Conclude celebration with cakes and wine.

Spring Equinox
(Equinozio della Primavera)

Items required (other than usual):

- Cauldron
- Torch to represent the "god light"
- Torch to represent the Goddess's returning light
- Offerings for the Goddess

- A small cloth (hand size)
- A length of red cord to bind statues together
- A small white cloth with a red stain (originally a wolf pelt)
- A pouch to hold offerings
- A pouch of soil
- A pouch of seed
- Seeds intended for blessing and planting (you can substitute symbols of your needs or desires)

1. Circle is cast in the usual manner, then place the God statue at the North Quarter, along with the pouch of seeds. Also, place the Goddess statue at the East Quarter, along with the pouch of soil.
2. Stand before the altar and say:

   "I mark now with this time of gathering, the beginning of the Ascent of our Lady from the Hidden Realm of Shadows. For this is the time of Her desire for the Light and Life of the World. I mark also the death of the Wolf God, and the splendor of the new young god, rayed in power, Lord of the Sky."

3. Perform the Rite of Union to the altar (gazing upon the statues or symbolic torches). Then, place the seeds upon the white cloth stained with a red mark and bless the seeds for planting by praying:

   Return pouch of seeds to North Quarter. Recite:

   The Myth of the Ascent: "Now it came to pass that Diana longed for the Light of the World, and for Her many Children. And she departed from the Hidden Realm, in secret, leaving the Dark Lord in His solitude.

   In the Hidden Realm of Shadows, Diana would bear the Child of the Great Dark Lord. And the Lords of the Four Corners came and beheld the newborn god. Then they spoke to Diana of the misery of the People who lived upon the World, and how they suffered in cold and in darkness. So Diana bid the Lords to carry Her son to the World, and so the People rejoiced for the Sun God had returned.

And it came to pass that Diana longed for the Light of the World, and for Her many Children. So, She journeyed to the World and was welcomed in great celebration.

Then, Diana saw the splendor of the new god as He crossed the heavens, and she desired Him. But each night He returned to the Hidden Realm and could not be see the beauty of the goddess in the night sky.

So, one morning the Goddess arose as the God came up from the Hidden Realm and She bathed nude in the sacred lake of Nemi. Then the Lords of the Four Corners appeared to Him and said "Behold the sweet beauty of the Goddess of the Earth." And He looked upon Her and was struck with Her beauty so that He eI have come to play beside your bath" He said, but Diana gazed upon the stag and said "You are not a stag but a god!" Then He answered "I am Faunus, god of the forest. Yet as a I stand upon the World I touch also the sky and I am Lupercus the Sun, who banishes the Wolf Night. But beyond all of this I am Dianus, the first born of all the Gods!" Diana smiled and stepped forth from the water in all Her beauty. "I am Fana, goddess of the forest, yet even as I stand before you I am Jana, goddess of the moon. But beyond all this I am Diana, first born of all Goddesses! And Dianus took Her by the hand and together they walked in the meadows and forests telling their tales of ancient mysteries. They loved and were One and together they ruled over the World. Yet even in love, Diana knew that the god would soon cross over to the Hidden realm and Death would come to the World. Then must She descend and embrace the Dark Lord, and bear the fruit of their Union."

4. At the North Quarter, hold up the statue of the God and say:

   "Where is my Lady?"

5. Set statue down and, beginning at the North, move to each

quarter, bearing a lighted candle, then (passing the North again) stop at the East Quarter.

6. Hold out the candle to the North and say:

"O' Dark One, Your Lady comes to me, and I welcome Her with great rejoicing. All living things do know that She is near, and the world stirs with Life again. The Lady journeys now to return Her Essence to the forest, field, and glen."

7. Pick up the statue of the Goddess and say:

"Hear me, for now I draw near! Hear me, all who sleep from Winter's embrace, awaken unto rebirth, come forth now. Receive now my essence and be full with Life, and the desire for Life."

8. Set statue down, extend palms over it, and say:

"O' Great Goddess of the Earth, return in Your fair nature, lovely Maiden of Youth, and Joy and Love. Only You can break the spell of Winter and enchant the Earth with Your Essence. Hail to the Great Goddess!"

9. Take the pouch of soil to attach it to the Goddess statue. Retrieve the God statue and seed pouch from the North Quarter. Set it next to the Goddess statue and attach the seed pouch to the God statue. Take a red cord and bind the statues together as a couple.
10. Open the pouch and pour a small amount of wine into it. Next, open the pouch of seeds and push some seeds into the damp soil. Then, take out the mixture and place it on a small cloth. Set the cloth into the cauldron (East Quarter). Place wand into cauldron, gesture the triangle of manifestation over the cauldron, and say:

"Blessed be the Plow, the Seed, and the Furrow."

11. Set the bound statues in front of the cauldron and say:

"Behold the Beauty of the Goddess, She who is Fana, Lady of the Earth; She who is Jana, Mistress of the Moon; She who is Diana, Ruler of the Universe!"

"Behold the Power of the God. He who is Faunus, Lord of the Earth; He who is Lupercus, Master of the Heavens; He who is Dianus, Ruler of the Universe!"

12. Place personal offering into the cauldron. Prayers, requests, or blessings may be offered now.
13. Take a lit candle and, beginning at the North, tread the circle to all points three times.
14. Gesture the triangle of manifestation over the cauldron and statues, saying:

"You are truly the Power in all things. You are the Earth, the sky, and beyond."

15. The celebration concludes with wine and cakes.

Afterwards, the items within the cauldron are collected and placed within a pouch or bag. Bury the pouch in a planting field (for increase of crops) or suspend it from a tree within the woods (for an abundant hunt) to *charge* the area with fertile energy. You can adapt this part of the ritual to your personal needs. For example, you may wish to carry the pouch hidden on your body when going for a job interview, seeking a home loan, or appearing in court.

Diana's Day
(La Giornata di Diana)

Items required:

- A small crown of flowers
- A small candle
- A fresh flower
- Ritual sword

Instructions:

1. Circle is cast in usual manner.
2. Give address at the altar:

"At this joyous time, I welcome the return of my Lady. That which began in the Time of Shadows has come to its fullness. Cycle unto Cycle, Time unto Time, Age unto Age. As it was in the time of the beginning, so is it now, so shall it be."

3. Move to the South Quarter and give address:

"By and by, all things pass, season unto season, year unto year. The Lady has come again to Her Hidden Children of Time. And the Goddess ever bestows love and peace, and guards and cherishes Her Hidden Children in Life.

In Death, She teaches the way to Her Communion, and in this world, She teaches the mystery of the magick circle, which is placed between the worlds of men and of the gods. And for this the Lady descended, in times of old, into the Realm of Shadows.

And the Lord of the Shadows was bewitched by Her Beauty. And He taught Her the mysteries of Death and Rebirth. And in love, He bowed before Her and gave Her all of His Power."

4. Place the crown of flowers on the head of the Goddess statue. Perform the Rite of Union facing the Goddess statue.
5. Lay down the sword in front of the statue and say:

"My Lady, all power is given to You, for this is so ordained. And with love there is submission to Your ways, and reign is given over into Your hands."

6. Recite *The Charge of Aradia:*

"Whenever you have need of anything, once in the month when the moon is full, then shall you come together at some deserted place, or where there are woods, and give worship to

She who is Queen of all Witches.

Come all together inside a circle, and secrets that are as yet unknown shall be revealed. And your mind must be free and also your spirit, and as a sign that you are truly free, you shall be naked in your rites. And you shall rejoice, and sing; making music and love. For this is the essence of spirit, and the knowledge of joy.

Be true to your own beliefs, and keep to the Ways, beyond all obstacles. For ours is the key to the mysteries and the cycle of rebirth, which opens the way to the Womb of Enlightenment. I am the spirit of Witches all, and this is joy and peace and harmony.

In life does the Queen of all Witches reveal the knowledge of spirit. And from death does the Queen deliver you to peace.

When I shall have departed from this world, in memory of me make cakes of grain, wine and honey. These shall you shape like the moon, and then partake of wine and cakes all in my memory. For I have been sent to you by the Spirits of Old, and I have come that you might be delivered from all slavery. I am the daughter of the Sun and Moon, and even though I have been born into this world, my Race is of the stars.

Give offerings all to She who is our mother. For She is the beauty of the Green Wood, and the light of the moon among the stars, and the mystery which gives life, and always calls us to come together in Her name.

Let Her worship be the ways within your heart, for all acts of love and pleasure are like rituals to the Goddess. But to all who seek her, know that your seeking and desire will reward you not, until you realize the secret. Because if that which you seek is not found within your inner self, you will never find it from without. For she has been with you since you entered into the ways, and she is that which awaits at your journey's end."[31]

7. Move to the East Quarter and recite:

---

31 Charles Godfrey Leland, "The Charge of Aradia," *Aradia: Gospel of the Witches* (David Nutt, 1899).

"Hail and adoration O' Great Diana! You who are the Great Moon Goddess, Queen of Heaven, Lady of the Earth, I welcome You and rejoice in Your presence."

8. Place a fresh flower before the Goddess statue, kiss the statue, and say:

"Blessed be all in the Goddess."

9. Then, take a chalice of wine, whisper the name of the Goddess upon the surface of the wine, and then drink.
10. Ritual celebration continues with cakes and wine.

Summer Fest
(La Festa dell'Estate)

Items required (in addition to standard ritual set-up):

- Flowers for procession
- Symbol for God and Goddess
- Cauldron
- Libation fluid (nectar/ambrosia)
- Four small bowls for libation (at quarters)
- Offerings (one for deities, and another for Nature spirits)
- Fennel stalk
- Sorghum stalk

1. Cast circle in usual manner.
2. Open a threshold at the Northeast point.
3. Pass through the threshold, tossing flowers as you enter.
4. Seal the threshold.
5. At the altar, recite:

"I come on this sacred night of Summer's Eve, and join myself to the powers and forces of this mystical season. On this night, the Folletti gather, as do all those spirits of Nature

to which I am kindred. For the Witch and the fata are of a similar Race. So, it was in the time of our beginning, so is it now, so shall it be."

6. Symbols of the God and Goddess are placed before the cauldron, which is set at the South Quarter. Then, recite:

    "Here is the Divine Couple, whose Union gives Life to the World. Blessed be all in the God and Goddess."

7. Perform the Rite of Union facing the symbols.
8. Place Deity offerings in the cauldron at the South Quarter.
9. Go to each of the four quarters and pour a libation of nectar into the bowls set there for libation.
10. Place Nature spirit offerings at the four quarters. Recite from the altar:

    "O' spirits of the Elemental forces, hear me, and receive these blessings. O' spirits of the Earth, O' powers that be, hear me and receive these blessings. Assist me on this sacred night to maintain the natural balance that keeps vital the essence of the earth. Let there always be clear, flowing water, freshness in the air, fertility within the soil, and abundant life within the world."

11. Perform the drama play of the struggle between the forces of Light and Darkness (the fennel stalk represents the powers of Light and the sorghum stalk represents the powers of Darkness.) Hold the stalks in an X formation out in front of you. Beginning at the East Quarter, walk around the circle, ending at the North. At the completion, the sorghum stalk is broken, and the fennel stalk is raised in victory. Then, present the fennel stalk at each quarter, saying:

    "Blessed be the power of Light. Blessed be the power of life."

12. Place the cauldron at the East Quarter. Snip off an inch or two of the fennel stalk and place it in the cauldron, along with some powered incense. Light the incense and recite:

    "I release the power of Light, the waxing force, whereby I charge You, O' Sacred Ether of our world. Be free of all evil and negativity. I charge you for the good of all life within our world."

13. Visualize the power of Light rising up on the smoke of the incense. Mentally direct the power up into the ether of the community.
14. End the ritual with celebration of cakes and wine. Close circle. Leave libation bowls out overnight for the Nature spirits. It is said that, on the night of Summer's Eve, all the spirits of Nature are in celebration. Faeries, Elves, and all the "little folk" gather in meadows, forests, and any secret or hidden place. If you see them or can find any evidence of their celebration the next day, then you will receive a special blessing. Should you come across any of their gathering sites, be sure not to disturb anything. Leave everything as you found it.

Cornucopia

Items required (other than usual ritual items):

- One cornucopia icon
- Offerings for the harvest
- Cornucopia incense
- Cauldron

1. Circle is cast in usual manner.
2. At the altar, recite:

    "I come on this appointed day in anticipation of plenty. I acknowledge the Grace of the Earth Mother and the Sky Father. From Him, have I received the Sacred Emanation, which the Mother has nurtured and delivers unto me."

3. Perform the Rite of Union to the altar/torches/symbols of God and Goddess. Place offerings at the South and recite:

   "It is good and right to give offerings to the Great God and Goddess. It is proper to give thanks of all that is good in my life. For the Great Ones provide for me, and I must."

4. Light the cauldron at the South Quarter and place a token of your needs/requests in the flames. They may be written on either parchment or cloth and burned in the cauldron fire. Place the cauldron before the altar and pour sweet incense into the cauldron flames, saying:

   "I call out to You, O' Diana and Dianus, and pray that You receive my wishes and desires as they rise up to you on the smoke of this incense. I ask that You grant my requests and bring them to their fullness, even as You bring forth the fruit from the seed. In your names, so be it done."

5. Sit before the cauldron and recite:

   "I speak now the words of Aradia, the Holy Strega: 'know that every action brings forth another, and that these actions are linked together through their natures. Therefore, whatsoever you send forth, so shall you receive. A farmer can harvest for himself no more than he plants. Therefore, let us consider what is good in our lives, and what is full. Let us also consider what is bad and what is empty. And let us meditate upon the reasons for all of these things."

6. Bless the ritual cakes and wine:
7. Lift up the wand, saying:

   "Blessed be the plow."

8. Then, lift up the chalice, saying:

"Blessed be the furrow."

9. Lower the wand into the wine, saying:

   "Herein is the Essence of the Union of Dianus and Diana, wherein all things are renewed and made vital."

10. Trace an X over the cakes, hold out palm of left hand over them, and say:

    "Here is the substance of the union of Dianus and Diana, wherein all things are established and renewed."

11. Place the cakes and wine on the altar, and say:

    "In the names of Diana and Dianus, blessed be these symbols. Blessed be the plow, the seed, and the furrow. Blessed be your mysteries."

12. Conclude ritual with celebration of wine and cakes feast.

Autumn Equinox
(Equinozio di Autunno)

Items required:

- A white candle to represent the "god flame"
- Ruta (sprig of rue)
- Receiving vessel for grain "essence"
- Cauldron for offerings (West Quarter)
- Grain and pouch
- Loaf of bread
- Red cord to tie around "god candle" on altar
- Oak leaves and vessel to contain them
- Slain God icon
- Goddess icon

1. Circle is cast in usual manner.
2. At the altar, recite:

"I come at this sacred time to rejoice for the abundance which has come into the world. Yet, also, to honor Dianus, the Lord who is sacrificed for my sake. The time has come when all things have grown into their fullness and are gathered by hunter and fieldsman. As it was in the time of our beginning, so is it now, so shall it be."

3. Stand at the East Quarter, and then move to the West, bearing the "god flame" candle and reciting:

"Farewell, O' Lord of Two Faces, who stands in the Light and within the Darkness."

4. Tie pouch of grain to waist cord, positioning it to hang above the genital area. Take the "god flame" candle and move around the circle three times, beginning at the North Quarter. Go to the West Quarter carrying the god flame. Remove the pouch suspended from your waist and place it in the receiving vessel set within the Cauldron of Offering. Extinguish the god flame with a spring of rue, then recite:

"The God has departed from His shining abode in the heavens, for the Season has come. And Death shall come to the world for the Winter draws near. The Lord of Light now becomes the Lord of the Shadows."

5. A vessel is brought out and placed in the West. Place some oak leaves within it and then taste some of the grain placed beside the vessel.
6. Recite:

"In the earliest times, the Lord and Lady lived in the ancient forest of Nemi. The Lady seduced the Lord and there did She receive the Sacred Seed from which all But the Lord knew

not the secret which only the Goddess understood, for She had drawn the Life from Him. And the World was abundant with all manner of animal, and that which grows from the earth. Now there came a time when all things grew to their fullness, and were to be gathered by Hunter and fieldsman alike. And in that time was the God slain and drawn into the Harvest."

7. Place Slain God icon at the North Quarter, along with the Goddess icon. Here, you will begin the sacred dialogue, holding up the appropriate icon in both hands as you recite:

   Goddess: *"I have come in search of Thee, is this where I begin?"*
   God: *"Begin to seek me out, and I shall become as small as a seed, so you may but pass me by."*
   Goddess: *"Then I shall split the rind, crack the grain, and break the pod."*
   God: *"But I shall hide beneath the earth, and lay so still, that you may but pass me by."*
   Goddess: *"Then I shall raise you up in praise, and place upon you a mantle of Green."*
   God: *"But I shall hide within the Green, and cover myself, and you may but pass me by."*
   Goddess: *"Then I shall tear the husk, and pull the root and thresh the chaff."*
   God: *"But I shall scatter, and divide, and be so many, that you may but pass me by."*
   Goddess: *"Then I shall gather you in, and bind you whole, and make you One again."*

8. Place the sacred bread loaf on the altar.
9. Holding ritual dagger pointed at the loaf, recite:

   "Behold the Harvest Lord. Blessed be the Lord of the Harvest."

10. Plunge the dagger into the loaf, and then cut the loaf into eight

pieces. Then recite:

> *"Behold the Lord, the Green Man, the Stag King, the Hooded Man. Now is he taken within, to be as One again."*

11. Eat one piece of the loaf, and drink a portion of red wine. Recite:

> *"With this I am now as One with Him. I am of the Sacred Blood. That which was, at the time of beginning, is now, and always shall be."*

12. Place a piece of the loaf at each of the four quarters. The remaining three pieces represent the three aspects of the God: Hooded One, Horned One, and Old One. Bury these in the garden, in a fertile field, or in the woods.
13. Celebration concludes with cakes and wine.

The rue used in this ritual is taken from the whole plant of which two pieces are used at the Autumn Equinox, and the rest dried and saved for Winter Solstice. It is the symbol of death and rebirth, waxing and waning, it is the "god-root plant." This plant is grown from the seed planted at the Spring Equinox.

Appendices

The Roots of The Old Religion

The cultural roots of Italian Witchcraft go deep into antiquity. They can be found in Ancient Greece, Etruscan, and Roman culture. The deepest roots extend into Old Europe in prehistoric times, as will be explored later in this chapter. It is by studying the commonality that we arrive at a fuller understanding of the heart and soul of Italian Witchcraft.

In the earliest writings in Southern Europe about Witches, we find glimpses of religious Witchcraft. One example is the Witch known as Medea, who is depicted as a priestess of Hecate. Specific elements of ritual Witchcraft also appear in these writings, where we find the use of the cauldron, wand, blade, altar, and ritual circle. Ritual nudity is also noted.

The ancient writings of such people as Homer, Lucan, and Ovid provide us with an overview of Witchcraft as depicted in Pagan society. Medea, for example, calls upon the power of the stars, Moon, mountains, and groves (as well as the deities associated with them). The Witch known as Canidia uses a book of enchantments by which she can "Draw Down the Moon." She calls upon the goddess Diana to aid her magick.

In the ancient writings of Homer, Lucan, and Ovid, we find a triformis goddess comprised of Hecate, Diana, and Proserpina. These goddesses share a long association with Witchcraft that spans many centuries. In this chapter and those following, these goddess-forms will be further explored and their natures more fully revealed.

Although most of the literature about Witches is written from a negative perspective, we must note that the practices of Witches involved common elements of the culture of their times. It is more often the motive of the Witch in the story that paints her as evil. As we shall see in the chapters of this book, there is a political agenda through which the Witch is intentionally maligned and depicted as evil.

The literary works on Witches and Witchcraft are fictional tales designed to tell a story or function as satire. Even though they are fiction, they still contain important information. A good fiction contains truth as well, and familiar settings are used, as well as known cultural elements. These things help the reader picture events and identify with situations. Therefore, it is important to note what is being said about Witches and Witchcraft in literary works. From this, we can discern known practices and beliefs. The task is to weed out bias from observation and truth from perspective. The old saying that there are two sides to every story is wise to keep in mind when we encounter the stereotypes of Witches as evil.

To understand the Witch, we must look to various elements related to her life. Early writers remark that the Witch lived outside the cities in remote rural settings. She harvested herbs that she used for healing, potions, and magickal purposes of all kinds. The Witch used a cauldron as a focus of her magick and also used a bronze knife and wand made from beech or olive trees. In various tales, her secret arts were available for hire.

One of the most common abilities ascribed to the Witch in ancient writings is her skill at communicating with spirits and departed souls. This was most often performed at the crossroads, which is associated with the goddess Hecate, as well as with Witchcraft in general. Crossroads were considered magickal because they represented a place "in-between," and such places were regarded as portals to other Realms. Hecate was, among other things, a goddess of doorways and gates.

It is in the association of the Witch with spirits of the dead that we find the ancestral connection. In this section, you will be introduced to *Lare* spirits, which, in archaic Roman religion, were ancestral entities that maintained a connection between past and present generations. We know from ancient writings that Witches were believed to communicate with the dead by offering drops of blood. The blood gave the dead the ability to speak to the living.

The ancient writer Pliny mentions a "holding stone" called a *synochitis* (similar to beryl) that allowed Witches to temporarily retain a spirit once summoned. This stone is the predecessor of the "holy stone," which is used to evoke Faeries, as well as being a charm stone. Another stone reportedly used by Witches was called a "compulsion stone" (*ananchitis*), which evoked the gods in rituals of *hydromancy* ("divination in water"). Writings such as these confirm an established tradition related to Witches and Witchcraft that reflects involvement with spirits and deities. The majority of these are associated with the night.

According to modern scholars on Greek and Roman Witchcraft, there were two types of Witches. One was the real person that could be encountered in the city, town, or village. The other was the Night Witch, a mystical and legendary figure. The Night Witch was believed to possess supernatural powers and could transform from human to animal form—the most common was that of a screech owl. From this rose the belief the Latin name *strix* also appeared as a term for a Witch.

As this exploration continues, we will look closer at all of these things in their proper context. It is through this that we can begin to unravel the misrepresentations of the Witch and dispel the misinformation about her and her Craft or religion. In doing so, we will see past the deliberate maligning of the Witch-figure and the distortions used to depict her as a poisoner and doer of evil deeds. Let us turn now to a look at the historical documentation.

Historical Background

In this section, we will explore the historical foundations and elements of the Old Religion. The material includes excerpts from various books by Raven Grimassi and is incorporated into this text because the concepts are foundational. Not everyone reading this has read the published material, so it is important to include this information here. For those who have read Grimassi's books, please be assured that excerpts from already published material are kept to a minimum in this text.

The origins of the Old Religion date back to the pre-Roman period of Italian history and beyond. Archeological evidence indicates that the early Italian people worshipped in grottoes or rock sanctuaries and practiced pictorial engravings as part of their religious ceremonies. In the book *Roman and European Mythologies* compiled by Yves Bonnefoy, we find that even into Roman times:

> *...traces survived of primitive conceptions and practices so distant from the rationality of the classical world that they sometimes provoked the astonishment and incomprehension of writers in the Hellenistic and Roman periods. Most striking are the suggestions of an animistic conception of the supernatural; the omnipresent importance of divine signs and divination; the high social and religious status of women (in Etruria and even in early Rome), which have been interpreted as survivals of matriarchy...*[32]

Many ethnic groups lived in Italy during the Villanovan period of the tenth century BC. The main groups were:

- Apuli
- Brutti
- Calabri
- Campani
- Etrusci
- Galli
- Hirpini
- Histri
- Latini
- Liguri
- Lucani
- Piceni
- Sabini
- Samniti
- Ursentini
- Veniti

32 Yves Bonnefoy, *Roman and European Mythologies,* Wendy Doniger, tr. (U of Chicago Press, 1992).

In the early mythos of these groups, a belief in an animal guardian of the clans arose. For example, the animal guardian of the Hirpini and Lucani was the wolf. The Piceni were protected by the woodpecker, and the Sabani by the bull. The guardian of the Ursentini was the bear.

The myth of the animal guardian of the clans was quite widespread in prehistoric Italy. These clan animal spirits were viewed as ancestors, providers of food, protectors, and guides. Clear archaeological evidence supports the validity of this relationship in the culture of the so-called "Apennine Bronze Age." It is even found in the oldest Latin and Roman legends. Examples of this are the legends of Aeneas and the sow, Romulus and Remus and the she-wolf, and so on.

Most scholars agree that the Etruscans appeared in Italy sometime around 1000 BC, possibly having migrated from the east, although sufficient evidence exists to argue that the Etruscans were not an Indo-European People. They subjugated the tribes of Italic peoples in North-Central Italy and reached the height of their civilization in the sixth century BC. The Etruscans were famous for their knowledge of the magickal and mystical arts. The Romans highly praised them for their ability to divine the future. The decline of their kingdom began around 300 BC, and they eventually fell to the expanding Roman Empire around 200 BC.

With the rise of the Roman Empire, other factors began to influence Italic religion. The Roman armies carried the Pagan religion of Italy into all parts of the known world and returned with aspects of all the religions with which they made contact. They also planted the seeds of Italic Paganism in every land that they conquered, which accounts for many of the similarities between Southern and Northern European practices. Roman religion went on to eventually become perhaps the greatest eclectic tradition in all of history. The Senate libraries of Rome contained the great mystery texts of *Etrusca,* along with the teachings of other lands conquered by Rome. This left Italy in a unique situation, for, in effect, she preserved the world's religious concepts and wove them into a living mosaic. Here, they have remained a silent testimony to the ways of our European ancestors.

In the far-off villages of the Roman Empire lived the rustics who had little contact with the ways of the Roman cities. Their religion was somewhat different than that usually associated with Roman mythology. They were not concerned with the Great Gods, such as Jupiter and Vulcan. Their gods were deities of the fields and forests upon whom the rustics still depended for their livelihood. This general theme is captured in the writings of Hesiod in a work titled the *Theogony*.

In the *Theogony*, Hesiod claims that the muses appeared to him and were sent directly by the high gods. In the tale, Hesiod is told to write down the teachings related to the lineage of the gods and the ages over which they ruled. It is here that we first learn of an almost forgotten race of gods known as the Titans. Hesiod tells us that the Titans preceded the Olympians in a misty past. In order to distinguish the teachings of the muses from the contemporary beliefs of the rustic people, Hesiod states that what he writes is "not of oak and boulder," but is received directly from the gods.[33] It is noteworthy here that the older teachings are referred to as "oak and boulder."

The idea of *oak and boulder* relates to the primal. It arises from pre-historical beliefs and practices rooted in the ways are distant ancestors perceived the world around them. The Titan gods, for example, appear to represent the great "untamed" forces of Nature in comparison to the Olympian gods, who reflect a society much like that of the ancient, yet advanced civilizations of the Mediterranean. In this light, the teachings of oak and boulder see the Divine reflected within the imagery of Nature, while the Olympian gods reflect the Divine through a depiction of human nature.

In Ancient Rome and Greece, we find a very clear distinction between the educated class and the rustic or peasant class pertaining to religion. For example, in order for a sect to be considered valid, it had to possess a temple, which meant that it needed funds to build and maintain it. The priests and priestesses also required funds in order to function in their role for the populace. The State granted a document to an established temple, which labeled it a *collegium* (an association). The Temple of Apollo, for example, would have been known as the *Collegium of Apollo* ("College of Apollo").

In *Witchcraft and Magic in Europe: Ancient Greece and Rome*, we find that sects without a collegium were designated as practitioners

33 Hesiod, "Theogony."

of illicit religion (something not acknowledged or sanctioned by the State). As stated in the book, the class of Witches, magicians, seers, and other "vagabonds" were assigned to the illicit category.[34] In Ancient Greek literature, Witches are specifically referred to as practitioners of illicit religion.

Historian Richard Gordon writes:

> *...the Roman world had already developed a number of words for negatively-marked use of religious power, nouns such as venefica, saga, local adjectives such as Marsus, also Sabellus, Paelignus, relating to the Sabellian people, traditional enemies, famous for being able to burst snakes open by magic, or Thessalus, borrowed from the Greek word commonly used for male witch...*[35]

Gordon further comments about Witches and other illicit practitioners:

> *...the practices of dominated groups such as wise women, herbalists and smiths, which are inaccessible to, and largely unaffected by, the processes of rationalization and moralization of the divine world which set in motion the formation of the city state.*[36]

This sets them apart from the functionality and acceptability of the temples and their attendees within the cities. Here, we see a distinct separation of religious practices and beliefs. Within the city, we find the common religion, which is widely known and accepted as the norm. Outside the cities, we find "illicit" religion and its practitioners who gathered at night in deserted places. As Gordon

34 Valerie Flint, et al. *Witchcraft and Magic in Europe: Ancient Greece and Rome.* Bengt Ankarloo & Stuart Clark, ed. (U of Penn Press, 1999).

35 Flint, et al. *ibid,* 165.

36 Flint, et al. *ibid,* 178.

notes, the customary view of the educated elite and the population at large held that any non-civic rituals were mere mumbo-jumbo, and saw the beliefs and practices of non-sanctioned sects as "marginal religions," which were regarded as absurd at best.

HIstorian Albert Grenier, in his book *The Roman Spirit,* writes of the vagabond classes that gather at the crossroads. Grenier places them under the protection of the Lare, Roman entities whose earliest role was the protection of boundaries. Grenier writes:

> *The Lares are friendly gods, without prejudices. About their altars on the cross-roads they collect all the vagabonds, all those who have no family, no hearth, no worship of their own. Their humble devotees combine to celebrate their feats as best they can, forming Colleges of the Cross-roads, collegia compitalicia.*[37]

Grenier notes of the College of the Crossroads sects:

> *History, being wholly aristocratic and political, hardly noticed them. For they lived outside of history, so to speak, content to be alive under a sunny sky, on a land which they loved. They needed no more than a few very simple ideas inherited from their forefathers and a few homey rites to give them confidence and joy. A loyal, courageous race, feeling no dread n the presence of the unknown and, at bottom, not caring much about it, when the thoughts and fancies of the Mediterranean came pouring in they kept alive the original conceptions and religious acts f the first masters of the Italian soil.*[38]

Historian Cyril Bailey, in his book *Phases in the Religion of Ancient Rome,* presents some interesting information regarding the Lare. The festival of the Lare was known as the "Compitalia," which refers to the crossroads. The crossroads were the traditional setting

37 Albert Grenier, *The Roman Spirit: in Religion, Thought, and Art,* M. R. Dobie, tr. (Alfred A. Knopf, 1926) 369.

38 Grenier, *ibid.* 370–371.

for the veneration of the Lare.[39] Scholar Georges Dumezil, in his book *Archaic Roman Religion,* mentions that the worship of the Lare included setting little towers with an altar placed before them.[40]

Archaeologists Lesley and Roy Adkins note in their book *Dictionary of Roman Religion* that the Lare shrine at the crossroads was: "open in all four directions to allow passage for the Lar."[41] The ancient writer Ovid, in his work titled *Fausti,* refers to the Lare as the "Night Watchmen." Here, we can see the theme of four towers associated with the four directions, as well as four Guardians of boundaries or demarcation.[42]

The concept of guardianship is also connected to the sacred sanctuary intimately linked to the goddess Diana, who is associated with Witchcraft by several ancient authors. Over the course of time, Rome outlawed magickal practices, along with the Dianic Cult associated with the King of the Woods at Lake Nemi. The priestesses of Diana took refuge among the isolated villages near Lake Nemi, and the Temple of Diana fell into ruins. Cultured and educated Romans looked down upon the country dwellers, who they viewed as uncouth simpletons. Yet, it was here in these rural villages that the Old Religion of Italy was maintained, separate and independent of Roman religion.

The writings of the Ancient Roman poet Horace are among the first historical accounts associating the goddess Diana with Witches and their practices. In the *Epodes of Horace,* written around 30 BC, he tells the tale of an Italian Witch named Canidia.

Horace's description of Canidia is less than kind, but does address the timeless association of Witches with spellcasting and

39 Cyril Bailey, *Phases in the Religion of Ancient Rome* (U of California Press, 1932).

40 Georges Dumezil, *Archaic Roman Religion: with an Appendix on the Religion of the Etruscans,* vol. 1, Philip Krapp, tr. (Johns Hopkins UP, 1966) 343.

41 Lesley & Roy A. Adkins, *Dictionary of Roman Religion* (Oxford UP, 1996).

42 Ovid. *The Fausti,* John Benson Rose, tr. (Dorrell and Son, 1866).

magickal practices (as well as "Drawing Down the Moon"). Horace goes on to say that Proserpine and Diana grant power to Witches who worship them, and that Witches gather in secret to perform the mysteries associated with their worship. He speaks of a Witch's "Book of Incantations" (*Libros Carminum*), through which the Moon may be "called down" from the sky. Other Ancient Roman writers, such as Lucan and Ovid, produced works which clearly support the same theme. This would seem to indicate that, during this era, such beliefs about Witches and Witchcraft were somewhat common knowledge. In Epode 5, we read: "*…Night and Diana, who command silence when secret mysteries are performed, now aid me; now turn your vengeance and influence against my enemies' house…* "[43]

In Epode 17, we find these words (addressed to Canidia):

> *Now already I yield to your mighty art, and suppliant beseech you by the realms of Proserpine, and by the powers of Diana, not to be provoked, and by your books of enchantments that are able to call down the fixed stars from heaven, Canidia, at length spare your magic words, and turn backward your swift wheel…*

Canidia replies:

> *…must I, who can move waxen images and call down the moon from the sky by my spells, who can raise the vaporous dead, and mix a draught of love lament the effect of my art, availing nothing upon you?*[44]

We know from the writings of Roman times that Proserpine and Diana were worshipped at night in secret ceremonies. Their worshippers gathered at night beneath the Full Moon and shunned the cities where the solar gods ruled. In secret ceremonies, they celebrated the ancient rites of the goddess Diana.

---

43 Horace, "The Witch's Incantation," *Epodes of Horace* (David McKay, 1884) V.

44 Horace, *ibid.* 177–178.

In his book *The World of Witches,* Julio Baroja writes of Southern Europe:

> *There seems to have been a flourishing cult of Diana among European country people in the fifth and sixth centuries AD, and she was generally looked upon as a Goddess of the woods and fields, except by those trying to root out the cult, who thought she was a devil.*[45]

In the author's notes for chapter four, he adds that the cult also worshipped a male deity called Dianum. The modern rendering of this name is Dianus.

In AD 906, Regino of Prum wrote in his instructions to the Bishops of the Kingdoms concerning Witches:

> *...they ride at night on certain beasts with Diana, goddess of the pagans, and a great multitude of women, that they cover great distances in the silence of the deepest night, that they obey the orders of the goddess... by speaking of their visions (they) gain new followers for the Society of Diana...*[46]

It is interesting to note that the label "Society of Diana" mentioned by Regino continues to be associated with Witches throughout the centuries in Italy, as recorded in Witch trials by the Italian Inquisition. It appears with greater frequency during the later part of the fourteenth through the late fifteenth centuries in trial transcripts of these periods. A brief chronology follows to summarize the unbroken chain of Italian Witchcraft through the centuries. These are taken from the book *Italian Witchcraft* and repeated here in this section because of their historical importance:[47]

---

45 Julio Caro Baroja, *The World of Witches* (U of Chicago Press, 1964) 65.

46 Baroja, *ibid.* 60.

47 Raven Grimassi. *Italian Witchcraft: The Old Religion of Southern Europe* (Llewellyn Publishing, 2000).

- **30 BC:** Roman poet Horace in his *Epodes of Horace* associates Witches with the goddess Diana in a mystery cult.
- **AD 314:** Council of Ancyra labels Witches as heretics who believe that they belong to a "Society of Diana." Council concludes that Satan deceives them.
- **AD 662:** Saint Barbato converts Romuald (Duke of Benevento) to Christianity. On Saint Barbato's bidding, Romuald has the "Witches' walnut tree" cut down. This walnut tree was the gathering place of Witches who worshipped Diana, well known in the region. In AD 680, Saint Barbato attended the Council of Constantinople, where he spoke out against the "Witches of Benevento."
- **AD 906:** Regino of Prum (acting under Papal direction), in his instructions to the bishops, claims that Pagans worship Diana in a cult called the "Society of Diana."
- **AD 1006:** Nineteenth book of the *Decretum* (entitled "Corrector") associates the worship of Diana with the common Pagan folk.
- **AD 1280:** Diocesan Council of Conserans associates the "Witch cult" with the worship of a Pagan Goddess.
- **AD 1310:** Council of Trier associates Witches with the goddess Diana (and Herodias).
- **AD 1313:** Giovanni de Matociis writes in *Historiae Imperiales* that many laypeople believe in a nocturnal society headed by a queen they call Diana.
- **AD 1390:** A woman tried by the Milanese Inquisition for belonging to the "Society of Diana" confessed to worshipping the "Goddess of Night" and stated that "Diana" bestowed blessings upon her.
- **AD 1457:** Three women tried in Bressanone confessed that they belonged to the "Society of Diana" (as recorded by Nicholas of Cusa).
- **AD 1508:** Italian Inquisitor Bernardo Rategno writes in his *Tracatus de Stigibus* that a rapid expansion of the Witch Cult had begun 150 years earlier. He concludes this from his study of trial transcripts from the Archives of the Inquisition at Como, Italy.

- **AD 1519:** Italian poet Girolamo Folengo associates a "mistress" known as Gulfora with Witches who gather to worship at her court in his poem "Maccaronea."
- **AD 1526:** Judge Paulus Grillandus writes of Witches in the town of Benevento who worship a goddess at the site of an old walnut tree.
- **AD 1576:** Bartolo Spina, in his *Quaestrico de Strigibus,* lists information compiled from confessions that "Witches" gather at night to worship "Diana" and have dealings with night spirits.
- **AD 1608:** Francesco Guazzo writes, in his *Compendium Maleficarum,* of Italian Witches who gather in a ritual circle, pass their Craft on to their children, and work with elemental spirits.
- **AD 1647:** Peter Pipernus writes, in his *De Nuce Maga Beneventana* and *De Effectibus Magicis,* of a woman named Violanta who confessed to worshipping Diana at the site of an old walnut tree in the town of Benevento.
- **AD 1749:** Girolamo Tartarotti associates the Witch Cult with the ancient Cult of Diana in his book *Del Congresso Nottorno Delle Lammie.* In his *A Study of the Midnight Sabbats of Witches,* he writes: *"The identity of the dianic cult with modern witchcraft is demonstrated and proven."*[48]
- **AD 1890:** Author Charles Leland associates the Witch Cult with the goddess Diana as a survival of the Ancient Ways in his books: *Etruscan Magic & Occult Remedies, Legends of Florence,* and *Aradia; Gospel of the Witches.*

What we see in the above citations is a theme of survival related to the concept of Witches and a goddess-figure within Witchcraft. The persistence of such elements strongly suggests a repressed history that continually reappears in fragments of commentaries, Church writings, and trial transcripts. Despite this, scholars insist that no such sect or belief ever existed.

48 Girolamo Tartarotti, *Del Congresso Notturno delle Lammie: Of the Nightly Meeting of Witches* (Giambatista Pasquali, 1749).

The Deities

The origins of the deity-forms that appear in Ancient Witchcraft are barely visible behind the veil of prehistory. One of the earliest deities to appear associated with Witches in Western literature is the goddess Hecate. She was one of the Titans, a prehistoric race of gods so old that their legends were but faint memories at the time the first myths were written down in ancient times.

The value of looking at the Titans is that they are the first entities that we can say with certainty were thought of by our prehistoric ancestors as gods and goddesses. They are not mute stones, etchings, or carvings left to our interpretation. It seems reasonable to assume that the Titans evolved from earlier ancestral beliefs traceable to the earliest attempts of humankind to conceive of deities. The Etruscans are said to be the heirs of prehistoric religion and, therefore, it is important to consider the religion of this ancient race.

In pre-Christian religion, there were many gods and goddesses with many names. The oldest name in Tuscan Witchcraft for the Goddess is Uni and for the God is Tagni, which appear to be derived from Ancient Etruscan religion. As we continue in this topic, we will look at the origins of the God and Goddess in Italian Witchcraft and how these deities are viewed today.

The Old Gods of Europe

The Old Gods of Europe originate from a pre-Indo-European culture that contrasted sharply with the ensuing patriarchal proto-Indo-European culture, which was superimposed on all of Europe, except the southern and western fringes. Between 4500–2500 BC, three waves of infiltration from the northeast swept Europe, replacing (in many cases) the matrifocal religions of Old Europe with the patrifocal religion concepts of the Indo-Europeans. What developed from this merging of traditions was a mixture of the two mythic systems of Old European and Indo-European religious cultures.

As early as the seventh millennium BC, villages were established in southern Europe that depended upon the domestication of plants and animals for continued survival. The inhabitants of Southern Europe seven thousand years ago were not the primitive villagers of the incipient Neolithic Era. During the period from the seventh to the fifth millennia, the farmers of Southern Europe had evolved an agricultural system (and corresponding cultural associations unique to themselves) that was contemporary with similar developments established in Mesopotamia, Egypt, Anatolia, and Syro-Palestine. By the fifth millennium BC, this culture had reached its peak in Old Europe, which is a region encompassing the Aegean and Adriatic, along with parts of Czechoslovakia, Poland, and Ukraine.

The region of Old Europe is significant for several reasons. The primary one is that it reflects primal concepts that are at the root of a unified pre-Christian system of beliefs and practices. These prehistoric elements were the foundation for the religious views that arose in the region of Old Europe. The symbols, animal images, and rudimentary ritual objects continue to appear in later periods. Owls, frogs, toads, snakes, and other creatures associated Witchcraft are all significant things that are featured in the prehistory of Old Europe. All of these appear in the myths and legends of various gods and goddesses associated Witchcraft in the Aegean Mediterranean cultures.

In Old Europe, the ancient Mythos of Deity was *not* polarized into feminine and masculine power, per se, as it appears to have been in the Indo-European peoples. Both aspects of deity were manifested side-by-side or pictured with their opposite genders in animal companion forms, which served to affirm and strengthen their respective forces (such as the goddess Diana with a stag or with hunting hounds). In the agricultural communities, humans began to more closely observe the forces of Nature than did those of the hunter-gatherer communities, for obvious reasons. Deities began to be "reshaped" into gods and goddesses of the fields and crops. They retained their ancient hunter-gatherer associations of both a magickal and religious nature, but often were renamed and appeared in a domesticated form (such as the Horned Stag God of the hunter-gatherer reappearing as the Horned Goat God of the agricultural community).

Dr. Marija Gimbutas, a former professor of European Archaeology at UCLA, writes in her book *The Goddesses and Gods of Old Europe:*

> *Significantly, almost all Neolithic goddesses are composite images with an accumulation of traits from the pre-agricultural and agricultural eras. The water bird, deer, bear, fish, snake, toad, turtle, and the notion of hybridization of animal and man, were inherited from the Paleolithic era and continued to serve as avatars of goddesses and gods. There was no such thing as a religion or mythical imagery newly created by agriculturists at the beginning of the food-producing period.*[49]

We can easily see that the earliest forms of those deities, which we readily recognize as the gods and goddesses, were originally powerful animal totems. Some of the most ancient and enduring of these animal forms are the bear, stag, boar, wolf, and goat. As early as 4500 BC, images of bears appear in ancient carvings and religious artifacts. The bear was a powerful image of the Mother Goddess; strong, nurturing, and protective. The stag appears as early as the sixth millennium BC, where carvings of deer appear in religious artifacts. In the fourth millennium BC, images of stags appear with lunar crescent symbolism, associating the deer with the Moon in early religious belief.

Gimbutas writes in *The Goddesses and Gods of Old Europe* (concerning the boar):

> *Sculptures of pigs are known from all parts of Europe and date from every period... The fast growing body of a pig will*

49 Marija Gimbutas, *The Goddesses and Gods of Old Europe: Myths and Cult Images* (U of California Press, 1974).

> *have impressed the early agriculturist... came to symbolize the earth itself, causing the pig to become a sacred animal probably no later than 6,000 BCE.*[50]

Images of dogs and wolves appear in carvings and paintings as early as the fourth millennium BC. Much of the symbolism is connected with themes of protection and hunting. Wolf heads worn by shamans and some Roman soldiers were symbolic of an atavistic connection with this ancient animal spirit. Wolf cults flourished for centuries, comprising both warrior and priest classes (remembered now only in legend and folklore as distorted stories of werewolves).

Goats have long been symbols of fertility and sexual virility. During the Middle Ages, female Witches were accused of having sexual intercourse with goats (an ancient practice in certain mystery cults originating in the regions of Egypt and Chaldea, and seen also in some Greek Mystery Traditions). Early forms of goat deification can be seen in the god Pan, as well as in the legends of satyrs in general. In Italy, Witches were said to have ridden to their ceremonies on the backs of goats, unlike the Witches of Northern Europe, who were said to fly on broomsticks.

The Horned God

In the Old Religion of Italy, the god-force is considered to have three aspects. These are commonly known as "the Horned One," "the Hooded One," and "the Old One." In this section, we will explore each of these aspects as they pertain to the religious concepts of the Old Ways.

In the early days of clan life, people were nomadic hunter-gatherers. Hunting game was very dangerous, because human weapons of that era required a hunter to get very close to the prey. The bravest hunter wore the skin of a stag, attempting by disguise to get very close to the herd. In order to accomplish this, he had to act like the very beast that he hunted. His bravery was much revered by his tribe, and he became a symbol of power. Out of this evolved

50 Gimbutas, *ibid.*

the belief that he must be in touch with (and favored by) a great spirit of the animal world (because of his skill at "becoming" the stag which he hunted).

The first male deity of the early Witch clans in Italy was "The Horned One," who was often referred to as *Cern,* which is Latin for "horned." In Italian Witchcraft, he is called Aplu or Dianus. He was believed to be the God of the Forests, providing food for the clan and animal hides for clothing and shelter. He was portrayed as half-human and half-beast, with stag antlers sported upon his head. This represented the power of the hero-hunter, a man who could merge with the animal world and become one with the beasts. Therefore, the God was a great spirit who could merge with humans and become one with them as well. Thus, the clan was under the protection of a greater power than themselves, a god.

Diana and Actaeon by Giuseppe Cesar

The second aspect of male deity was "the Hooded One," *Rex Nemorensis* ("King of the Woods"), who was commonly known as Virbius. He evolved out of the figure of the Horned One as religious concepts began to mature in human religious thought. The Hooded One is, therefore, considered to be the *son* of the Horned One. He represents the plant kingdom in very much the same way that the Horned One represents the animal kingdom. The Hooded One is said to be *hooded-in-the-Green;* that is to say that he is covered with the green of the forest. As humans began to rely more upon plants, learning to grow and harvest crops, the god who provided for their needs began to change as well. He went from being the Lord of the Woods to being the Lord of the Harvest.

The third aspect of the God is "the Old One," who is commonly known as Mantus. This aspect encompasses the other two, representing another stage in the evolution of human thought. The Old One is more human in appearance and is portrayed as an Elder. He carries a staff that sports a pair of antlers and, around which, is entwined a living vine. He does not appear as a man in the decline of old age, but rather as a powerful, experienced, and wise man, transformed by the years he has lived.

The Slain God—Divine King

In ancient times, the law of "only the strong survive" was a very true, and a very experienced, reality. Today, with modern medicine and technology, we as a society keep alive those who Nature would have allowed to perish. Where the age of elders in our own time is often a matter of modern medicine, in ancient times, it was a matter of personal prowess.

In our early tribal states, hunters and warriors held a very significant place in society. The bravest of these were honored among the tribe and came to be looked upon as a leader. In many cases, the wellbeing of this individual affected the wellbeing of the tribe. This is a theme that we find present in the King Arthur Mythos. Merlin tells Arthur that if he succeeds, the land will flourish, but if he fails, the land will perish. Arthur asks "Why?" and Merlin replies, "Because you are King!"

Even today, with our own presidents, we find that their ailments are always downplayed and that they are always reported as recovering well. To understand this intimate relationship, we must look at certain aspects and connections. For, as Merlin tells Arthur, "You are the Land, and the Land is you," let us journey back to the past to uncover these roots.

Before humans learned to farm and to herd, the hunt was essential to life. Without successful hunters, the clans would perish. Hunting was dangerous, for humans had not yet successfully removed themselves from the food chain. As previously noted, early weapons required that the hunters be quite close to the prey, and injuries were common. Many hunters lost their lives or were lame as a result of the hunt. In time, the hunter became the warrior, risking his life for the sake of his tribe. The needs of the tribe, whether it was for food or defense, required sending out the best the tribe had to offer (hunter or warrior). In time, this concept formed along with humankind's religious consciousness.

Over the course of time, the concept of Deity and its role in life and death began to form into ritual and dogma. Eventually, the idea arose of sending the best of the tribe's people directly to the gods in order to secure favors. This was the birth of human sacrifice (those who went willingly were believed to become gods themselves). Offerings were nothing new, many times food and flowers or game were laid out before the gods. To offer one of your own was considered the highest offering the tribe could make. Among human offerings, the sacrifice of a willing human was the height of all possibilities. Surely, it was believed, the gods would grant the tribe anything if someone would willingly lay down their life in order to appear before them.

In his book, *Western Inner Workings,* renowned occultist William Gray addresses many aspects of this cult theme. One of these has to do with sacred bloodlines. Here, he writes:

> *Something drove them toward Deities not from fear or for seeking favors, but because they sensed a degree of affinity between themselves and the invisible Immortals. In a remote way they realized they were distantly related to those Gods and wanted to improve that relationship. This trait in specific members of the human race shows some evidence of genetic lines leading back to the "Old Blood" which originated from outside this Earth altogether.*[51]

51 William G. Gray, *Western Inner Workings,* Sangreal Sodality Series, vol. 1 (Samuel Weiser, 1983).

Mr. Gray goes on to show how, eventually, kings or rulers were sacrificed (being the "best" of the clan) and how bloodlines were an important consideration. The rulers of Ancient Rome and Egypt were considered to be descended from the gods or gods themselves.

Gray also gives an account of how the blood and flesh were distributed among the clan and into the land. Parts of the body were buried in cultivated fields to ensure an abundant harvest. He writes, "They gave their late leader the most honorable burial of all—in their own stomachs" (all of this can also be found in Christian Mythology within the Rite of Communion). After these practices ended, Mr. Gray notes that the custom remained to burn them in a funeral pyre.[52] Remnants of this practice can be seen in the effigy burning of Befana, a custom still observed in parts of Italy today.

Bloodlines are still very important among hereditary Witch families. Witch blood (or being "of the blood," as it is called) is traditionally considered essential to the passing on of Craft secrets. This is performed on November Eve and involves (in part) a meal of fava bean soup and the pricking of a finger with a sharpened bone spur. Such things are rarely made known to people outside of the bloodlines, and, in fact, most families in the "Old Country" will not even discuss Witchcraft with someone who is not of the blood. This is one of the most difficult obstacles in trying to teach (and maintain) the true Old Religion for future generations.

In the Divine King/Slain God Mythos, sacrifice is only part of the story. Sacrifice is the sending of your best, but what about getting them back? In common Craft verse, we find a passage which reads "...and you must meet, know, remember, and love them again." To such an end, rituals were designed to bring about the rebirth of those who personified the Slain God as a willing sacrifice, and bloodlines were carefully traced. Special maidens were prepared to bring about the birth, usually virgins who were artificially inseminated so that no human male was known to be the father.

As human consciousness matured and evolved, human sacrifice turned to animal sacrifice (the scapegoat ritual of killing an animal), and this was eventually replaced with plant sacrifice. The same Ancient Mythos applies to plant sacrifice, and we find the "eating of deity" in the ritual of cakes and wine (symbols of flesh and blood) within traditional Craft rituals. Although the meaning and preparation have been lost to most "reconstructed" systems, they have still been preserved by hereditary traditions.

---

52 Gray, *ibid.* "The Cult of Kingship."

In the Ancient Tradition, it was through the connection of the body and blood of the Slain God that the people were made *one* with Deity. This is essentially the concept of the Christian Rite of Communion or Eucharistic Celebration. At the "Last Supper," Jesus reportedly declares to his followers that the bread and wine is his body. He then declares that he will lay down his life for his people and bids them to eat of his flesh and drink of his blood (the bread and the wine). This is an ancient concept within the Old Mystery Traditions, which seems to have been adopted by Early Christianity.

Blood was believed to contain the essence of the life force—the death of the king freed the sacred inner spirit. By the distribution of his flesh and blood (in the people and the land), Heaven and Earth were united, and his vital energy renewed the kingdom. Remnants of these practices can still be clearly seen in the Old Religion, although they are veiled and highly symbolic.

The Divine King/Slain God appears in various aspects throughout the Ages. His essential image can be seen in such figures as the Jack-in-the-Green, the Hooded Man, the Greenman, and the Hanged Man of the Tarot. He is the Lord of Vegetation, he is the Harvest Lord, and in his wild (or free) aspect, he is the Lord of the Forest. He does not take the place of the Earth Mother, nor does he usurp her power, he is the compliment to her and remains her consort.

The popular Greenman image probably best summarizes the Divine King/Slain God. He is the spirit of the land manifesting in all plant forms. He is the procreative power, the seed of life. His face is obscured within the foliage, but he is always outwardly watching. The Greenman signifies the relationship of man to Nature. Author William Anderson, in his book *Green Man,* writes: "He sums up in himself the union that ought to be maintained between humanity and Nature. In himself he is a symbol of hope: he affirms that the wisdom of man can be allied to the instinctive and emotional forces of Nature."[53]

This is, in effect, our bridge between the worlds. He is one with Heaven and Earth, and to be one with him is to be one with the Source of All Things.

---

53 William Anderson, *Green Man: The Archetype of our Oneness with the Earth* (HarperCollins Publishers, 1990).

The subject of the Divine King/Slain God is far too vast to cover in the format of a single section. It is presented here simply to lay the foundation for understanding this concept. Further study into it can be found in many books still available today. A few suggestions are *Western Inner Workings* by William Gray, *The God of the Witches* by Stewart Farrar, *Earth Rites* by Janet and Colin Bord, and *Green Man* by William Anderson.

The Crescent-Crowned Goddess

In the Old Religion of Italy, the feminine aspect of Deity is viewed as having four individual aspects. Since the Old Religion is a Lunar Cult, each of these aspects is associated with one of the four phases of the Moon. In this section, we will explore each of these goddess-forms: Umbrea, Diana, Losna, and Manea.

When the Moon is dark and unseen (for three days), this phase is associated with the goddess Umbrea, whose name means "shadow." When the Moon is new (forming a Waxing Crescent), we associate this phase with the goddess Diana. When the Moon is full, it is associated with the goddess Losna. When the Moon is a Waning Crescent, we associate this phase with Manea (who is a goddess of night spirits and departed souls).

Umbrea

Umbrea is the name of the Goddess in her Underworld aspect. She is the consort of the god Dis, who is the God of the Dead. Umbrea is a Goddess of Shadows and Secrets, and all things that are hidden and obscure. Whenever the Moon cannot be seen, for whatever reason, it is said that Umbrea is present. She is considered to be the Enchantress, a goddess who can shapeshift at will, or can go unseen as she pleases. Although Umbrea is assigned to the Dark Moon, she is actually not fixed to this phase. Umbrea does not have a formal consort, but is often paired with the god Dis. He is an Underworld god.

Diana

Diana is the most common name associated with Italian Witchcraft. In common lore, she is the Goddess of the Poor and Oppressed. Diana is also viewed in circles as the Goddess of Outcasts and all those who are rejected by society (those who do not "fit in" within the mainstream). In classical lore, Diana is a Moon Goddess and is viewed as the Maiden aspect of feminine divinity. However, she is also a huntress and an Amazon warrior.

An entire Cult of Witches devoted exclusively to Diana flourished in Italy up through the Middle Ages. They viewed her as the only goddess and acknowledged three aspects within her: youth, maturity, and old age. In modern terms, this can be expressed as the *Maiden, Mother,* and *Crone.*

In the esoteric tradition, Diana is a great goddess-figure. She is discussed separately in this text as we continue. In Italian Witchcraft, she is called Artimiti or Atimite. Her consort is Aplu.

Losna

Losna is an old Etruscan name for the Moon Goddess. They also called her Leukothea. Losna was literally "the Moon," as the early Etruscans believed that the Moon itself was a living goddess. And so, Losna *is* the Moon as a living deity, rather than a goddess *of* the Moon. Leukothea was an aspect of the Moon Goddess and was associated with the ocean and the tides. Therefore, Leukothea is a Goddess of the Power or the Light of the Moon (which, to the Etruscans, was the same thing).

When the Moon is full, we associate this phase with Losna, the Mother Goddess; the fertile essence of moonlight light. Uni is the universal aspect of the Goddess, encompassing all goddesses. Therefore, Uni contains all goddesses and is the "One Great Goddess." In Italian Witchcraft, Losna is paired with her consort Virbius.

Manea

Manea is the Goddess of Night Spirits and Spirits of the Dead. In Classical Roman mythology, she is the Goddess of the Dead and the Mother of the Lares and the Manes. Manea is the Crone aspect of the Goddess and rules over decline and death. When the Moon begins to wane following the Full Moon, we associate this phase with Manea. In Italian Witchcraft, Manea is paired with her consort Mantus.

Diana, as the Great Goddess

Most contemporary Witches readily acknowledge that the goddess Diana is one of the main goddesses associated with Witchcraft. Many ancient sources also point to this fact, along with other writings from the fifth and sixth centuries AD and beyond, which record the existence of the Witches' sect and its focus upon Diana. Even as far back as 30 BC, the goddess Diana has been associated with Witches and Witchcraft in many public writings. The Ancient Roman poet Horace, in his *Epodes,* associated Diana with secret mysteries performed at night and enchantments that could "Call Down the Moon." He notes these aspects of the Cult of Diana in a dialogue that takes place with a woman he calls Canidia the Witch. [54]

Italian scholars have been able to present evidence of the antiquity of Diana and the Witch Cult in the very distant past. The most famous image of Diana of Ephesus contains a visual history of the ancient Cult of Diana, which is reflective of Neolithic, if not Paleolithic, imagery. Covering her body are images of various animals, all of which are sacred within the Witch Cult of Old Europe. The farther back we go in our research of Diana, the nearer we come to the animal totems that pre-dated her human form.

From archaeological and anthropological studies of ancient clans, we know that the first deities to be worshipped appeared in animal form. Among the early forms of Artemis/Diana, we find a bear, and it was not until much later in time that images of her human form began to appear. In the book *Woman's Mysteries,* author M. Esther

---

54 Horace, *Epodes of Horace.*

Harding writes (concerning the evolution of images associated with deities of the Moon):

> *First the moon deity was an animal, then the spirit of the god is an animal. Later the god or goddess is attended by animals. Later still these animal attendants were replaced by human beings who wore animal masks, performed animal dances, and were called by animal names...the animal attendants and animal emblems surrounding the goddess in her shrines must have constantly reminded the worshippers of later days, of those wilder aspects of her nature from which she had in part evolved. Her animals she still kept near her, for she could not be comprehended except in the light of her past.*[55]

The classical image of Diana in Rome was that of a young woman dressed in a hunter's tunic. She is a young, powerful virgin: a huntress and a warrior. In early statues of Diana, she is pictured standing with a stag; her bow in one hand, and the other reaching for an arrow from the quiver worn upon her back. In later art forms, she is shown with hunting dogs (remnants of an archaic association with wolves). From these ancient symbols, we can conclude that these animals are reflections of her power and spirit animal nature. Her association with the bear seems to have survived in one of her other names: Callista.

In Southern Europe, it was observed that vegetation flourished, for the most part, due to the coolness of night and the accumulation of dew, which served as a substitute for the lack of rain during the dry months. Ancient people were aware that the dew was most plentiful when the sky was clear and moonlight fell upon the fields. This, in part, served to connect the Moon Goddess with fertility of the crops. It was also one of the links of the Moon Goddess with wetlands, lakes, wells, and other bodies of water. The effect of the Moon upon the tides was also noted, of course, as was the Moon's influence upon menstrual cycles.

---

55 M. Esther Harding, *Woman's Mysteries: Ancient and Modern* (Longmans, Green & Co., 1935).

Diana never lost her earliest associations from the hunter-gatherer period and, even in the agricultural communities, she was believed to roam at night through the forests and groves with her nymphs and satyrs. The presence of the Full Moon gave light to the Earth, and Diana was viewed here as the protector of travelers and herds (as wild animals were more easily observed and defended against when the moon lit the night). The moon, however, was dark at times and, thus, Diana was also viewed with a dark side. She was seen as the Goddess of Wild Animals, as well. In classic mythology, stories of Diana give accounts of her punishments to those who needlessly slay a stag or other forest creatures.

In Arcadia, the Goddess was known as Calliste and worshipped in the form of a bear. As the Bear-Mother, she nursed, reared, and protected her children. Young girls were sometimes called "bears" in allusion to their patron goddess. When they reached puberty, it was customary for them to dedicate their girdles to Diana. Due to the fact that the pure, serene light of the Moon naturally suggests the idea of modesty or an "unblemished" nature, the Goddess was also viewed as the "chaste" goddess in her Maiden aspect.

Well-bred Athenian women of marriageable age danced as bears in honor of Artemis of Brauronia and, during the rites of cult initiation, "became" bears (wearing animal masks and acting like beasts). The girls and women of Lakedemonia performed orgiastic dances to glorify Artemis and were later joined by the men in a fertility dance. Offerings to Artemis included phalli and all species of animals and fruits, for she was protector of all life, bestowing fertility upon humans, animals, and fields. Goats and stags were highly valued as offerings to the goddess, as was the hare.

The Etruscans called her Atimite or Artimiti. Atimite was the Goddess of the Forests and Wild Animals, chaste and untouched by men. Atimite has been characterized as the Goddess of the Free Wildlife, in which, as huntress, she dominates the animal world. This is a symbolic projection of her role as ruler over the unconscious powers that still take on animal form in our dreams.

Central Deities in Italian Witchcraft

Dianus and Diana

The most popular deities associated with Italian Witchcraft are the mated pair known as Dianus and Diana. In many artistic renditions, Dianus is commonly depicted as the pastoral god playing his lyre, and Diana is depicted as the woodland goddess, dressed in hunter's clothing.

Faunus and Silvanus

The woodland deities known as Faunus and Silvanus are more primal aspects of the god Dianus. Faunus possesses oracle powers and delivers dreams about the future to those who sleep in a sacred grove. Silvanus is specifically a God of Uncultivated Land and Forests, in particular.

Hecate

One of the earliest goddesses to be connected to Witchcraft is Hecate. She is collectively described by Ancient Romans (such as Horace, Ovid, and Lucan) as a triformis goddess consisting of three natures: Hecate, Diana, Proserpina.

Hecate is a goddess intimately connected to the crossroads and is the gathered of wayward souls who are prevented (for whatever reasons) from passing into the Afterlife. In this capacity, she assumes the role of the guardian of the threshold between the worlds.

Janus and Jana

The gods Janus and Jana are the gatekeepers. In many popular depictions, they're portrayed as head with two faces that can see all entrances and exits. In classic mythology, they are guardians of any threshold and hold the key to allow passage, as well as the rod to drive off those who may not pass.

Hestia

The Goddess of the Divine Flame was known by the Greeks as Hestia, while the Romans called her Vesta (but, unlike the Greeks, never gave her a form). Fire was among the earliest representations of divinity and was used in grotto worship, as well as within sacred groves. The fire within the hearth was also sacred and kept under the protection of women whose duty it was to ensure that it never died out.

Lupercus

Sometimes referred to as the "Great Golden Wolf" is the god known as Lupercus. In his primal form, he was known as Lupus. Lupercus is a solar deity associated with protection against the forces of darkness, secret enemies, and theft.

Ceres

The Goddess of the Mysteries is known as Ceres, and she is typically portrayed holding a sheaf of wheat grain, which symbolizes the dying and rising god known as the Harvest Lord. The torch is a symbol of her lunar nature, associated with night, the Moon, and the Underworld or Otherworld.

Dis

The Underworld aspect of the God is known as Dis. In Ancient Etruscan and archaic Roman art, he is often depicted wearing a wolfskin headdress.

Key Plants in Italian Witchcraft

There are many plants that are intimately associated with Italian Witchcraft. Some of them are herbs, and others are trees. Each has its own lore which connects it to mystical or magickal themes. Let us look at some of the key plants that appear in Witchcraft traditions:

- **Rue:** Rue is associated with the goddess Diana and with the Faery race. It is from this plant that the charm known as the "cimaruta" takes it basic design. It is used in initiation rites and, afterwards, carried as a charm.
- **Vervain:** This plant is sacred to the Faery race, and its blossom appears on the Witch's cimaruta charm. This represents an ancient covenant between the Witch and the Faery. It is used in ceremonies of oath.
- **Fennel:** Fennel appears in ancient legends associated with fire and light. In one myth, a bundle of dried fennel stalks are used to steal fire from the gods, which is then brought to humankind.
- **Ivy:** Ivy is associated with binding and oaths. It is utilized in initiation rites and is used in its dry, crushed form to sprinkle around ritual circles.
- **Camphor:** This tree is sacred to the Moon and Moon Goddess. Its scent is used in ritual incense and magickal incense related to lunar themes.
- **Laurel:** This tree is sacred to the Sun and the Sun God. It is used in offerings and for protection spells. It is also used as a

charm for oracle divination and, when placed under a pillow, it can encourage dreams about the future.

- **Belladonna:** This plant is used in chthonic magick and as offerings to Hecate-Diana-Proserpina. It is poisonous and very dangerous if ingested, so avoid doing so.
- **Wolfbane or Monkshood:** This plant is used in chthonic spells and for war magick or hex breaking. It is deadly, and great care must be taken when handling. Do not touch the bare roots, as it is extremely dangerous if the juice gets into the bloodstream (death is likely).
- **Foxglove:** This plant is sacred to the Faery race and is often planted as an offering. It is used in love spells and work related to relationships in general.
- **Madder:** This plant is used to produce dyes used for sigil and symbol-making, as well as for staining spell bags.
- **Gypsywort:** This plant is used to produce a black dye suitable for staining ritual robes and for making symbols and sigils.
- **Oak:** This tree is sacred to the God, and acorns are often placed as offerings. The oak is considered to be a powerful and protective tree. Oak logs are used in the Winter Solstice celebration, where three candles are placed upon a log to denote the Child of Promise figure that is born at this season.
- **Pomegranate:** This tree is sacred to both Proserpina and Hecate. Pomegranate fruit is often used as an offering to the Goddess and for spells and rituals of a chthonic nature. The seeds are sometimes eaten before performing divination or oracle work. A walnut liqueur known as "Nocino" or "Nocello" was traditionally consumed at the Summer Solstice festival.
- **Walnut:** This tree is associated with the goddess Diana and the goddess Proserpina. It features strongly in Italian Witchcraft legends connected to the ancient city of Benevento. According to legend, this was the site of a great walnut tree where Witches came from all parts of Italy to celebrate their ways.
- **Wormwood:** This plant is sacred to the goddess Diana and is planted as an offering. Traditionally, three leaves are placed in a bottle of wine, which is drunk on the May Celebration.
- **Fava:** This plant produces the fava bean, which was used in ancient times for divination. The lore of the fava associates it

with the Underworld. The fava blossom is pure white with a dark stain on the petal, which is said to be the fingerprint of the Lord of the Underworld. The fava bean has a mark on it resembling a mouth which, according to lore, is the mouth of a departed soul (thus, the beans speak from the Underworld and provide oracle).

Italian Spirit Lore

The first fairytales to be written down in Europe were those of Italy. These early tales were collected directly from the old storytellers in towns and villages that had kept the oral traditions alive, which had been passed down to them over the centuries. Unfortunately, many of the favorite fairytales have been altered over the passage of time for political reasons. Therefore, only the oldest tales are useful for the purpose of discovering authentic bits of old Italic lore related to spirits. The oldest written recordings of Italian tales come from around 1637 and were collected by Giambattista Basile. Another famous collector was Giovanni Francesco Straparola. These are the fullest accounts.

One of the primary features in old Italian lore is a Faery woman appearing as either a Maiden or a Crone figure. Also featured are many magickal creatures, snakes in particular. Negative associations are largely absent in the early tales, but they become much like the Grimms brothers' stories by the nineteenth century, where such creatures are beings are of ill intent. It is here in the common folk-tales that the inner mysteries once preserved in the original tales fall victim to distortion among the populace. Such is always the fate of the esoteric in the hands of the common people.

In the original tale of Cinderella, the fairy godmother is actually the departed mother who has become a fairy woman. Cinderella's father returns from a trip to Sardinia and brings Cinderella a tree as a gift. The tree has been taken from the grotto of the faeries, and, when Cinderella waters and cares for the tree, out comes the fairy woman to aid her in times of trouble.

In the tale of Pinocchio, the fairy is actually the departed wife of Geppetto who died without having birthed a child. Pinocchio is made from the wood of a tree sacred to the fairy. Eventually, the fairy grants life to the wooden puppet, who becomes the child that she and Geppetto never had, but always wanted.

The following tales contain some of the older and veiled lore that testifies to pre-Christian elements that survived hidden within the storyline. Let us turn now in this chapter and look at a few of these very interesting fairytales. Here, we will find many of the early elements of esoteric lore.

Malconseil

Far away, shining brightly under the rays of the Italian sun, stand the snowy peaks of the Alps. Just below the level of the eternal snow, the rocky surface is dotted with the loveliest flowers, perhaps sown by the Fae after their midnight dances. Amongst these flowers, there is a little lake called Our Lady of the Snows, whose waters are such a clear, deep blue that they say it is a bit of sky dropped there by accident.

The lake is so beautiful and calm, and the landscape so daunting to traverse that it is almost impossible to disturb the peace of the place. And yet those waters, as transparent as crystal, have a secret as deep and mysterious as themselves. This secret is known to the four winds, who only tell it to the larches in the vast wood below, or to the Lady of the Snows, who sits on her throne higher up, between two rocks, very near the sky. This secret I am going to tell you as I heard it whispered by the breeze on fine night as I sat on a stone by the lake.

Long ago, there was a little grey stone cottage surrounded by a small field on the hillside below the larchwood. In the cottage lived old Magna Martric and her handsome son Renzo. They were quite well off, having several sheep and goats, two cows, a pig, and numerous chickens.

On every fine spring and summer day, Renzo used to take his sheep and goats up to the larchwood and, while they grazed, he would rest on the grass and listen to a wonderful sound in the air. It was a music that came from afar, sounding more like an echo than like a real voice—a song so sweet and tender, so full of harmony, that it could not be the expression of a mortal, but rather that of a fairy. Each day, he would search in vain for the musician who played such beauty.

One evening, as he lay in the grass, the Shepherd's Star shone bright above the snowy peak. Renzo felt deeply sad and returned home to his mother. Magna Martic asked him why he was so sad. After he explained what happened on the mountain each day, she warned him, saying: "Be careful my son, there is magick afoot there, and the Fantina has an eye on you!"

Reniz asked: "Who is the Fantina?"

Magna Martric replied that it was dangerous to talk of such things and said that one day, when he was older, she would explain. This only served to increase his curiosity. The next day, Renzo returned to the mountain with his flock. It so happened that one of the goats wandered off, and Renzo climbed in search of the goat until he discovered the secret lake.

Suddenly, the mysterious music began to play, and Renzo looked across the lake to see a woman of wondrous beauty. Fair as might be all the maidens of the valley, not one had he ever seen so lovely as this. Her long, glorious hair rippled in wonderful curls almost to her knees. Her mouth resembled a red carnation, and her eyes were the color of the bluest sky. There she stood, loveliest of the lovely, smiling at Renzo, who gazed in ecstasy at the entrancing vision.

He longed to go to her, but the lake was too deep and wide, and he had no boat. The woman stretched out her hand and called to him to come to her. Suddenly, the water turned to ice so that Renzo could walk upon it. Renzo was so taken with the vision of the woman that he forgot his mother's warning. He began to walk across the frozen surface of the lake when, halfway out, the ice suddenly vanished.

Renzo was drawn through the deep waters by a mysterious force. The Fantina also disappeared from the banks and, soon, her beautiful white arms were around Renzo's neck, and she was kissing him. Here, below the lake, the Fantina showed Renzo to the magnificent grotto where she had made her home.

And, once a year, on a fine summer evening, while the Shepherd's Star shines bright above a snowy peak and the sky is reddened by the glow of the setting Sun, if you look straight down through the clear, blue waters of the Malconseil, you can see quite distinctly, far below, two young people, one fair, the other dark, and they are kissing each other. It is Fantina and Renzo, who are still together.

Viola

Long ago, there lived three beautiful sisters named Rosa, Garofana, and Viola. Despite being beautiful themselves, the two sisters were envious of Viola for being even more beautiful. Each day, the three sisters sat on a balcony; one would spin, the other weave, and the third sew.

It so happened that a handsome prince rode by each day and complimented the women on their beauty, giving special attention to Viola. This became unbearable for the older sisters, who then plotted to be rid of Viola.

In those days, thimbles were very precious and rare, and Viola possessed one that was given to her by her father. He had brought it to her from a far-away land. The thimble was made of gold, set with rubies and diamonds. Viola cared for it more than anything in the world. So, the sisters stole the thimble and threw it into a garden owned by an Ogre who loved to eat young maidens.

When Viola was unable to find her thimble, she lamented to her sisters. Rosa said she would look into her magic mirror and see if she could discover where the thimble had gone. Rosa shortly returned and told Viola that the ring was in the garden of Bruttaccio, the terrible Ogre.

Her sisters then told Viola that they would lower her into the Ogre's garden with a rope and then pull her safely back up once she had retrieved the thimble. Viola agreed to the plan, but, as she was lowered halfway down into the garden, the sisters cut the rope and left Viola behind.

Then, the Ogre came upon Viola, but he thought she was too thin to eat, so he decided to keep her as a maid servant until he could fatten her up. Now, it happened that the prince who used to flirt with Viola had a pet parrot. One day, when the parrot did not return from its daily outing, the prince went in search of it. It was then that he came upon a wall and, looking over it from his horse, he saw Viola in the window of the cottage.

The Ogre always slept with one eye open, which made it impossible for Viola to move about undetected. So, the prince decided to go into the forest and ask his godmother for help. He rode until he came to vast and ancient oak tree, where the Faery known as Merlina lived within its deep and large hollow. The prince called out "Mama Merlina, Mama Merlina, pretty Viola has fallen into the hands of Bruttaccio. What can I do to have her safely back with me?"

Then, Merlina went inside the oak to consult the Book of Words and presently came out, holding a distaff, a clew of thread, and a comb. These she gave to prince Lionello, saying: "When you are in danger of Bruttaccio catching you, throw first the distaff, then the clew of thread, and finally the comb, saying at the same time: 'Merlina, Merlina, come and help us!' and all will be well."

Lionello thanked his fairy godmother and kissed her hand, after which, having carefully put away the charms, he rode back to town. That night, he went to Viola's window and told her that he had a charm to protect them against the Ogre and to come down at once, so they could escape. Viola used the rope that her sisters had left behind and let herself down to the garden. The prince scooped her up in his arms, put her on his horse, and away they rode.

Bruttaccio knew at once what had occurred and he sprang to his horse in pursuit. Lionello heard the sounds of the horse's hooves behind him and turned to see the Ogre gaining on him. The prince then threw the distaff over his shoulder and shouted: "Merlina, Merlina, help, help me!"

Suddenly, sharp swords protruding from the ground all around him hindered the Ogre's path. This slowed the Ogre down for a short time, but, soon, he passed the obstacles and galloped even faster after the prince. Next, the prince tossed the clew of thread and called again upon Merlina to render aid. Immediately, a fast-rushing stream separated the prince and the Ogre. But the Ogre forced his way through the water and continued the chase.

As the Ogre was almost upon them, the prince threw the comb over his shoulder, shouting to Merlina to help him. Suddenly, a very high mountain made of soap arose in front of the Ogre and, every time he tried to get his horse to climb, the poor creature slid back down. The Ogre then tried to climb the soap mountain himself, but he slid off and fell to his demise.

The prince took Viola to his palace, where they married. Afterwards, he called for Viola's sisters and rendered a punishment for their actions against Viola. The couple then lived happily from that day forward under the protection of Mama Merlina.

Biancabella and the Snake

A long time ago in Monteferrat, there was a wealthy nobleman who had no children. He and his wife prayed for a child, but the years passed without producing one. Then, one day, his wife went into the garden to rest and fell asleep on the ground beneath a tree. As she slept, a small snake crawled beneath her clothes, entered her vagina, and nestled in her womb. All of this went unnoticed by the wife.

In a short time, the wife found herself to be pregnant, much to her surprise and delight. When the child was born, it was a baby girl. However, everyone was shocked to see her born with a snake wrapped around her throat three times. The midwives were very frightened, but the snake did no harm to anyone and simply untwined itself and slipped away into the garden.

After midwives cleaned and bathed the baby girl, they noticed a delicate, gold necklace around her neck. It seemed to radiate from beneath the skin, and the necklace went around the baby's neck three times. The midwives remarked that this was just the way the snake was wrapped around the baby's neck.

The baby was named Biancabella ("beautiful, blonde girl") and lived a happy childhood. Such was her beauty in her nature that some people remarked that she was more divine than human. On her tenth birthday, a nurse took her to a balcony where she had never been before. From there, she saw a garden and asked who it belonged to, and the nurse answered that this was the mother's garden.

Biancabella wanted to visit the garden, so the nurse took down there and sat under a beech tree, while Biancabella gathered flowers. Soon, Biancabella felt tired and laid down under a tree in the garden and took her rest in its shade. Within a few moments, a snake appeared and moved to her side. Biancabella was afraid, but the snake spoke to her: "Be quiet and don't move. You need not have any fear because I am your sister. I was born on the same day as you, and my name is Samaritana."

The snake then instructed Biancabella to do as she bids and good fortune will follow. However, the snake warned her that, if she refused, then ill fortune is sure to follow. Samaritana told Biancabella to bring two buckets on the following morning. One bucket was to be filled with pure milk, and the other with fine rose water.

Enlisting the aid of the household servants, Biancabella delivered two basins, each filled as directed. Biancabella entered the garden and sat down beside the buckets. As soon as she did, the snake appeared and approached her. Biancabella was then directed to remove all of her clothing and to step naked into the bucket filled with milk. Biancabella complied, and the snake washed her from head to toe in the milk and licked her all over with its tongue, which cured her of all defects. After Biancabella stepped out of the milk, she went into the bucket of rose water and was given a scent that made her feel very fresh.

The snake then instructed Biancabella to put her clothes back on and not to tell anyone (even her parents) what had taken place in the garden. It was the snake's intention that Biancabella was not to be matched in beauty and grace by any other woman. So, the snake endowed her an infinite number of qualities, and then, she departed.

When Biancabella returned home, her beauty startled her mother, and she asked Biancabella what had happened to her. Biancabella did not know what to say, so she remained silent. Her mother then began to brush Biancabella's hair, when, suddenly, out fell pearls and precious stones. When Biancabella went to wash her hands, rose, violets, and all kinds of bright flowers tumbled from them with such sweet fragrance that the room was like the earthly paradise.

Upon seeing all of this, the mother ran to the father and told him what she had observed. The father did not believe it, and he had to see it for himself. Upon witnessing these wondrous things, he declared that no man was worthy of marrying Biancabella. But, very soon, the fame and glory of Biancabella spread across the land, and many kings, princes, and dukes came from all over the world to wed Biancabella. However, each of the suitors was deemed to be unworthy. At last, Ferrandino, the King of Naples, arrived, and his prowess and illustrious name radiated like the Sun among the smaller stars. Seeing Ferrandino, the father consented to the marriage, and it took place without delay.

No sooner were the marriage rites completed than Biancabella recalled the loving words that her sister Samaritana had said to her. So, she withdrew from her husband under the pretext that she had certain things to do and went to her chamber, locking the door. Then, she walked through a secret passage into the garden, where she began to call Samaritana in a low voice. However, the snake did not answer, and Biancabella was distressed that Samaritana did not reply because she was offended in some way with Biancabella.

After their wedding night, the king and Biancabella left for Naples and went to live in the king's castle. Now, it so happened that Ferrandino had a stepmother who had two ugly and nasty daughters, and she has hoped to marry one of them to the king. Upon seeing Biancabella, the stepmother felt that all hope was taken away. So, the stepmother then began to make plans to kill Biancabella.

As it happened, the king had to leave to fight a war against a rival, and Biancabella was left with his stepmother. Immediately, she arranged for two of her loyal servants to kill Biancabella and bring some proof of her death. These were men who never hesitated to so some evil deed. So, they told Biancabella that they wanted to show her a beautiful place in the woods. Upon arriving, the men were so overcome with her grace and beauty that they could not bear to kill her. However, fearing the stepmother's wrath, they cut off Biancabella's hands and blinded her. Then, they returned to the stepmother with the evidence, saying that Biancabella was dead.

As fate would have it, an old man came upon Biancabella in the woods and, feeling pity for her, took her home to his cabin in the woods. When his daughters attended to her, brushing her hair, out fell pearls, rubies, diamonds, and precious jewels. Biancabella then asked for a bucket of water to wash her face, and arms, roses, violets, and other flowers tumbled from her. This event caused the poor family to believe that Biancabella was a divine person and certainly not human. In any case, the family was relieved that their poverty was ended.

Biancabella asked the old man to take her back into the woods where he had found her and then to return at dusk to take her back to the cabin. When she was alone, Biancabella decided to take her own life, because she could not bear her condition. Remembering a nearby pool of water, Biancabella decided to drown herself. However, when she reached the water, a voice called out to her to stop. The voice was that of the snake, her sister Samaritana.

The snake then gathered some herbs and went to Biancabella, spreading them on her eyes, and this restored her sight. Then, the snake touched Biancabella's arms, and her hands were restored as well. When this was accomplished, the snake shed its skin and revealed itself as the beautiful maiden Samaritana.

As the Sun began to lose its light, the old man returned to fetch Biancabella. When he arrived, he saw her sitting in the company of a Forest Nymph. Biancabella explained that this was her sister and that she had healed her. The old man was delighted and he bid both of the women to return with him to the cabin.

Many days later, Samaritana and Biancabella, along with the old man and his family, decided to move to Naples. They found a vacant place near the king's palace and decided to make this their home. Samaritana took a laurel twig and hit the ground with it three times and said certain words. No sooner had the sounds of the words faded than the most beautiful palace arose from the ground.

The next morning, King Ferrandino looked out of his window to see a great palace across the way. In the window, he saw two beautiful women, one of which looked very much like his lost Biancabella. So, the king decided to pay them a visit, and he took the stepmother and her daughter along with him. When they arrived, Biancabella and Samaritana insisted on presenting them with a feast.

After dinner was over, Samaritana had a maiden named Silveria play a lyre for the king and his company to entertain them. While the music played, Samaritana sang the tale of Biancabella from beginning to end without ever mentioning the maiden's name. When the song was over, she asked the king what would be a fitting punishment for those who could do such evil to a fair maiden. The stepmother and her daughters felt a doom fall over them.

The stepmother, who thought she might cover her guilt by answering herself, did not wait for the king to reply and said that the guilty people should be cast into a burning furnace. Then, Samaritana's face grew red as embers, and she said: "You are the very wicked and cruel woman who caused all these terrible things to happen, and you've condemned yourself by your own words."

Samaritana had the daughters of the old man brush Biancabella's hair, and the king saw the pearls and jewels fall out, as he had on other occasions. Then, she showed the king Biancabella's white neck where the gold necklace appeared, wrapped three times. The king knew then that this was his beloved Biancabella. He ordered the stepmother and her daughters to be thrown into a burning furnace as punishment for what they had done to Biancabella. Then, Ferrandino, Biancabella, and Samaritana live a long life together and left heirs to inherit the kingdom.

The Walnut Faeries

There was, at Benevento, a poor family whose members gained their living by going about the country and getting fruit, which they sold. One day, the youngest son was roaming, trying to see what he could find, when he beheld a walnut tree—but one so beautiful 'twas hardly credible what nuts were on it! Truly, he thought he had a good thing of it, but, as he gathered the nuts, they opened and from each came a beautiful little lady who, at once, grew to life size. They were gay and merry, and so fair they seemed the eyes of the Sun. Sweet music sounded from the leaves, they made him dance; 'twas a fine festa.

However, he did not for all that forget why he had come there and that the family at home wanted bread. But, the ladies who were Faeries (fate) knew this, and, when the dancing was over, they gave him some of the nuts. And they said: "When you shall be at home, open two of these, keep a third for the king's daughter, and take this little basket full to the king. And tell the queen's daughter not to open her walnut 'till she shall have gone to bed."

When he had returned and opened his nut, there poured from it such a stream of gold that he found himself richer than the king. So, he built himself a castle of extraordinary splendor, all of precious stones. Upon opening the second nut, there came from it such a magnificent suit of clothes that, when he put it on, he was the handsomest man in the world. So, he went to the king and was well received. But, when he asked for the hand of the princess, the monarch replied that he was very sorry, but he had promised his daughter to another prince. For this other, the princess had no love at all, but she was enamored with the youth.

So, she accepted the nut and went to bed; but oh, what wonder! What should come out of it but the young man who had asked her in marriage! Now, as she could not help herself and, moreover, had no special desire to be helped, she made the best of it and suffered him, only to remain, but to return, which he did zealously, full many a time; with the natural result in the course of events, the princess found herself with child and declared that something must be done.

And this was arranged. She went to her father and said that she would never marry the prince to whom he had betrothed her, and that there should be a grand assembly of youths, and they should agree that, lest her choose whom she would, they would support her choice. So, it was done, and there were feasts, balls, and, at last, a great assembly of young men. Among them appeared her own lover, the man of the walnuts. He was dressed like a poor peasant and sat at the table among the humblest who were there. The princess went forth from one to the other of those who wished to marry her. And she found some fault in everyone, 'till she came to her own lover, and said: "That is the one who I choose," and threw her handkerchief at him—which was a sign that she would marry him.

All who were present were enraged that she should have selected such a peasant, or beggar, nor was the king himself well pleased. At last, it was arranged that there should be a combat and that, if the young man could hold his own, he might marry the princess. Now, he was strong and brave, yet this was a great trial. But the ladies of the walnut tree helped their friend so that all fell before him. Never a sword or lance touched him in the fray, he bore a charmed life, and the opposing knights went down before him like sheep before a wolf. He was the victor and wedded the daughter of the king; and, after a few months, she gave birth to a beautiful babe who was called, in gratitude to the Faery ladies, the "Walnut of Benevento." And so, they were happy and contented.

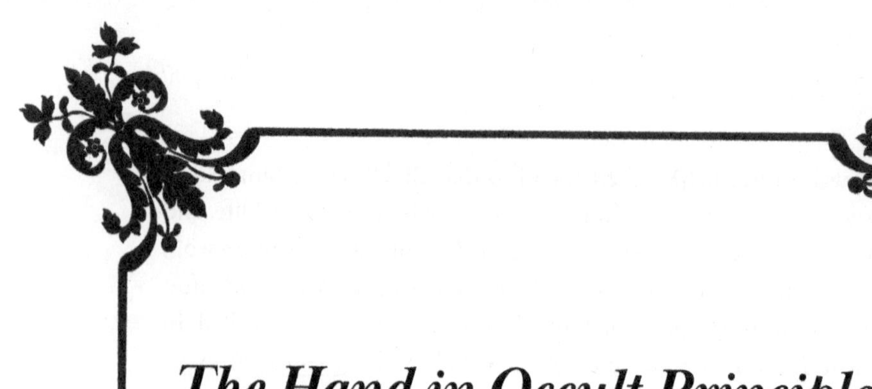

The Hand in Occult Principles

The art of palmistry has helped to preserve some of the old teachings associated with the human hand. Palmistry is linked to planetary forces and stellar properties. The old teachings tell us that the Sun, Moon, and planets exercise a distinct and particular influence upon our race. The influences are established at conception, mature during gestation, and are set in place upon birth. It is this final process that anchors the character of the individual for their own life experience. This does not remove free will, but it does establish the core personality.

The stellar influences that are set in any individual affect not only the life experience, but also influence daily thoughts and actions. This is conveyed through what occultists call the "Astral Light." This etheric material is comprised of seven vapors that emanate from the seven planets of our solar system. However, the Sun and the Moon temper and modify these emanations as they pass through the atmosphere (both inner and outer).

According to occult teachings, the influence of each planet passes into us through specific areas of the hand. These receptors were established during the gestation period as the hands were forming under stellar influence. This is also part of the inner knowledge of palmistry.

The planetary currents emanating through the Astral Light combine and flow through the individual along the lines of the hand. In essence, they first establish the lines, then flow through them like canals. Over the course of time, they leave signs of what has taken place in a person's life, as well as what is to come in the future. As with any form of divination, the future is defined as "the probable outcome," if nothing intervenes to affect its course.

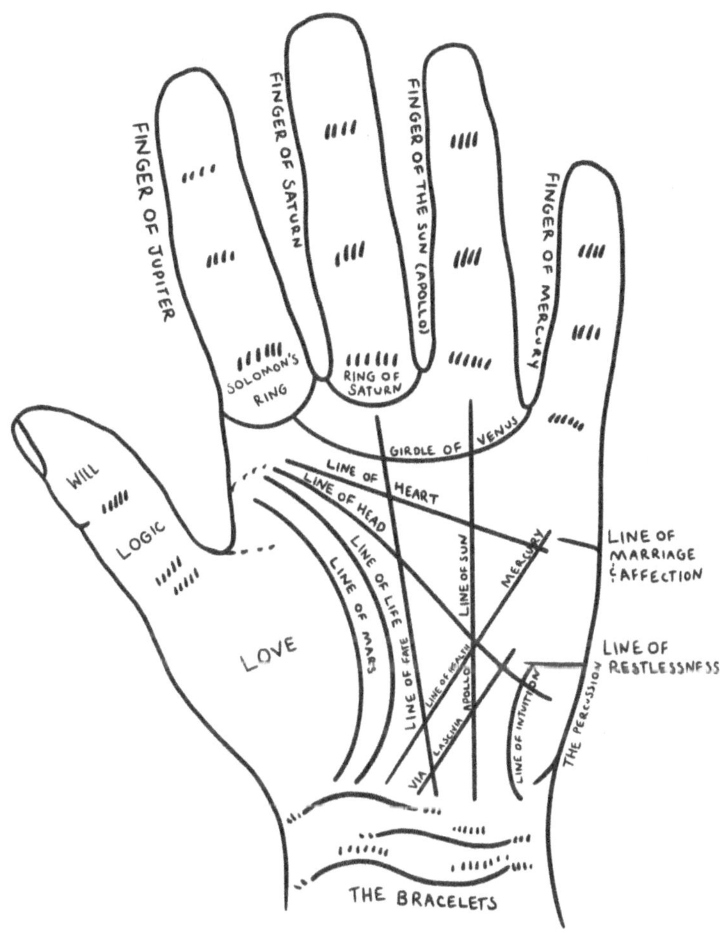

In essence, the hand is the past record, the current moment, and the future, all existing within a single energy imprint revealed in the lines of the hand. For one who knows how to read the signs, the future is as clear to them as is the past to a historian with accurate records.

In the occult arts, the hand is associated with healing, and this is typically performed by laying hands upon the ill or injured person. Such an act might be considered instinctive, as we naturally touch other people when they are injured or ill to console them. But, from an occult perspective, this is an alignment, a means of seeking both the ailment and the cure (for all things are connected).

In magickal terms, the stellar properties at the command of the fingers can be directed in spells and rituals. Certain combinations of gestures with the hand and fingers created alignments. These alignments create links to astral forces that can be drawn and tapped for magickal intentions.

Magickal and Ritual Gestures

Ritual and magickal gestures are very traditional in Italian Witchcraft. Some of them have leaked out into common folk magick traditions and are, therefore, very well known today. The two most common gestures are the *cornuto* and the *mano in fica.*

Cornuto and Mano in Fica

The *cornuto* is used when evoking the Horned God of Witchcraft. It is also used as a symbol of protection and, when displayed, it announces that one is under the protection of the Horned God. The *mano in fica* (or *mano fica*) is used in sex and fertility magick, and its symbol is not made public. In common folk traditions, the meaning takes on different intentions and is usually a negative or insulting expression. As a charm, it protects the life force and prevents enemies from drawing power away from the wearer.

Some gestures possess religious or spiritual symbolism. One example is the sign of the Triple Goddess. The thumb represents Proserpina in the Underworld. The index finger represents Hecate and is symbolic of the ancient Pillar of Hecate that stood at the center of the crossroads. The middle finger of the hand is Diana (next to the two bent fingers representing the waxing and waning forces over which she reigns). Together, all three fingers are a symbolic crossroads (three roads dividing).

The Sign of the Triple Goddess

Another example of a religious or spiritual gesture is that of the Moon Altar. This gesture is used to pray to the Goddess of Night, the Moon Goddess, or Queen of the Heavens. The fingers are slightly curved to represent the opening of a grotto or cave. This is one of the most ancient sites of Goddess worship. The thumbs are pressed together and inserted into the opening of the hands. Here, they form an altar. To use this gesture, the hands are positioned so that the Moon seems to sit on the thumbs (the altar). Traditionally, only the left eye is used to view the Moon through the opening of the hands.

The Ancient Magick

Witchcraft in ancient times is almost exclusively assigned to women. In Ancient Greece, it was referred to as an illicit religion, as well as feared system of magick. The history of Witchcraft includes not only charges of magick, but also combines prostitution and banned sexuality. At the core of such laws and prohibitions is a deep-rooted male fear of female sexuality and its power over men.

Among the earliest appearances of a Witch in ancient writings, we find the figure known as Medea. In the tales associated with Jason and the Argonauts, Medea is depicted as harvesting herbs with her dress undone and open. In other writing she is depicted nude, as is the Witch known as Pamphile. The ancient writer Apuleius writes of her as a Thessalian Witch who removes all of her clothing and smears her body with an ointment.[56]

Nudity continues to be associated with Witches well into the Christian era. Historian Jeffrey Burton Russell writes, in his book *Witchcraft in the Middles Ages: "A woman named Marta was tortured in Florence about 1375: she was alleged to have placed candles round a dish and to have taken off her clothes and stood above the dish in the nude, making magical signs."*[57]

---

56 Apuleius, *Metamorphoses: The Golden Ass,* 3.15–25.

57 Jeffrey Burton Russell, *Witchcraft in the Middles Ages* (Cornell UP, 1972).

Historian Ruth Martin, in her book *Witchcraft and the Inquisition in Venice 1550–1650,* notes that it was a common practice for Witches of this era to be "naked with their hair loose around their shoulders" while reciting conjurations.[58] In addition, there are several examples of nudity appearing in various seventeenth century woodcuts that depict Witches dancing naked.

One dominating feature of Ancient Witchcraft is the ritual and magickal cauldron. The cauldron has long been associated with women and feminine symbolism in general. Scholar Erich Neumann, in his classic work titled *The Great Mother,* wrote:

> *The vessel of Transformation–viewed as magical can only be effected by the woman because she herself, in her body that corresponds to the Great Goddess, is the cauldron of incarnation, birth, and rebirth. And that is why the magical cauldron or pot is always in the hand of the female mana figure, the priestess and later the witch.*[59]

In the ancient tales of Medea, the cauldron is depicted as a vessel of transformation. As such, it can renew life and vitality, as well as draw it back into its depths. In many regions of Europe, we find tales of the cauldron associated with such goddess-figures as Ceres and Ceridwen. In these ancient tales, the cauldron often appears hidden in a cave, a dungeon, or in the Underworld. This speaks to its secret or hidden nature, as well as its connection with the Otherworld. As a tool associated with life and death, the cauldron is intimately connected to souls of the dead. This is one of the reasons why the skull often appears with the cauldron (as well as bones in general).

---

58 Ruth Martin, *Witchcraft and the Inquisition in Venice 1550–1650* (Basil Blackwell, 1989).

59 Erich Neumann, *The Great Mother: An Analysis of the Archetype, Ralph Manheim,* tr. (Princeton UP, 1955).

In ancient times, the cauldron was suspended within the hearth. The hearth is the symbol of the sacred grotto where the Goddess was originally worshipped. The stones of the hearth represent this ancient setting. The opening of the hearth symbolizes the cave, the ancient entrance into the Underworld. The fire burning within the hearth is the divine flame, the oldest representation of the Goddess in her purity without human form. This is one of the reasons why the goddesses of Witchcraft carry lighted torches. The other reason is that goddesses of the torch-bearing classification are connected to the Moon, and torches represent light in the darkness.

Fire, as a representation of the Goddess in her primal nature, symbolizes her as unclothed and liberated. The flicker of torchlight on the nude bodies of Witches conveys the liberating power of the Goddess to her followers. This meaning is reflected in the text known as *The Charge of Goddess,* where we find this passage:

> *Whenever you have need of anything, once in the month when the moon is full, then shall you come together at some deserted place, or where there are woods, and give worship to She who is Queen of all Witches. Come all together inside a circle, and secrets that are as yet unknown shall be revealed. And your mind must be free and also your spirit, and as a sign that you are truly free, you shall be naked in your rites. And you shall rejoice, and sing; making music and love. For this is the essence of spirit, and a knowledge of joy. Be true to your own beliefs, and keep to the Ways, beyond all obstacles. For ours is the key to the mysteries and the cycle of rebirth, which opens the way to the Womb of Enlightenment.*

Drawing Down the Moon

Ancient pre-Christian writings of Greece and Rome depict Witches performing acts of magick associated with the Moon. One dominant theme portrays Witches as being as able to "Draw the Moon Down" from the sky. Various ancient authors held differing views as to what this meant.

As historian Daniel Ogden points out in his book *Magic, Witchcraft, and Ghosts in the Greek and Roman Worlds,* the act of Drawing Down the Moon incorporated erotic attraction magick. This is another reason for ritual nudity.[60] The long-standing tradition of the Moon as a fertile agent, and romance connected to the Full Moon, are remnants of this ancient tradition.

In the ancient text of the *Metamorphoses (of Apuleius),* we find the idea that Drawing Down the Moon leaves a deposit of foam on the ground, which is called the *virus lunare,* or "moon-juice." This substance is used for magickal purposes.[61] Unknown to the ancient scholars, the substance was actually the morning-dew left on lichen

60 Daniel Ogden, *Magic, Witchcraft, and Ghosts in the Greek and Roman Worlds: A Sourcebook* (Oxford UP, 2002).

61 Apuleius, *Metamorphoses: The Golden Ass.*

that grows on rocks. The lichen was a grayish-white color, and the spots of it on the rocks looked much like the patterns one sees with the naked eye when looking at the surface of the Full Moon.

According to oral tradition, the moisture of the heavy dew following the night of the Full Moon was scraped and collected onto leaves, which were used to pour the drops of dew into a small container. The dew was then used in magickal spells, as well as for blessings, healings, and anointings.

The connection of the Moon to water is also noted in the teachings regarding the Moon's reflection on the surface of lakes and the ocean. At Lake Nemi, Italy, where the Temple of Diana once stood, the lake was known as "Diana's Mirror." This was because of the Full Moon's reflection on the surface of the quiet lake, which could be easily seen from the temple itself. It is noteworthy that Diana was known in ancient times also by the epithet of "the Dewy One."

The Roman poet known as Horace writes (in his work *The Epodes*) that Witches use a book by which they can "call down the Moon" with incantations. He also depicts Witches calling upon Diana to aid them in their night dealings. Horace refers to a Witch's book known as the *Libro Carminun,* which means "Book of Songs," or "Book of Enchantment." In the text, we find these Latin words spoken by the Witch known as Canidia: *"Nox, et Diana, quae regis silentium cum arcana sacra fiunt; nunc, nunc adeste: nunc vertite iram atque numen in hostiles domos" ("Night and Diana, who command silence when secret mysteries are performed; now, now aid me: now turn your vengeance and influence against my enemies' houses").*[62]

It is noteworthy that, in the writings of Charles Leland on this subject, we also find this theme related to Italian Witchcraft. Leland portrays Aradia (in the personage of the daughter of Diana) as a Witch who fights against the oppression of peasants by the noble class. This theme is also found in the words of the closing prayer in the Full Moon ritual:

"Give us power, O' Most Secret Lady, to bind our oppressors. Receive us as Your children, receive us though we are earthbound. When our

62 Horace, "The Witch's Incantation," *The Epodes.* V.

bodies lie resting nightly, speak to our inner spirits, teach us all Your Holy Mysteries. I believe Your ancient promise that we who seek Your Holy Presence will receive of Your wisdom."

In this text, we also find the idea of a covenant between the Witch and their deity. At the core is a promise and, therefore, a trust of that promise. In the following ancient incantation, there appears a mention of the night as the keeper of secrets. There is also mention of the stars and the Moon bearing witness to the deeds of the Witch:

Night, trustiest keeper of my secrets, and stars who, together with the moon, follow on from the fires of the daylight, and you Hecate of the three heads, who know all about my designs and come to help the incantations and the craft of the witches, and Earth, who furnish witches with powerful herbs, and Breezes, Winds, Mountains, Rivers, and Lakes, and all the gods of the groves and all the gods of the night, be present to help me. Night-wandering queen, look kindly upon this undertaking.[63]

The observation or witnessing of these rites is a very old theme. Remnants of it appear in archaic Roman religion (itself derived from Etruscan religion). We know from ancient sources that Witches gathered at the crossroads to perform their rituals and magick. In early Roman religion, the crossroads were also the place where veneration of the ancestral Lare spirits took place. Ovid, in his *Fausti,* calls the Lare the "Night Watchmen."[64] Scholar Georges Dumezil states that the Lare were associated with points of demarcation and towers, as well as being associated with the agricultural seasons.[65] This ancient theme appears to be reflected in the Modern Wiccan concept of the Watchers and the Watchtowers.

63 Charles Godfrey Leland, *Aradia: Gospel of the Witches* (David Nutt, 1899).

64 Ovid. *The Fausti,* John Benson Rose, tr. (Dorrell and Son, 1866).

65 Georges Dumezil, *Archaic Roman Religion: with an Appendix on the Religion of the Etruscans.* vol. 1, Philip Krapp, tr. (Johns Hopkins UP, 1966) 343.

Witchcraft at the Crossroads

Since ancient times, the crossroads have been intimately linked to Witches, Witchcraft, and the goddess Hecate. Hecate is one of the oldest goddesses associated with Witchcraft. It was the custom in ancient times to erect a wooden pole called a *hekataion* or *hekataia.* The *hekataion* is described as a tree trunk placed at the center of the crossroads, which represented her triple nature.

Hecate is often equated with Enodia, a Greek goddess whose name means "In-the-Road," and who guarded entrances. The key was a cult symbol among Enodia's worshippers, as it also was for Hecate. In ancient times, the threshold of a doorway or gateway was a liminal area, which means a place in-between. This was also true of the crossroads, for the place where the roads came together was "in-between" the paths.

It was an ancient belief that souls who passed from life through a tragic, unjust, or violent death found it difficult to cross over into the Otherworld. These souls were believed to gather at the crossroads, a place between the worlds. Hecate assembled the lost souls under her protection and guidance at the crossroads.

One of the legends attached to Hecate portrays her leading this band of lost souls in night processions. This may well be the origin of the Church Canon called the "Canon Episcopi," which warns against the belief that some women have of traveling with the goddess Diana across great distances at night. Here is an excerpt from the canon:

> *Some wicked women are perverted by the Devil and led astray by illusions and fantasies induced by Daemons, so that they believe that they ride out at night with Diana the Pagan Goddess...to a meeting to commune and do, Her will flying across great distances...Many other people also believe this to be true although it is a Pagan error to believe that any other divinity exists than the one true God...He [Satan] shows her deluded mind strange things and leads it on weird journeys.*

> *It is only the mind that does this. But faithless people believe that these things happen to the body as well.*[66]

This text appears to be an attempt to discredit Pagan beliefs and practices, while, at the same time, bringing in the Judeo-Christian Devil-figure to further distort and discourage adherence to the Old Religion.

We know from ancient sources that Roman Witches favored the crossroads for their night rituals and works of magick. A skull was placed there, along with two crossbones, to call in the ancestral spirits. Pomegranates, when in season, were special offerings to Hecate and to the spirits gathered at the crossroads. Coins, grain, and wine were given as offerings to the chthonic deities. Spelt "cakes" were tossed up into the night sky as an offering to the entities of the night, the stars, and the Moon.

For works of magick, a large Y was etched into the soil with a beech wand, and, in the opening of the Y, a symbol was placed to indicate the desired intent of the spell. The Y symbolizes the female power, as it represents the female genitalia (and, therefore, the vessel of generation). As the spell was recited, a circle was etched around the Y with the handle of a broom (clockwise) to enclose it as the power was being raised or drawn. Once fully formulated, the spell was released by sweeping the circle away with a broom (in a counterclockwise manner). The broom was then lifted upward and swung around to "fling" the power off towards the direction of the target of the spell.

The practice of ancestral veneration is noted in the use of poppets at the crossroads. Witches danced at the crossroads with their ancestors by tossing the poppets back and forth in merriment while dancing and singing. Following the dance, the poppets where placed in the cauldron in a belief that this aided the rebirth of the ancestral souls. It may be the case that this act, when viewed by spies from a distance at night, made onlookers believe that the Witches were

66 "Canon Episcopi," *Council of Ancyra* (314 BC).

putting babies in the cauldron. By flickering torchlight, the limp poppets may have looked like dead babies.

To invoke the ancestors, the Witches pricked themselves and offered drops of their blood. This was done in the belief that the dead required blood in order to animate in the world of the living. Therefore, the blood gave them vitality when they were drawn to the Witches' rituals. Feasting was also part of the ritual, and places were set for the dead to partake of the festivities.

The assemblies of Witches were all under the auspices of Hecate. Her hekataion was the sacred tree of the worlds, which touched the Realms beneath the Earth and above it, as well as dwelling within the Mortal Realm itself. Around the tree, the Witches danced beneath the Full Moon, joining with the spirits of those who danced before them in the distant past. It was at the crossroads where magick poured in from the Otherworld, pooled, and then poured back into its source.

The Magick of Moonlight

An ancient belief held that the light of the Full Moon possessed magickal properties. This appears in old folk beliefs about moonlight falling upon the crops to make them fertile. A related belief is that if a woman slept nude in a field beneath the Full Moon and awoke covered with the morning dew, that she would be made fertile. During the Christian era, the Church sought to instill negative views about the Moon. This is the era in which we find writings that, if the moonlight falls upon a person while asleep, insanity may occur. This is also the period of writings on the Full Moon turning people into werewolves.

We know from ancient sources that the light of the Full Moon was considered to be both sacred and magickal. The reflection of the Moon on Lake Nemi was viewed as the face of the goddess Diana. In magickal and ritual practices, mirrors were used to reflect the Moon's light for certain intentions. These mirrors were made of polished silver, bronze, or copper. One technique involved reflecting the light of the Full Moon onto the forehead of a priestess. She stood with the Moon behind her, and the assistant knelt and angled the mirror to reflect the light. A series of mirrors was also used to reflect light into a bowl or a box. It was believed that the magickal essence of the Moon's light could be captured and stored in this way. This allowed access to the powers inherent in the Full Moon, despite the phase of the Moon during any particular time of the month.

The light of the Full Moon was used to magically charge rings, talismans, amulets, potions, and ritual tools. This could be performed by "snatching" the Moon's light, which involved using the left hand left like a bird's talons while looking at the Moon with the right eye closed. The moonlight was captured in the talons with a circular sweeping motion of the hand, and then the light of the Moon was dragged downward and directed into the object to be charged. This required releasing the light by opening the fingers and pressing down on the object with the fingertips.

A tradition grew around this practice, which then associated the placement of the Moon in one of the Zodiac signs. This was believed to enhance the Moon's power at such a time. The following are the traditionally assigned occult influences when the Moon passes into a particular Zodiac sign:

- **Moon in Aries:** amplifies forces, brings additional power
- **Moon in Taurus:** draws personal favor from others
- **Moon in Gemini:** enhances receptivity in any matter
- **Moon in Cancer:** stirs the subconscious, influences dreams
- **Moon in Leo:** influences and enhances one's social position
- **Moon in Virgo:** brings focus and organization (attention to detail)
- **Moon in Libra:** stabilizes partnerships and relationships
- **Moon in Scorpio:** cloaks, maintains secrecy, keeps things unrevealed or obscure
- **Moon in Sagittarius:** brings about reform and change
- **Moon in Capricorn:** enhances logic and reason
- **Moon in Aquarius:** influences change and enhances projected image

- **Moon in Pisces:** enhances psychic energy and stimulates the emotions.

Aradia, The Holy Strega

In some traditions of Italian Witchcraft, Aradia is called "The Holy Strega." Here, she features strongly as a Holy Woman or Wise Woman, in the time-honored sense. Such figures appear throughout time, from the ancient sibyl of the Etruscans and Romans, up through the village healers of the Middle Ages and Renaissance periods. In other traditions, Aradia is thought of as a goddess-figure who is the offspring of the goddess Diana.

Within those traditions that view Aradia as a type of human avatar, she is thought of as a mystic. In this light, Aradia delivers teachings designed to reveal the hidden mysteries. Because the tradition of Witchcraft is lunar in nature, the teachings focus on night and the Dream World. Here, the Moon becomes the symbol of enlightenment in the places of darkness. This, of course, makes the Full Moon highly significant in the Realm of Witchcraft.

In the Mystical Tradition, there are two types of consciousness, one "worldly" and one "Otherworldly." The former is our conscious mind, which concerns itself with the tasks of daily life. The latter is our subconscious mind, which concerns itself with the inner spirit. Like the Sun and the Moon, they rise and disappear in their cycles, never quite meeting, except for one brief moment of transition. The Sun and the Full Moon sit opposite on the horizon, and the *awake mind* and the *dream mind* reflect one another just at the point of falling asleep or waking up. This is the twilight phase, when we are not yet awake, but not quite free of the dream.

One of the oldest teachings in Italian Witchcraft is that we are taught while we sleep, meaning that secrets are passed to us in the dream states of consciousness. This is because the guardian mind of the conscious state is not the master in the Dream World, and we can accept the reality of a Realm in which things can take place that are impossible in the Material World. In dreams, we can fly, breathe underwater, and so on. It is here that the ways of magick are real experiences in the fullest sense. We need only add moonlight to this and, thereby, bring enlightenment to the Subconscious Realm.

In one of the classic texts found in Italian Witchcraft, we can see the formula outlined in a magickal prayer. This prayer mentions Aradia and the Realm of Dream teachings. The verse also refers to *the appointed time,* which appears in *The Charge of the Goddess* as the night of the Full Moon. The prayer is part of the closing of the Full Moon ritual and reads as follows:

"O' Great Lady, Queen of all Witches, hear our songs of adoration. Hear our voices when we speak your praises. Receive our words as they rise heavenward, when the Full Moon brightly shining fills the heavens with your beauty. See us as we gather before you, when we reach our arms up towards you. When the Full Moon shines upon us, give us all your blessings.

O' Great Goddess of the Moon, Goddess of the Mysteries of the Moon, teach us your ancient mysteries, ancient rites of invocation that the Holy Strega spoke of, for I believe the Strega's story; when she spoke of your shining glory, when she told us to entreat you, told us when we seek for knowledge to seek and find you above all others.

Give us power, O' Most Secret Lady, to bind our oppressors. Receive us as your children, receive us though we are earthbound. When our bodies lie resting nightly, speak to our inner spirits, teach us all your Holy Mysteries. I believe your ancient promise that we who seek your holy presence will receive of your wisdom.

Behold, O' Ancient Goddess, we have gathered beneath the Full Moon at this appointed time. Now the Full Moon shines upon us. Hear us. Recall your ancient promise. Let your glory shine about us. Bless us, O' Gracious Queen of Heaven. So be it done."

There exists another text that is sometimes referred to as *The Charge of Aradia.* A heavily modified version of the original appears in Leland's Aradia material, and a modified version of Leland's text appears in Gardnerian Wicca. This version contains insertions of Celtic themes, along with those found in the Aegean/Mediterranean. In essence, the Charge is written as Aradia speaking to her followers in a parting speech. She leaves a set of instructions regarding the time and place for ritual meetings, along with codes of conduct. Aradia speaks of her mission and shares her mystical nature and background in a way that she felt her followers could understand. She asks to be remembered through a ritual meal at the time of the Full Moon. In closing, Aradia reveals the inner nature of the Goddess and provides clues to the alignments through which initiates can commune with her. The Charge concludes with a mystery teaching that directs the initiates inward, where the Divine Spark of the soul can meet with the source of light from which it originated.

The Charge of Aradia

Whenever you have need of anything, once in the month when the Moon is full, then shall you come together at some deserted place, or where there are woods, and give worship to She who is Queen of all Witches. Come all together inside a circle, and secrets that are as yet unknown shall be revealed. And your mind must be free and also your spirit, and as a sign that you are truly free, you shall be naked in your rites. And you shall rejoice, and sing; making music and love. For this is the essence of spirit, and a knowledge of joy. Be true to your own beliefs, and keep to the Ways, beyond all obstacles. For ours is the key to the mysteries and the cycle of rebirth, which opens the way to the Womb of Enlightenment.

I am the spirit of witches all, and this is joy and peace and harmony. In life does the Queen of all Witches reveal the knowledge of spirit. And from death does the Queen deliver you to peace. When I shall have departed from this world, in memory of me make cakes of grain, wine and honey. These shall you shape like the moon, and then partake of wine and cakes, all in my memory. For I have been sent to you by the spirits of Old, and I have come that you might be delivered from all slavery. I am the daughter of the sun and the moon, and even though I have been born into this world, my race is of the stars.

Give offerings all to She who is our mother. For She is the beauty of the green earth, and the white moon among the stars, and the mystery which gives life, and always calls us to come together in Her name. Let Her worship be the ways within your heart, for all acts of love and pleasure are like rituals to the Goddess. But to all who seek her, know that your seeking and yearning will reward you not, until you realize the secret. Because if that which you seek is not found within you, you will never find it outside of you. For she has been with you since you entered into the ways, and she is that which awaits at your journey's end.[67]

An Italian Legend, La Pellegrina delta Casa al Vento *(The Female Pilgrim of the House of the Wind)*

There is a peasant's house at the beginning of the hill or ascent leading to Volterra, and it is called the House of the Wind. Near it, there once stood a small place wherein dwelt a married couple who had but one child, a daughter, whom they adored. Truly, if the child had but a headache, they each had a worse attack from fear.

Little by little, the girl grew older, and all the thought of the mother, who was very devout, was that she should become a nun. But the girl did not like this and declared that she hoped to be married like others. When looking from her window one day, she saw and heard the birds singing in the vines and among the trees all so merrily and said to her mother that she hoped someday to have a family of little birds of her own, singing around her in a cheerful nest. At this, the mother was so angry that she gave her daughter a cuff. And the young lady wept, but replied with spirit that, if beaten or treated in any such manner, she would certainly soon find some way to escape and get married, for she had no idea of being made a nun against her will.

At hearing this, the mother was seriously frightened, for she

67 Charles Godfrey Leland, "The Charge of Aradia," *Aradia: Gospel of the Witches* (David Nutt, 1899).

knew the spirit of her child and was afraid, lest the girl already had a lover and would make a great scandal over the blow; and, turning it all over, she thought of an elderly lady of good family, but much reduced, who was famous for her intelligence, learning, and power of persuasion. She thought, "This will be just the person to induce my daughter to become pious and fill her head with devotion and make a nun of her." So, she sent for this clever person, who was at once appointed the governess and constant attendant of the young lady, who, instead of quarrelling with her guardian, became devoted to her.

However, everything in this world does not go exactly as we would have it, and no one knows what fish or crab may hide under a rock in a river. For it so happened that the governess was not a Catholic at all, as will presently appear, and did not vex her pupil with any threats of a nun's life, nor even with an approval of it.

It came to pass that the young lady, who was in the habit of lying awake on moonlit nights to hear the nightingales sing, thought she heard her governess in the next room, of which the door was open, rise and go forth on the great balcony. The next night, the same thing took place and, rising very softly and unseen, she beheld the lady praying, or at least kneeling in the moonlight, which seemed to her to be very singular conduct, moreso because the lady kneeling uttered words which the younger could not understand and which certainly formed no part of the Church service.

Being much exercised over the strange occurrence, she, at last, with timid excuses, told her governess what she had seen. Then, the latter, after a little reflection, first binding her to a secrecy of life and death, for, as she declared, it was a matter of great peril, spoke as follows:

I, like thee, was instructed when young by priests to worship an invisible god. But an old woman in whom I had great confidence once said to me, "Why worship a deity whom you cannot see, when there is the Moon in all her splendour visible? Worship her. Invoke Diana, the goddess of the Moon,

> *and she will grant your prayers." This shalt thou do, obeying the Vangelo, the Gospel of (the Witches and of) Diana, who is Queen of the Fairies and of the Moon.*

Now, the young lady, being persuaded, was converted to the worship of Diana and the Moon and, having prayed with all her heart for a lover (after learning the conjuration to the Goddess), was soon rewarded by the attention and devotion of a brave and wealthy cavalier, who was indeed as admirable a suitor as anyone could desire. But, the mother, who was far more bent on gratifying vindictiveness and cruel vanity than her daughter's happiness, was infuriated at this and, when the gentleman came to her, she bade him begone, for her daughter was vowed to become a nun, and a nun she should be, or die.

Then, the young lady was shut up in a cell in a tower without even the company of her governess and subjected to strong, hard pain, being made to sleep on the stone floor, and would have died of hunger, had her mother had her way.

Then, in this dire need, she prayed to Diana to set her free; when lo! She found the prison door unfastened and easily escaped. Then, having obtained a pilgrim's dress, she travelled far and wide, teaching and preaching the religion of Old Times, the Religion of Diana, the Queen of the Faeries and of the Moon, the Goddess of the Poor and the Oppressed.

The fame of her wisdom and beauty went forth over all the land, and people worshipped her, calling her *La Bella Pellegrina.* At last, her mother, hearing of her, was in a greater rage than ever, and, in fine, after much trouble, succeeded in having her again arrested and cast into prison. And then, in evil temper indeed, she asked her whether she would become a nun; to which she replied that it was not possible, because she had left the Catholic Church and become a worshipper of Diana and of the Moon.

In the end, it was the mother, regarding her daughter as lost, who gave her up to the priestess to be tortured to death, as they did all who would not agree with them or left their religion.

But the people were not well pleased with this, because they adored her beauty and goodness, and there were few who had not enjoyed her charity.

However, by the aid of her lover, she obtained, as a last grace, that, on the night before she was to be tortured and executed, she might, with a guard, go forth into the garden of the palace and pray.

This she did, and standing by the door of the house, which is still there, prayed in the light of the Full Moon to Diana that she might be delivered from the dire persecution to which she had been subjected, since even her own parents had willingly given her over to an awful death.

Now, her parents and the priests, along with all who sought her death, were in the palace watching, lest she should escape.

When lo! in answer to her prayer, there came a terrible tempest and overwhelming wind, a storm such as man had never seen before, which overthrew and swept away the palace with all who were in it; there was not one stone left upon another, nor one soul alive of all who were there. The gods had replied to the prayer.

The young lady escaped happily with her lover, wedded him, and the house of the peasant where the lady stood is still called *La Casa al Vento,* or the House of the Wind.[68]

---

68 Leland, *ibid.*

The Hidden Italian Tradition

There is a certain degree of debate today over whether the Magician of the Tarot as we *now* know him is the same figure as depicted on the early Tarot decks. In the Tarot, the traditional placement of the Magician follows the Fool card. Two of the earliest images appearing on Tarot cards in this position within the Major Arcana depict either a cobbler (shoemaker,) a juggler, or a curious figure sitting at a table with a variety of objects spread out before him. This latter figure is often referred to as the slight-of-hand-artist, or the swindler. The most common image of this is the shell game, where a pea is hidden under one of three walnut shells, which are quickly mixed, while the performer talks to distract the onlooker.

Some modern commentators feel that these early characters were not of an occult nature and represent a different figure from the Magician altogether. In exploring the origins of the Magician card, we will examine the early character of the cobbler/shoemaker and look at the other characters as well. The word "cobbler" comes from the Middle English word *cobeler.* The archaic meaning of the word is "a bungler" or "one who is clumsy." This seems, at first glance, to be an odd association with the shoemaker. The word "clumsy" is ultimately derived from the Scandinavian *clomsen* and the Icelandic *klunni.* Interestingly, these are the roots words of the clown, buffoon, and jester, as well. The word "jester" is ultimately derived from the Latin *gestusus,* which means "to gesticulate." *Gesticulation* is "to make gestures, especially while speaking." This is the art employed by the slight-of-hand expert.

But why was the cobbler associated with the concept of being clumsy? The answer may lie in an ancient magickal tradition that features the sandal. From the ancient writings of Empedocles and from those written about him, we enter into the Cult of Hecate. Here, we find the bronze sandal as a symbol of the magician of Hecate, possibly linked to silver sandals appearing in sixth century Babylonian practices associated with the god Adad and his wife, Shala. In *Ancient Philosophy, Mystery, and Magic* by Peter Kingsley, we read: *"[The bronze sandal]...was the magical 'symbol' par excellence of Hecate. Worn or held by the magician, it was the 'sign' of his ability to descend to the underworld at will."*[69]

Legends surrounding Empedocles as an initiate of the Cult of Hecate insist that he wore a bronze sandal. To move about in a bronze sandal would indeed, at the very least, give the appearance of being clumsy, if not define the concept of clumsy itself. It is interesting to note that, in Norse lore, we find a legendary blacksmith known as Wayland the Smith. He was lamed by command of King Nidud of Sweden so that he could not escape and was compelled into his service. In his earlier tales, Wayland is actually King of the Gnomes and produced metal amulets and magickal swords. The association of Gnomes with earthen caverns and the association of Hecate's magician with the Underworld is equally noteworthy in our discussion. On a side note, it is curious that the Latin and Scandinavian words for "clumsy" are both from cultures in which we find figures whose feet are encumbered due to their office, who make shoes, and who are connected to metal in a magickal way.

By the end of the sixth century BC, we find writings by Heraclitus of Ephesus that attack magicians as swindlers and tricksters who use deception to persuade people into believing they have magickal power. Despite this, magick continued to thrive over the centuries, and magicians were viewed as theurgists. A *theurgist* is one who performs divine actions chiefly with the aid of magickal symbols. This is the image of the Neoplatonic Magician, who was considered to possess the ability to make rain, stop plagues, and to

69 Peter Kingsley, *Ancient Philosophy, Mystery, and Magic* (Oxford UP, 1995).

both extract and replace the soul of an individual at will. According to Kingsley, Neoplatonic theurgists also had "visionary encounters" with Hecate.[70]

Now that we have seen evidence of an occult tradition associated with the shoe, what about the slight-of-hand artist? One of the earliest images of this Tarot-figure depicts a table set with a cup and several round balls. Commentators are unsure what the balls are, but most suggest something akin to bread. It is quite likely that these balls are the type used in aleuronmancy. *Aleuronmancy* is a form of divination in which various outcomes or situations are written on small strips of paper. This was popular in the temples of Apollo who, as patron of this art, was known as Aleuromantis.

In aleuronmancy, each strip is then folded and rolled up in a small ball of dough (very much like a fortune cookie). Each ball of dough is then covered with a walnut shell. Walnuts were attributed by the Greeks and Romans with oracle properties. The shells are mixed nine times, and then people pick a shell and retrieve the strip of paper to learn of their fortune. So, here we see a possible connection of the early Tarot image of the slight-of-hand artist as an oracle of the god Apollo, an association with divination. Divination itself has long been the providence of Underworld deities, which brings us back to Hecate and the magician/priest.

One of the sacred cult objects of Hecate was a triangular plaque with a rod rising up from the center. Mounted on the rod was a flat disk laying horizontally. This tool was actually the standard design in ancient times for the working surface of the cobbler. On the disk, leather was placed to be worked; the rod allowed height so that sandal straps could hang down and be laced around the disk to the other side of the sandal. Since, in the Cult of Hecate, the sandal was the sign of the Magician's ability to descend into the Underworld at will, it may be that the polished disk also doubled as a type of scrying mirror for divination.

Professor Kingsley depicts the tradition of Empedocles and the Neo-Platonist theurgists as heirs of the mystical sect of Hecate and

70 Kingsley, *ibid.*

the associations discussed in this section.[71] With the renewed interest in Hermetics during the rise of the Renaissance era in Italy, it is likely that the theurgist recognized the symbolism of the cobbler in the Tarot symbolism, the secret revealed only in symbolism, not in name. Within a short period, the Tarot symbolism would change to rightly reflect the cobbler and the slight-of-hand artist as representative of the theurgist/magician.

---

71 *Ibid.*

Bibliography

Adkins, Lesley & Roy A. *Dictionary of Roman Religion.* Oxford UP, 1996.

Anderson, William. *Green Man: The Archetype of our Oneness with the Earth.* London: HarperCollins Publishers, 1990.

Apuleius. *Metamorphoses: The Golden Ass.*

Bailey, Cyril. *Phases in the Religion of Ancient Rome.* Berkeley: U of California Press, 1932.

Baroja, Julio Caro. *The World of Witches.* Chicago: U of Chicago Press, 1964.

Bonnefoy, Yves. *Roman and European Mythologies.* Trans. Wendy Doniger. Chicago & London: U of Chicago Press, 1992.

Burdick, Lewis Dayton. *Magic and Husbandry: The Folk-lore of Agriculture; Rites, Ceremonies, Customs, and Beliefs.* Binghamton: Otseningo Publishing Co., 1905.

Campbell, Joseph. *The Hero with a Thousand Faces.* New York: Pantheon Books, 1949.

"Canon Episcopi." *Council of Ancyra.* 314 BC.

d'Alviella, Goblet. *Migration of Symbols.* Westminster: Archibald Constable & Co., 1894.

Dumezil, Georges. *Archaic Roman Religion: with an Appendix on the Religion of the Etruscans.* Volume One. Trans. Philip Krapp. Baltimore & London: Johns Hopkins UP, 1966.

Ennemoser, Joseph. *The History of Magic.* Trans. William Howitt. London: H. G. Bohn, 1854.

Fletcher, Richard. *The Barbarian Conversion: from Paganism to Christianity.* New York: H. Holt & Co., 1998.

Flint, Valerie, et al. *Witchcraft and Magic in Europe: Ancient Greece and Rome.* Ed. Bengt Ankarloo & Stuart Clark. Philadelphia: U of Penn Press, 1999.

Frazer, James George. *The Golden Bough: A Study in Magic and Religion.* London & New York: Macmillan & Co., 1900.

Gimbutas, Marija. *The Goddesses and Gods of Old Europe: Myths and Cult Images.* U of California Press, 1974.

Ginzburg, Carlo. *Ecstasies: Deciphering the Witches' Sabbath.* Trans. Raymond Rosenthal. New York: Penguin Books, 1992.

Gordon, Linda Duff. *Home Life in Italy: Letters from the Apennines.* London: Methuen, 1908.

Gray, William G. *Western Inner Workings.* Sangreal Sodality Series, Vol. 1 York Beach: Samuel Weiser, 1983.

Grenier, Albert. *The Roman Spirit: in Religion, Thought, and Art.* Trans. M. R. Dobie. New York: Alfred A. Knopf, 1926.

Grimassi, Raven. *Italian Witchcraft: The Old Religion of Southern Europe.* Llewellyn Publishing, 2000.

Harding, M. Esther. *Woman's Mysteries: Ancient and Modern.* London, New York, & Toronto: Longmans, Green and Co., 1935.

Heaton, Eliza Osborn Putnam. *By-Paths in Sicily.* New York: E.P. Dutton & Co., 1920.

Hesiod. "Theogony."

Horace. *Epodes of Horace.* David McKay, 1884.

Inman, Thomas. *Ancient Pagan and Modern Christian Symbolism.* New York: J. W. Bouton, 1875.

Kingsley, Peter. *Ancient Philosophy, Mystery, and Magic.* Oxford UP, 1995.

Leland, Charles Godfrey. *Aradia: Gospel of the Witches.* David Nutt, 1899.

—. *Etruscan Roman Remains: in Popular Tradition.* London: T. Fisher Unwin, 1892.

Lethbridge, T.C. *Witches.* New York: Citadel Press, 1962.

Levi, Eliphas. *The Great Secret, or Occultism Unveiled.* 1868.

Magliocco, Sabina. "Who Was Aradia? The History and Development of a Legend." *The Pomegranate: The Journal of Pagan Studies,* Feb. 2002. Issue 18.

Martin, Ruth. *Witchcraft and the Inquisition in Venice, 1550–1650.* Oxford: Basil Blackwell, 1989.

Mormando, Franco. *The Preacher's Demons.* Chicago: U of C Press, 1999.

Murray, Alexander. *Who's Who in Mythology.* New York: Crescent Books, 1988.

Neumann, Erich. *The Great Mother: An Analysis of the Archetype.* Trans. Ralph Manheim. Princeton UP, 1955.

Ogden, Daniel. *Magic, Witchcraft, and Ghosts in the Greek and Roman Worlds: A Sourcebook.* Oxford UP, 2002.

Ovid. *The Fausti.* Trans. John Benson Rose. Oxford: Dorrell and Son, 1866.

Rategno, Bernardo. *Tractatus de Strigibus.* 1508.

Russell, Jeffrey Burton. *Witchcraft in the Middles Ages.* Ithaca: Cornell UP, 1972.

Starke, Mariana. *Travels in Europe for the Use of Travellers on the Continent, and Likewise in the Island of Sicily.* Ed. 9. Paris: A. & W. Galignani and Co., 1836.

Stevens, Walter. *Demon Lovers—Witchcraft, Sex, and the Crisis of Belief.* Chicago: U of C Press, 2002.